Praise for
Embracing Paradox, Evolving Language

Many modern scientists and philosophers have come full circle to an ancient and indigenous view of the world as a radically interconnected whole. But Indo-European languages, of which English is the most widely spoken, are inherently dualistic. They are based on subject/object relationships that separate. We have a budding awareness of our radical interconnection, but a language that handcuffs us from doing much about it. What to do? Enter L.E. Maroski. Maroski has written a richly evocative book about a new language for the future—a book that not only recognizes the world as radically interconnected and the English language as incapable of describing it, but does something about it. She re-examines English in relation to paradox and metaphor and proposes many potential ways to transform the language into a more inclusive, relational way of communicating. She asks lots of generative questions throughout the book, and she grapples with real world examples of changing the language to accommodate a shifting worldview. What she has done in this book is immensely important. Not since David Bohm's short-lived attempt at shifting English into a more verb-based language rheomode, based on the Greek rheo (to flow), has anyone tried to remedy this foundational dilemma of language being out of touch with reality.

She asks: "How much do we have to ruin life on Earth before we change our beliefs and their concomitant behaviors? How many species must die, how many rivers must dry up…?" While she cannot answer the timing of this question, she does propose a solution: an emergent, integral form of both/and consciousness not unlike an emulsion of oil and vinegar that holds the integrity of the difference within a unified container. You might call it sacred mayonnaise. Or use Maroski's own words: "interconnected opposites, interpenetrating ideas, and dynamic interdependence." This is exactly what the world needs now.

—**Glenn Aparicio Parry**, author of *Original Thinking: A Radical ReVisioning of Time, Humanity, and Nature* and *Original Politics: Making America Sacred Again*

Embracing Paradox, Evolving Language is a rich exploration of the impact of language on our ability to live sustainably. Maroski argues that our language is a significant barrier to achieving a more holistic approach towards addressing our role in the destabilization of the Earth's ecological system.

She highlights the dualistic perspective that underpins our language—either/or logic, the split between subject and object, the separation of 'me' and 'not me'—which has resulted in a mechanistic approach to fixing the damage rather than working with life on its own terms. Opposites remain polarized rather than being seen as mutually interdependent. Paradox is not antithetical to logic and life, it is an indicator of the capacity of life.

Maroski's use of multiple sources provides rich perspective and insights into the consequences of language as an indicator and window of progress. This enjoyable read challenges us to think differently and opens the door to the subliminal work required to shift our engagement with life.

—**Bill Reed**, Regenesis Group, co-author of *The Regenerative Design Handbook*

Embracing Paradox, Evolving Language

EXPRESSING THE UNITY AND COMPLEXITY OF INTEGRAL CONSCIOUSNESS

L.E. MAROSKI

Untimely Books

Untimely Books
untimelybooks.com
An imprint of Cosmos Cooperative
PO Box 3, Longmont, Colorado 80502
info@untimelybooks.com

Cover image: *Fourth Coniunctio*, by John Dotson
Illustrations by Cate Mulligan
Book design by Kayla Morelli

Publisher's Cataloging-in-Publication Data
Names: Maroski, L.E., 1964-, author.
Title: Embracing Paradox, Evolving Language: Expressing the Unity and Complexity of Integral Consciousness / L.E. Maroski.
Description: Longmont, CO : Untimely Books, 2024. | Includes bibliographical references and index. | Summary: The author proposes that humanity is poised on the cusp of a transformation of consciousness that requires not only a shift in values and perspectives, but also a shift in a basic technology we take for granted—language. Because we use language to create social structures and institutions, including education, governance, and our most intimate relationships, the structure of our language contributes to the way we structure those creations. Maroski questions the cultural assumptions that are built into the structure of language, primarily English, and invites the reader to imagine and ultimately to help develop novel structures of language that arise from different assumptions. To do so, she shows how we can draw inspiration from paradoxical topological forms, such as the Möbius strip and Klein bottle, as they embody both unity and duality/multiplicity. By seeing our reality not simply in terms of either/or but also in terms of both (many)/and, perhaps our feelings of fragmentation and the stultifying oppositions that have polarized society can transform into appreciation for the wholeness of all existence.
Identifiers: LCCN 2023947809 | ISBN 978-1-961334-10-6 (hb) 978-1-961334-05-2 (pb) 978-1-961334-06-9 (ebook)
Subjects: LCSH: Language and languages – Philosophy. | Linguistic change. | Thought and thinking. | BISAC: PHILOSOPHY / Language. | LANGUAGE ARTS & DISCIPLINES / Linguistics / Semantics.
Classification: DDC 401
LC record available at https://lccn.loc.gov/2023947809

Man acts as though he were the shaper and master of language, while in fact language remains the master of man.
—Martin Heidegger

The supreme paradox of all thought is the attempt to discover something that thought cannot think.
—Søren Kierkegaard

Speak a new language
so that the world
will be a new world.
—Rumi

I dedicate this book to the Kogi people, with the hope that it will help younger brother become like elder brother.

Contents

Acknowledgments

I thank my Accountability Group partners, Helen J. Kessler and Gerald H. Thomas, for providing ongoing support and encouragement, as well as needed critiques and reality checks; the Monterey Friends of C. G. Jung and the Sunday Jung Study Group; my Cosmos Co-op clan—Marco V Morelli, John Davis, Douglas Duff, Michael Stumpf, Ed Mahood, and Heather Fester—for believing in this and helping me birth it; and friends who commented on early drafts, including June Gorman, John Quijada, and Grégory Brun. Thanks also to my clients who gave me projects that directly contributed to the content. I thank Dr. Fergus Shanahan for checking the material on the microbiome, Bill Reed for the Regenesis stories, Andreas Quast for creating new German words, Cate Mulligan for the graphic design, and Juan Quintana for copyediting. Chapter 16 was previously published in *Cosmos and History*. For that chapter specifically, I thank John Dotson, Robert Schrauf, and Steven M. Rosen for critically commenting on the manuscript, and the anonymous reviewer who provided helpful guidance on how to improve and strengthen the arguments. I was enormously influenced by and am grateful to Glenn Aparicio Parry, Leroy Little Bear, and the participants of the Language of Spirit conferences in Albuquerque. I thank all my teachers, both formal and informal, especially Mike Lieber, who introduced me to systems thinking, cared enough to push me deeper into my ideas, and has been supportive for over 30 years. Lastly, I am ongoingly grateful to John Dotson for walking beside me through all this and for his skill in applying heat to my half-baked ideas. Thank you.

Introduction[1]

This book has big dreams and wants you to dream, not just the familiar nighttime adventures of your soul, but to dream all-the-time adventures with what-is-possible. This book also hopes to inspire you to imagine—as that is where the future begins. Imagining the future begins with questions—the greatest invention language users devised. First among them is "what if...?"

The imaginings of a few creative people come to life for billions of others through books, movies, and other media. In that way, fiction can become reality. But when our imaginings of nightmares, apocalypse, or war become real, we must ask ourselves, "Is that really the kind of future we want to bring to life, the legacy we want to leave for our children and grandchildren?" If not, why do we keep doing that?

Do you remember going to the old 3D movies where you'd put on the dorky blue-and-red glasses that enabled you to see an extra dimension leaping out of the screen at you? This book wants to be those glasses for us, with one difference: this book wants us to be able to see not just an enhancement—something that's already there in 2D—but rather something that we haven't been able to see before.

The previous paragraphs, starting with the first sentence, are—by current linguistic and cultural standards—grounded in a category mistake. We all know that books don't have dreams, right? They're inanimate. By means of that same category mistake, we're going to question the "it-ness" of some *things*. If poets and cartoonists can, we can too.

This book is not a thing. It might seem that way to you now, especially if you are holding a paper or digital facsimile in your hands. This book is a being—not a human being like you, but an idea being. Like other beings, it will develop and grow, and hopefully it will yield fruit or reproduce in its own unique way.

This book wants to be a springboard for you, for me, for all of us to dive into realms yet to be imagined. Dream. Imagine. Invent new ways to language a world of idea beings into existence. Let this book open that door for you.

∞

The preceding text is what came to me when I asked the question, "What does this book want to say by way of introduction?" This type of active imagination, as Carl Jung called such dialogues with dream images and other entities, can be a useful way to bridge the realms of psyche and matter, to find the numinous in the mundane, the sacred in everything. That is the adventure this book will take us on.

The mindsets and paradigms emerging from the Industrial Revolution tended to exclude Life from matter. The developments from that revolution, which continued into the information revolution, helped to deliver us to where we are now—on the brink of a sixth mass extinction event and in political and economic chaos, ill health, and facing global climate change. In other words, we are facing a crisis of crises—a metacrisis. This situation did not happen recently just because someone came up with a catchy name for it. Wise people have seen it coming for decades at the very least.

Although philosophers, physicists, and poets have been urging a change of mindset for decades, one thing that seems to have eluded many of the prophets of the past is how deeply embedded the current mindset is in the very structures of language—not just the words, but the structures that shape how words and other elements of language can and cannot be combined. Although humanity has been through several mindset shifts in the past few millennia, they have all occurred within a set of assumptions foundational to language structures that have not changed (or have not changed much) during that time. Just as words have sets of assumptions associated with them, linguistic structures such as syntax and logic do too. Although that is not news to linguists, it seems to have eluded many people who seek to solve today's problems by using the same mindset that created those very problems. Solving problems using the same mindset that created them is like trying to fix a leaky pipe by using a tool that causes more leaks.

How do we extricate ourselves from such a vicious cycle? Because both the problem and potential solutions are expressed in language that uses the same underlying assumptions, to shift the mindset we must also shift, alter, or invent novel forms of language grounded in a different set of assumptions. That is the insight that this book presents, as a possibility for all of us to take up.

For example, it does not work to try to bring peace by using metaphors that call to mind war. It does not work to try to express wholeness by using language structures that reify separateness. If we want to regenerate living systems, it will not work to continue treating them as an inanimate "it" rather than "we."

Language consists not just of words but of intricately interconnected systems of systems, including syntax, semantics, logic, category structure, and culture. We will need to invent new forms and structures for *all* those interdependent aspects of language.

I do not propose an answer or solution—intentionally—because language is a phenomenon of the collective. Neither I nor any individual can revise by oneself the language that a group uses, as language requires agreement among users in order to be useful. Instead, I ask a lot of questions as a way to stimulate our imaginations. Unfortunately, questions have been abused lately, pressed into the service of sophistry. Instead of being asked from a place of authentic inquiry, some media personalities have yoked questions to the propaganda wagon. They use questions as would a trial lawyer who principally wants to introduce reasonable doubt, but they simply want to sow doubt, not reason or even reasonableness. When I ask questions, I do so sincerely. They are intended to help us examine our own and our society's heretofore unexamined beliefs and assumptions. I hope that this book helps you uncover assumptions you didn't know you had.

This book is structured as a journey. Much like a drive across country, we will only stop at certain places—important historical sites, beautiful vistas, good restaurants. Some of the stops we will make might induce a little vertigo.

If so, just relax and finish the journey later. Several years ago, I was on a trip across Canada, and one memorable stop was at a park that provided a view of an engineering marvel of a train tunnel. The train entered the tunnel at a low elevation, made a complete loop inside the mountain, and emerged at a higher elevation. If the train was long enough, you could simultaneously see both the front end at one elevation and the back end at another. Sometimes our journey might seem like that: going into the tunnel and then stepping out to see both ends of the tunnel, and in your imagination seeing through the mountain.

Here is our itinerary.

First, some important cognitive foundations for the rest of the journey are introduced, namely, the curious topological structures of the Möbius strip and the Klein bottle. They will serve many functions during this journey—as intellectual monuments, as templates, and even as a map of the terrain covered in this book. Their paradoxical and self-referential nature is key to understanding the relationships among many topics of this book, particularly language and consciousness (Chapter 1). Another paradoxical device, the kōan, is introduced and subsequently used throughout the book (this entire book could be likened to a long kōan) to snap you out of old, habitual ways of thinking. Kōans help one look at what is not there, at the hole in the whole (Chapter 2). To start from where we are, we take stock of our "default" settings for being human (Chapter 3) and how we parse subjects, objects, and space (Chapter 4).

Other writers have suggested that to get someplace other than where the current mindset is taking us, we need to tell a new story about ourselves and our future. But can we tell a truly new story using the same old language structures? A new story requires not just new plots or new characters but radical shifts in what we think we are in relation to everything else. In Chapter 5, we explore how we might create language that expresses a radically new conception of ourselves in which we no longer leave our own evolution to chance, as if we were creatures without creative power. Rather, we look at how we can consciously shape our own evolving. In light of the intimate relationship between language and consciousness, perhaps we can influence our own cultural evolution by using language differently or creating different language. For example, what might language be like if it does not reify the world into some*things*? Might we then be able to live in a world of some*ones* (Chapter 6)?

In fact, each of our bodies is a galaxy of someones, as each one of us is home to millions of microbes, each with their own will to live (Chapter 7). By seeing ourselves in different types of part/whole, whole/part, and whole/whole relationships, we can begin to see our connectedness across scales of magnitude and levels of organization. As our microbes are to us, perhaps we are to Earth, and as we are to Earth, perhaps Earth is to the Milky Way, and so on. Given such complexity, it becomes clear that existing language is not structured to handle multiple scales and perspectives, not to mention the other forms of consciousness of symbiotes.

One way to see ourselves and our world differently—to shift perspectives— is by distinguishing our everyday facet consciousness from a more integral diamond consciousness. Such a shift not only alters our way of perceiving, but also shows us a profound way to question our assumption of separateness (Chapter 8). From there, we question how assumptions of separateness are embedded and embodied in the structure of language. A perspective grounded in either/or ways of thinking is then challenged by one that accounts for both/ and as well as neither/nor. How can we build all/both/and *and* neither/nor into the structures of language (Chapter 9)?

To answer that question, it is necessary to look at how language functions as an invisible architecture of culture. As buildings provide structure and boundaries for physical spaces, language provides structure and boundaries for psychic spaces. However, because we use language mostly unconsciously, we fail to see how it structures our thinking, as well as everything else we create through language, such as our laws, institutions, and relationships (Chapter 10). A simple example of a language structure that subtly influences our understanding of the world is the reflexive verb. Reflexive verbs illustrate a recursive relationship with oneself (Chapter 11).

Chapter 12 shifts our inquiry from "what is" to "what could be." If language has helped to keep us operating in facet consciousness, what would it take to expand language to enable us to operate and communicate from diamond consciousness? For example, how might metaphors be revised to enable us to convey our interconnectedness (Chapter 13)? And how might we overcome difficulties in holding opposites in consciousness simultaneously (Chapter 14)?

Many spiritual and psychological leaders speak *about* wholeness, so in Chapter 15 we ask what it would take to speak *from* wholeness, and in Chapter 16 we begin to answer that question. We look specifically at the many facets of language that operate together, from words and syntax through semantics to the category structures embedded in a language by the culture that uses that language. After analyzing those aspects of language, I use an ancient Gnostic text to show an early attempt to express unity and wholeness using ordinary language. Next, by using Jean Gebser's concepts of *transparency* and *diaphaneity*, we continue to examine that same text vis à vis integral consciousness and its expression in language (Chapter 17).

Chapter 18 addresses the growing community of people who enjoy inventing new languages. I hope to inspire not just conlangers but anyone who is interested in inventing new linguistic structures for expanding consciousness and better expressing complexity in existing languages.

Our path, a language-consciousness Möbial continuum, comes full infinity-sign now. Using Carl Jung's descriptions of the psychic process of *coniunctio*, integrations that occur in an individuating consciousness, I speculate on how similar integrations could occur in language. If consciousness and language are like two "sides" of a one-sided Möbius strip, then integration of consciousness could foster a concomitant transformation of the structure of language and vice versa. As users of language, we need to make that happen. I share my early, albeit incomplete, attempts to do that (Chapter 19).

Our cultural institutions have their foundations in language and language is essential to all our activities, from thinking to governing to educating, even to marrying. Therefore, in order to re-form (re-structure) cultural habituations that no longer serve us, it will be necessary to re-form the repository of their being, namely, the structure of the language by which we created them. To illustrate differences in assumptions, I provide examples of practices that are based on assumptions of separateness and others based on assumptions of profound interconnectedness (Chapter 20). Lastly, we must each confront the Big Question—Why? I share my *why* and ask you to consider yours. My answer is existential. We are facing a perfect storm of crises, not the least of which is climate weirding: CO_2 stoked by the hurricane winds of artificial intelligence soaking us with retweeted memes, blinding us with dis/information that floods our screens and thunders through our communities, drowning democracy.

To continue playing the (infinite) game of life, let's look at what has survived the test of time. Ancient wisdom, for example, emphasizes that both poles of a polarity are necessary and interdependent. For example, freedom requires responsibility; growth must be balanced by death; as above, so below. The old mystics used poetry and paradox to verbalize their visions of a both/and world. As a modern mystic, I propose that we build both/and-ness into our language and consciousness, as they are Möbial, after all. From a both/and perspective, we can then expand into a more complex pluriverse, a multiperspectival all/and world of many worlds.

To begin that process, I have put in the margins some glyphs that join opposite pairs of concepts that are discussed in the accompanying text. They are *not* what I mean by "novel structures of language," but they might inspire us to get there. For now, they are intended as a re-*mind*-er to simultaneously hold in mind interdependent pairs of polarities. It is a skill we must relearn. Because many such interdependent concepts have been separated and given distinct words, we have come to assume that they are ontologically separate when, in fact, they are inseparable. Need proof? Try exhaling without inhaling.

In our quest for new structures of language, let us not content ourselves with new content words or a new shade of meaning for a dilapidated concept. Let us not even look to new alphabets. Let us embrace our patterning instinct to its fullest extent to create entirely new forms and functions for language, because patterns activate our trans-rational capabilities. How can new patterns, both phonemic and graphic, enable us to express the heretofore unexpressible? (The inexpressible must remain silent, but there are plenty of experiences for which we simply have not yet conceived of expressions.) David J. Peterson, creator of many constructed languages (conlangs), sees the vast "uncharted territory" of what is possible to create linguistically. "The possibilities of what to encode and how to encode it are endless, and in about one thousand years of active language creation, we've barely scratched the surface of what's possible."[2] Our endeavor involves more than resuscitating desiccated concepts or reconstructing archaeolinguistic structures; it involves resacralizing language and resacralizing the world.

Welcome to the Möbius Strip Club

1

Forty years ago, Douglas Hofstadter's book *Gödel, Escher, Bach: An Eternal Golden Braid* blew open my mind to pondering the mysteries of the paradoxical topological structures known as the Möbius strip and the Klein bottle.[3] In the late 1800s, German mathematicians August Möbius (1790–1868) and Felix Klein (1849–1925) described, respectively, the Möbius band (or Möbius strip) and the Klein bottle, a higher-dimensional relative of the Möbius band. Those paradoxical structures gave me a way to envision the both/and-ness I saw around me. A pendulum only goes back and forth from one extreme to another until it stops. The same pendulum can be made to spin around in revolution after revolution, like seasons revolving in their appointed order, modeling cyclicity that doesn't change. The Möbius and Klein structures, however, integrate opposites; hence, I use them because they embody paradox. In contrast to semantic paradox, such as "this sentence is false," embodied paradox shows what it says. By embodying both/and, such as inside and outside, these topological forms give us a way to represent complementarity and paradox, which will enable us to reform language to better express both/and-ness.

The Möbius Strip

The simpler structure of the two, the Möbius strip is a two-dimensional surface that requires three dimensions for its existence. A two-dimensional flat plane could exist in a two-dimensional space; however, because the Möbius surface has a twist in it, it requires three dimensions in order to exist. In other words, it's a plane surface that is not flat. The twist adds a dimension, but that is not all it does.

Although it can be constructed from a piece of paper that has two sides, the Möbius strip has only one side. Locally, that is, at any point on its surface, it seems to have two sides. However, when you consider the entire Möbius strip globally, there is only one side.

Figure 1. Möbius Strip

To make a model of a Möbius strip, take a piece of paper that is longer than it is wide. (You can cut off a half-inch-wide strip from the last page of this book.) Join the narrow ends together, as if making a loop, *except* give one end a half twist just before you join it to the other end. Then tape the ends together. As a result of the half twist, the Möbius strip has only one side and one edge.

Test it for yourself by drawing a line down its center until you return to your starting point. Did you ever cross an edge? Or, hold the edge of the Möbius strip against the tip of a felt-tipped pen. Color the edge of the Möbius strip by holding the highlighter still and rotating the Möbius strip around. You were able to color "both" edges without lifting the pen, right? To reveal something completely different, cut the Möbius strip along the center line that you drew. You just made a lemniscate. Then draw a line down the center of the resulting band and cut along it. What happened? (Take a peek at Figure 10.)

The Klein Bottle

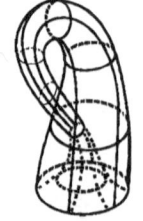

Figure 2. Schematic diagram of a Klein bottle

If you had flat, stretchy material and glued together two Möbius strips along their edges, one with a left twist and one with a right twist, you would create a Klein bottle. It would take a bit of dimensional trickery because the Klein bottle is a three-dimensional surface that requires four dimensions. Because we don't live in a world with four (spatial) dimensions, a Klein bottle is not as easy to imagine as a Möbius strip. The twist in a Klein bottle results in it looking like it goes through itself, like you'd have to cut a hole in the material it's made of. However, that is not the case if we are not limited to three spatial dimensions and further limited by drawing the Klein bottle in only two dimensions. Think of the difference between the drawing of the Klein bottle in Figure 2 and a real Klein bottle as being like the difference between looking at the painting by Marcel Duchamp called "Nude Descending a Staircase #2" and seeing a full 3D holographic movie of a nude descending a staircase.[4]

Like the Möbius strip, the Klein bottle embodies a continuum that encompasses a seeming duality. It, too, is one continuous surface that twists by curling in on itself; hence, "inside" and "outside" are not distinctly bounded but are one continuous unity. I like to use the Klein bottle as a model for the unity of complementarity because by its very nature it requires a higher dimension that is not part of our everyday three-dimensional reality. It points to the mystery of our existence, to the existence of the unknown, the n+1 dimension.

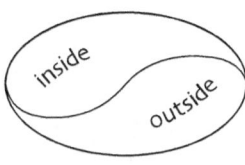

Although mathematicians describe the extra dimension needed for the Klein bottle not to self-intersect as another spatial dimension, topological phenomenologist Steven M. Rosen maintains that the extra dimension is the depth dimension, as described by the philosopher Maurice Merleau-Ponty, which is a psychophysical dimension. Unlike the three spatial dimensions, which Heidegger characterizes as pure exteriority ("outside-of-one-another"), the depth dimension is an interior dimension, the first dimension that contains all the others as well as itself. It is self-containing.[5] Thus, the depth dimension allows for complementarities to co-exist, for the movement and flow of process, for the unification of inner and outer, of light and dark, of self and other, for example. It allows for Möbial and Kleinian structures to be more than just mathematical curiosities. Indeed, the depth dimension provides a way to integrate matter and psyche. By bringing psyche into the picture in this way, we can begin to heal the old Cartesian split between mind and matter.

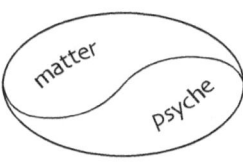

The Klein bottle shows how the labels of a duality or polarity are only labels of aspects of a whole that are not, in fact, separate. It exemplifies the concept of a merging continuum or union of opposites. It embodies the type of paradox that could be incorporated into language to be able to speak into being a world in which us *and* them; old *and* young; rich *and* poor; conservative *and* liberal; black, white, red, yellow, *and* brown are distinct but interdependent. Möbius strips and Klein bottles factor into the rest of this book in important ways—as signs that integrate a local context and a global (or higher-level) context, as ways of embodying both/and and all/and, and as a new type of linguistic container.

Let's consider how we might create Kleinian linguistic structures. How does a Kleinian structure work? According to Rosen,

> the Klein bottle, as a living symbol of integral consciousness (a "four-dimensional sphere"), brings unity and diversity together in such a way that neither is deficient. In its deficient expression, "diversity" amounts to mere atomization or fragmentation, with parts being disconnected from each other (as in the negative form of postmodernism). This is sheer discontinuity. In the deficient expression of "unity," we have a totalistic, monological uniformity. As I understand Kleinian integrality, it isn't enough to have both atomistic diversity and totalistic unity complementing each other. Rather, unity and diversity must interpenetrate each other in the Kleinian fashion in which they are different yet, paradoxically, they are a unity. The simplest example of this is given in the way the sides of a Möbius strip flow completely together while retaining their distinctness.[6]

I use these topological forms to structure the journey through this book. First we start, like the ants in M. C. Escher's drawing *Möbius Strip II (Red Ants)*, by walking on the surface of the Möbius strip. As we walk, first we seem to be on the inside; eventually that same path seems to be outside. Correspondingly, first we'll talk about consciousness, and those discussions will flow into various aspects of language. After that we must leap up so that we can see the entire surface of the discussions, that is, how one side seems to be two sides, how language and consciousness seem to be different sides of the same coin. Apperceiving one's perspective is a defining part of perceiving.

Logic Less Traveled

Complementary pairs such as being and becoming, reason and emotion, have been debated since the beginning of recorded philosophy as if one member of the pair must win the debate. This is because we do not have a convenient way of expressing the paradoxical unity of opposites, such as that afforded by

Möbial and Kleinian structures. From Parmenides and Heraclitus to Plato and Aristotle, polarities have been part of the Western philosophical canon, albeit polarities that have been split into monovalent concepts.

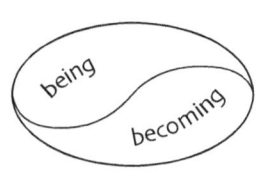

To see the utility of uniting polarities into a bivalent concept, let's examine the famous "becoming" claim by Heraclitus of Ephesus that all is in flux. Specifically, he said, "Into the same river we both step and do not step. We both are and are not" (fragment 81 [49a]). This aphorism is usually interpreted to mean that nothing in the world is fixed and unchanging from moment to moment. We might not be able to perceive the change macroscopically, but change is occurring. Heraclitus believed in the unity of opposites—not that they are the same but that they are inseparable—and that the strife of opposing forces is at the core of creativity and transformation. Thus, night is inseparable from day because of the temporal continuity from one to the other, and "disease makes health pleasant and good, hunger satiety, weariness rest" because it is not possible to know one fully without having experienced the other. In biology we see such opposing forces maintaining homeostasis and homeodynamics and thus life itself.

Modern scholars have advanced an interpretation of that fragment to align more with our Möbial/Kleinian structure:

> If this interpretation is right, the message of the one river fragment is not that all things are changing so that we cannot encounter them twice, but something much more subtle and profound. It is that *some things stay the same only by changing* [emphasis added]. One kind of long-lasting material reality exists by virtue of constant turnover in its constituent matter. Here constancy and change are not opposed but inextricably connected. A human body could be understood in precisely the same way, as living and continuing by virtue of constant metabolism—as Aristotle for instance later understood it. On this reading, Heraclitus believes in flux, but not as destructive of constancy; rather it is, paradoxically, a necessary condition of constancy, at least in some cases (and arguably in all). In general, at least in some exemplary cases, high-level structures supervene on low-level material flux.[7]

Hence, the unity of opposites is what balances constancy and change in an ongoing dance. If they were not united, we might not grow, or we might grow uncontrollably until we become too much to sustain ourselves.

Although Heraclitus never systematized his philosophy and all we have from him is a collection of fragments, several key ideas can be gleaned from them. First, for Heraclitus, dynamicity was not something to be explained; rather, it was explanatory of other things. Second, processes can form higher-order systems and can be measured. Third, he saw that dynamic alterations could be seen as fostering both change as well as "permanence" (as described above).

Other Greek philosophers developed opposing positions. Most notably, Parmenides developed a philosophy of stasis, centered in there being one Being, unchanging, that cannot be perceived with the senses. I can think or speak of a dog today and a different dog again tomorrow, and even though those events might or might not involve an actual dog, there is something eternal and unchanging about [dog] that allows me to reference it at different times and in different contexts. Aristotle argued that what is unchanging about [dog] is its "essence," which makes things what they are and restricts the kinds of changes they can undergo. Indeed, a puppy will become a dog, but a dog will never become a cat or a tree.

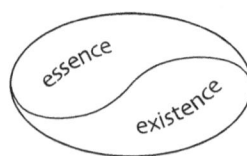

The different ways in which Heraclitus and Parmenides dealt with paradox still form the core of much of Western philosophy and the natural sciences that derive from it. Hence, we are still somewhat locked in debates about being versus becoming, structure versus function, nature versus nurture. This is partly because current modes of logical thought follow in the footsteps of Aristotle. Is that why we in the West have mostly wanted the poles of a polarity to be independent of each other and for one pole to have supremacy over the other? Why do we need one concept to win an imaginary "fight" between the opposites?

In the East, this issue was handled quite differently. Philosophers there saw the interdependence of one on the other, and they saw how one pole can become its opposite when pushed to its extreme. In China, the symbol for the ongoing dynamics of opposites is the taiji or yin-yang symbol ☯. Although that symbol has been found in old European cultures, the better-known Western symbol is the ouroboros, the snake (or dragon) eating its tail. It is not quite as suggestive of the interpenetration of opposites as yin-yang. In indigenous cultures of the Americas, there is also the concept of Quetzalcoatl, the plumed serpent of Mesoamerican cultures; and the heyoka, a contrarian, in North American indigenous cultures.

I have often wondered why English doesn't have concepts like yin-yang, since there is evidence for the symbol's existence in Western culture.[8] Why is there no systematic way to integrate opposites in Western languages? I believe we must try. In what follows I make the intellectual case for building the interdependence of opposites into concepts themselves. Although I experimented with developing image-based paradoxical concepts in my novel, *The One That Is Both*, I now realize that I cannot do it alone. No one person is capable of completely revising the structures of language, logic, and thought. Language is a phenomenon of the collective and as such requires agreement among its users. A new form of language will require the users—ourselves—to develop it together. Let's do it consciously, with input from the unconscious.

More importantly, however, we humans have a curious resistance to new ideas. If you doubt it, look at the history of science. Many of today's scientific truths were initially ignored, ridiculed, or dismissed until enough evidence confirmed them. In turn, they might fall to newer ideas in the future. In physics, for example, it was shown that light can be measured as both a wave and a particle simultaneously. In biology, with the ascendancy of epigenetics, which studies how the environment affects the expression of genes, the nature/nurture debate is finally shifting from either/or to both/and.[9]

A language in which complementarities form a new type of concept will require new logics, new graphic structures, and ultimately, a new consciousness. It will not work to impose the ideas about language presented here onto a consciousness that has not developed sufficiently to grok them. Hence, I treat language and consciousness as the "sides" of our Möbius strip wherein it seems like there are two sides, but there is only one. Which side you see, or both, depends on your perspective and on your ability to shift perspectives and hold the possibility of both.

Similar to opposites that define one another and hence cannot be separated from the other, pairs or groups of concepts, such as language and consciousness, also share an intertwined type of relationship. In fully functioning human beings, language cannot be separated from consciousness any more than one side of a piece of paper can be separated from the other.[10] Unlike an ordinary piece of paper, however, language and consciousness more resemble the seemingly different sides of a Möbius strip that really are just one side.

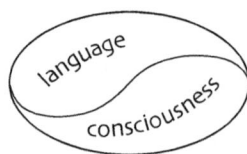

Where Does a Möbius Strip Begin?

2

Kōans mess with rational thinking. They are used in Zen training to shock you out of your habits of mind. "What is the sound of one hand clapping?" cannot be answered by thinking everyday thoughts. If I could write this book entirely in kōans, I would; in any case, it might seem that I have written this book almost entirely in questions (with a few kōans as chapter titles)! Ludwig Wittgenstein suggested writing a philosophy book consisting entirely of *jokes*. He never did, but perhaps he was imagining something like Lewis Carroll's adventures with Alice and friends in Wonderland, which takes up, with humor, many of the same conundrums of language and logic with which Wittgenstein wrestled. In the spirit of Alice, participate with this book as you would a long kōan. Don't just read it, let it undo you, redo you, or turn you inside-out. Jump out of your usual thinking. Pop out of your normal context. Expect to feel upside-down and backwards.

What is always evolving but does not change on its own?

In *The Unfolding of Language*, Guy Deutscher describes the evolution of language: "The most important discovery we have made so far is that language is in a perpetual state of flux. While no one in particular seems to be going about changing it, a few deep-rooted motives that drive all of us (economy, expressiveness, analogy) create powerful forces of change and ensure that sounds, meaning and even structures are always on the move." [11]

Different languages have different inherent abilities to facilitate their own creation. In English, for example, many a word-botanist has hybridized existing concepts—bittersweet, brunch, frenemy, mockumentary, for example. German, however, is much more flexible in enabling users to create new combinations of syllables into words that would be understandable by other German users, even if they had never encountered that word before. For example, I asked a German friend if there was a word that means something like "the ability of a language to create new words." He replied, "We have the word *Wortneuschöpfung*, which means essentially 'word-creating' or 'neologism,' and from that we could create *Wortneuschöpfungsgabe*, which would apply to someone who has the gift of being able to coin new words, and *Wortneuschöpfungsmöglichkeiten*, which would apply to the possibility that language has for creating new words." We just saw *Wortneuschöpfungsmöglichkeiten* in action.

I suggest that we plant seeds for new language forms by digging into the depths of the soil, the infinite fertile loam of the soul. This is our challenge—can we use words, the words we have, as I am doing here, to inspire us to create language that goes beyond these types of words?

Language users change language when they use it in novel ways, regardless of whether the new use was done consciously. Most new uses of language occur unconsciously. They are not planned, and they occur for reasons profound and mundane. For example, linguists study different types of unconscious changes in language, such as vowel drift, as when "ye" became "you". The evolution of the term "woman" reveals that the "wo" affix was not simply an addition to "man." The linguist John McWhorter explained that "the word 'woman' did not begin as a reference to a 'wo-' kind of man or male person. In Old English, at first, a male was a 'wer,' which is why a mythical man who can transform into a wolf is called a werewolf. A female was a 'wif,' and though that word looks and sounds like 'wife,' it didn't refer exclusively to a woman's marital status—holding on in terms such as 'midwife' and 'fishwife.' 'Woman' started as 'wif-man,' but 'man' first referred to people of either the male or the female gender. The word thus began as referring to a type of person, a woman-person, and not a type of man. Over time, the 'f' in 'wif' fell away and the result was a word we now pronounce as 'wimmin.' There was no 'woman.' Yet. The singular 'woman,' as opposed to the plural 'women,' came about in Middle English, as what some would have heard as a mistake or a quirk: Sounds have a way of changing in order to be more like ones near them. This is why, for instance, many pronounce 'tree' as 'chree,' with the 't' sound inching up closer to the front of the mouth where the 'ee' sound is going to be pronounced."[12]

In contrast, intentional changes were instigated by the LGBTQIA+ community regarding words used to refer to people who love others of their same sex and later by a variety of other words. They rejected the derogatory slurs and connotations of "homosexual" that criminalized and/or pathologized them, because such words turned real people with their own experiences of love into objects of derision. Those early activists replaced terms such as "homo" and "fag" with "gay" then "queer" and "trans." Descriptors such as "nonbinary," "two-spirit," or "gender-fluid" are also used now, and plural pronouns (*they, them, their*) have been expanded to include individuals who feel that they embody both/all aspects of gender. Language in this arena continues to evolve and blossom.[13] I recently learned the term "sapiosexual," which refers to someone who finds intelligence sexually attractive. Terms like that show how there are many different ways that we connect meaningfully with one another.

> You never change things by fighting the existing reality. To change something, build a new model that makes the existing model obsolete.
> —R. Buckminster Fuller

The examples above illustrate Buckminster Fuller's directive to create a new model, that is, new language that renders the old form of language obsolete. Although that type of linguistic evolution is important, it involves two hands clapping, one against the other, the new against the old, an "us" and a "them." But there is only us, all of us, yet there are distinctions that render each of us unique.

Despite the seeming complexity in the flowering of new language around gender issues, Deutscher explains that languages tend to shift from being more complex to less complex. Case in point, English used to require users to use gendered nouns, as French, German, Spanish, Hebrew, and many other languages still do. In the 1200s, gendered nouns were simplified out of English.[14] These days, we can see the forces of linguistic entropy operating in the simplifications introduced by texting. Letter-sounds have replaced words (e.g., "u" for

19

"you"), and phrases are reduced to acronyms. Such changes in message form emerged from the constraints of the medium (e.g., the 280-character limit of Twitter messages). Mainly they are shortcuts for clichés.[15]

When a complex system begins to undergo processes of simplification, it could indicate that it is dying (as when heart rhythm becomes too regular) or undergoing a transformational process (as happens to caterpillars when they lose their form and become imaginal cells before they transform into butterflies). When language becomes simpler, how do we save it from becoming like George Orwell's Newspeak? Should we address those entropic forces by adding complexity to language, by embracing the crumbling of the old form and welcoming in new forms—a kind of Linguistic Spring, or some other way, perhaps a Möbial or Kleinian way that could open an entirely new path for languages and their users?

Just as one can use the heel of a boot to hammer a nail, one can use a noun to modify another noun or use a new metaphor to characterize a familiar process. Similarly, a mind shift precedes using words in new ways, as poets strive to do. Because we are currently in the midst of a profound shift in consciousness, we will consider how language might change[16] in tandem with a specific change in consciousness, namely, the increasing awareness of our profound interconnectedness with everything else. As we come to understand this already-always connectedness, from the quantum level to the cosmic level, we might, for example, alter the *structure* of language so that it no longer perpetuates the assumption of separateness.

In the past, our ancestors faced a similar type of shift in their consciousness, one which seems obvious to us today: they shifted from thinking the Earth was flat to thinking the Earth is round. Today we are faced with a similar but qualitatively different shift—from thinking that we are each separate from one another and from our environment to thinking that we are already always interconnected with all-that-is. As we shift in who we know ourselves to be—from separate persons to an interconnected supraorganism—we must also ask, how do we correspondingly speak and write from this new perspective?

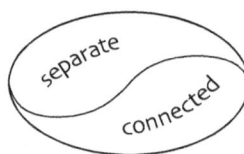

With this shift comes an opportunity to be creative, to invent new ways to speak and write, even entirely new ways to communicate. What does such a shift in consciousness make possible that wasn't previously possible? The Wright brothers (and others) noticed that humans couldn't fly; they saw an opportunity to create the ability to fly. Early alchemists sought to understand transformations in the material world and turned their gaze both inward and outward. Scientists remember them as failed chemists, but Jungians see the alchemists as protopsychologists. Working on that continuum between psyche and matter, the alchemists harnessed the language of symbols. The more adept ones understood that their quest was not to change actual lead into gold, rather leaden consciousness into light-filled consciousness.[17] We have a similar opportunity to expand our horizons in thought, word, and deed. This means not only transformations in consciousness and language, but also applying these changes to new ways of relating to each other and to the world.

Humans always get creative when forced to. When survival is at stake, people change their ways. The addict hits rock bottom. After husband and wife both have affairs, sometimes they can then imagine a new way of being together in relationship. Whether it comes to changing one's habits when faced with a devastating diagnosis or changing one's business model when faced with declining revenues, many of us prefer complacency until it is clear that the status quo will kill us. We are at that point as a species. Our complacency has put Earth at risk, and she will eliminate us to rebalance her own systems. How can we instead be creative with her? Although biomimicry studies are flourishing, they likely will not be sufficient to address the metacrisis constituting the context of the sixth, i.e., our current, Holocene (Anthropocene?) mass extinction event. We have cheated on Earth with fiat currency. How can we now shift our relationship with her?

Fortunately and unfortunately, humans do not perceive the same things or events the same way. We each have our contextualities and peculiarities. When presented with a doughnut, some people see the doughy part and some people see the hole. Some people study the qualities and characteristics of what exists in exquisite detail, and others see what's missing. Lao Tze said this about seeing the hole:

> Thirty spokes are joined together in a wheel,
> but it is the center hole
> that allows the wheel to function.
> We mold clay into a pot,
> but it is the emptiness inside
> that makes the vessel useful.
> We fashion wood for a house,
> but it is the emptiness inside
> that makes it livable.
> We work with the substantial,
> but the emptiness is what we use.
> —from the *Tao Te Ching,* translated for public domain by j. h. mcdonald

It's easier to critique something that exists than to create from nothing. It's easier to describe something that is than to imagine what does not yet exist. My task here is to keep pointing to what's not there and speculating on what could be created. Perhaps that will inspire you, dear reader, to create something—if not a new form of language perhaps new thoughtforms and multivalent expressions of those thoughtforms.

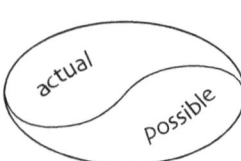

Novel language often emerges concomitant with a paradigm shift in science and/or a cultural shift in consciousness; in particular, new content words are added to the lexicon. The term *paradigm shift* was introduced by philosopher of science Thomas Kuhn[18] to describe the events in the history of science in which a radical new understanding of the world emerged, one based on different fundamental assumptions than the previous way of understanding. In contrast to the view that science makes gradual, incremental additions to the knowledge base, Kuhn noticed that sometimes there are discontinuities—big shifts—that introduce a different set of fundamental assumptions, which allow for entirely new types of questions to be asked and new words to be generated. Einstein suggested that the biggest shift was from a point-based understanding (classical mechanics) to a field-based understanding (Maxwell's equations) of the world.[19]

The Swiss philosopher and poet Jean Gebser provides broader terminology than Kuhn does, by describing what is happening in society as a shift in consciousness.[20] Whereas a paradigm shift affects a particular field of study, such as physics, biology, or art history, it does not necessarily affect other fields. However, a shift in consciousness affects most humans within a particular culture. Gebser noted how linguistic shifts accompany, perhaps even portend, the shifts in consciousness that he considers to be both ontogenetic and phylogenetic (Figure 3).[21] (More will be said about Gebser and these structures of consciousness later.) How might we shift both language and consciousness interdependently, enabling us to hear the sound of one hand clapping?

For either paradigms or consciousness to shift, someone needs to see what is missing from the existing paradigm or form of consciousness. That is why I like the passage quoted from the *Tao Te Ching*. We will need to develop the ability to see what's missing as much as the ability to see what's there.

Imagine, for example, being back in the 1970s (bell bottoms and platform shoes, go-go boots and miniskirts), and Steve Jobs of the future shows up at your door asking you to give him money to develop what he calls an iPhone, which is a telephone without a cord, without a rotary dial, but with a television screen that is so small that you could even carry it around with you all the time in your pocket or purse—and it could do all sorts of other things, too, like give you restaurant reviews, directions to just about anywhere, and be used to purchase stuff at the store or even at a "virtual" store, one that doesn't physically exist. In 1970, my first reaction would likely have been, "I don't want to carry a phone around with me all the time, especially when I don't want to be bothered." (The idea of carrying a phone with you while shopping or camping was ludicrous. But the car phone, originally a large, heavy box that one lugged around, changed all that.) To which our imaginary Mr. Jobs might have said, "But your phone—with a human-like voice—would tell you who is calling, so you can decide whether to answer it or not." If I had been an adult in the 1970s, I might have written him off as crazy. Times were different back then.

Just as Jobs had an intuition that more was possible for the humble telephone, I have a similar sense that something more is possible not just for the technological media by which we convey meaning—but for language itself. Marshall McLuhan famously proclaimed that the medium is the message,[22] and I am saying that the form our messages themselves take can also change, particularly with the new media being invented. Thanks to Motorola, Microsoft,

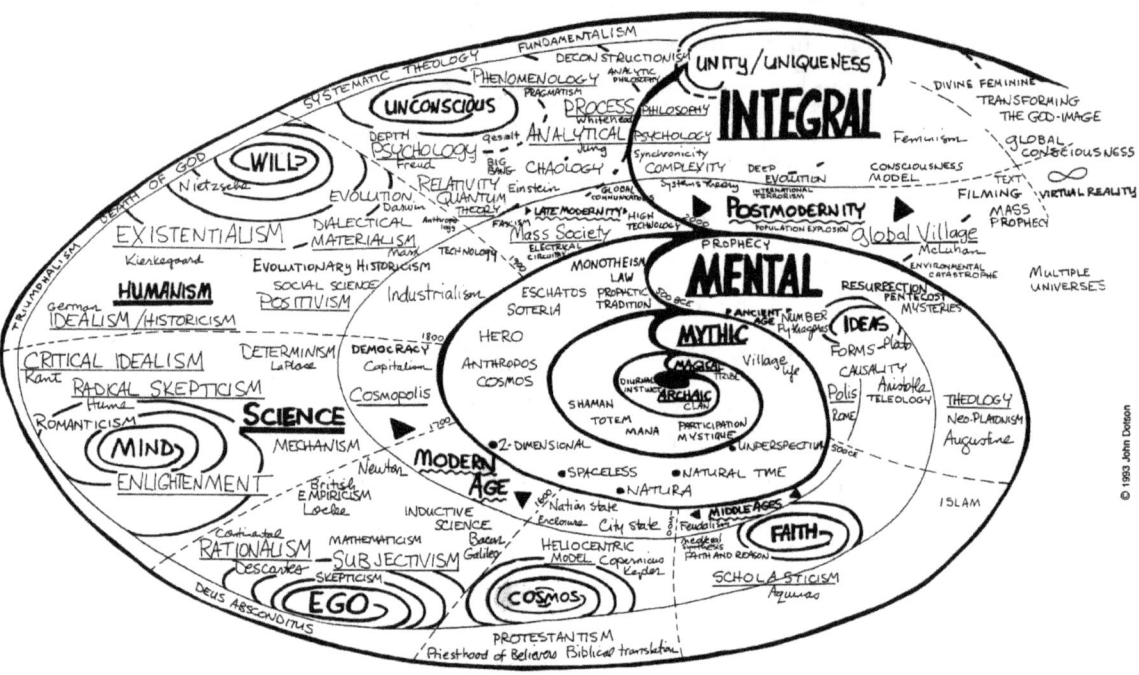

Figure 3. Graphic depiction of Jean Gebser's structures of consciousness—archaic, magic, mythic, mental, and integral. This graphic shows them emerging from origin while also being ever-present. Specific examples of personal and cultural expressions of each structure of consciousness are given. They are distinct but not separate, as are the chambers of a nautilus, the inspiration for this depiction. Briefly, archaic consciousness is undifferentiated, magical consciousness has differentiated but is in the flow of life, not trying to understand or explain it. Mythic consciousness begins to try to understand by means of stories. Mental consciousness wants to explain, look for causality, and integral consciousness sees the world through all the structures to the wholeness. For more description of each structure of consciousness, see note 44. Image created by John Dotson. Used with permission.

and Apple, as well as McLuhan, for laying crucial foundations for what we are undertaking here, this language+consciousness project is now possible. Without the shift to image-based, spreadsheet-like tables of contents (the home screen on your smartphone consists of a grid of icons, not rows of words) and the underlying technology that allows for images and their gestalts, perhaps a new form of language would not be possible. McLuhan's thesis that our new electronic media have shifted the message can be recursively applied to itself to suggest that these new media are also enabling us to develop new types of messages.

In our current era of wanting quick fixes and next-quarter return on investment, I want to caution that I am not proposing a quick fix. Rather, I see myself as planting a seed. If I see it sprout in my lifetime, that would be gratifying. I hope others will continue to water it, fertilize it, prune it, and eventually enjoy its fruit. The ideas proposed here by definition cannot be a fully fleshed-out system, just plug and play. These ideas—and language itself—will need to be tinkered with; fortunately, language is designed for tinkering. I am suggesting that we add new types of parts to tinker with—parts that are more complex, more dynamic. Let's find ways to melt the parts of language so that we might reshape them into something more dynamic or more fractal or more adaptable to different contexts, perspectives, and so on.

Before we change anything about language and/or consciousness, we should first look at the status quo—the default state of being human. What consciousness-state are we changing from?

Instructions for Being Human: Changing the Default Settings

3

"What have we come to accept as the default state of being human?" Arjuna Ardagh answers his own question:

> Most agree that human consciousness is characterized by an unnatural sense of separateness, a sense of a "me" and a "not me." We act as though we are separate from the source itself, from the divine. On the basis of this feeling of separation stands everything else that feels abhorrent to the heart—child abuse, domestic violence, people lying to and cheating each other, environmental degradation, war. All of these things arise from this feeling of "me" and "them" as separate, or "me" and "the planet" as separate.[23]

That statement echoes a passage that Alan Watts wrote thirty years earlier:

> We suffer from a hallucination, from a false and distorted sensation of our own existence as living organisms. Most of us have the sensation that "I myself" is a separate center of feeling and action, living inside and bounded by the physical body—a center which "confronts" an "external" world of people and things, making contact through the senses with a universe both alien and strange.[24]

Although neither Ardagh nor Watts mentions being thrown out of the Garden of Eden, the default state of feeling separate goes back a long way and never seems to be resolved for most of us, perhaps only for a few lucky or dedicated spiritual leaders.

I find myself wondering, "does this 'hallucination' mean that all my efforts to become a pillar of individuality have been in vain?" I hear a voice in my head answer:

No, that's not what he means. And your sarcasm is noted. Your efforts to become an individual are part of the process.

Who are you?

That little voice in your head.

Yeah, I know. But *who* are you?

Oh, you need me to be a "separate center of feeling and action" too? I'm not. I'm that part of you that is not suffering from the delusion of being separate; I'm the part that is still fully connected and has no sense of separation.

How can you be part of me when you seem separate from me?

Parts, wholes, you, me—you're getting us all confused! Your finger is part of you though it may seem separate. Same with your stomach. Same with every cell in your body, though they have all been replaced many times over, yet you are still you.

And what do you mean that my efforts to become an individual are "part of the process"?

The process of becoming your Self.

I *am* myself. Why do I have to *become* myself?

You are more than just an ego acting and reacting in spacetime. Your Self is infinite. Your Self is uncontained. Your Self, as Mr. Watts says in that same book you quoted, is who you really are. As long as you feel separate, you have forgotten who you really are.

I have felt very separate for most of my life.

And you think you're the only one who has felt this way? My dear, that is the default state of humans existing in spacetime.

Is there something other than the default state that I can experience while existing in spacetime?

Of course. And there are many ways to access it. Choose the one that's right for you.

Well, what is there, then, if there isn't a "me" and a "you"?

There is only Love, Cosmic Love, experiencing itself—or not.

Each of us has a little voice in our head. Sometimes it's benevolent and sometimes it's not. That's why we can even feel separation within ourselves, not just between us and others. There might even be several voices—the internalized voice of a parent, the presumed voice of God, or the "opponent." We might call that voice "intuition." I often joke that writers are just people who listen to the voice in their head and take notes. I think that my voice was trying to convey that there's a correspondence between the voice and "me," and me and "them." I can argue with the voice, which amounts to arguing with myself. Or I can argue with them, which also amounts to arguing with myself, if I understand that "they" are not separate from "me."

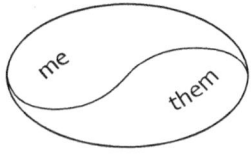

Both Watts and Ardagh suggest that we would not do the awful stuff we do to each other if we just realized that we are not separate egos, that we are instead like different fingers on the same hand. But because we think we're separate, we act like the thumb fighting with the pinkie for blood. From that perspective, some of our competitiveness seems crazy, because the differences between us as members of the same species are minimal compared to our similarities and because we are inherently interconnected. If I can see you in me and me in you, then I would be less likely, for one, to be afraid of you, to judge you, to fight you for something that in fact connects us. I might even be compassionate or loving.[25] Ardagh and Watts are saying that the feeling of separation leads to (or perhaps comes from) feelings of fear, and we definitely do bad s*&@# out of fear.

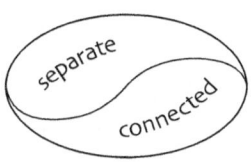

In the hallucination of "me" and "not me" people's actions can be rather unloving. The psychologist Carl Jung would maintain that the "not me" (anyone who is an "other") becomes a screen onto which we project our own shadow. One's shadow consists of the parts of oneself that one wants to deny or disown. You have probably heard the little voice in your head saying, "I'm not racist." "I'm not greedy." "I'm not… [fill in the blank]." Those are the shadows that you are disowning, the aspects of yourself that you have "othered." We do it whenever we think "I'm not X; he/she/they are X." Given different circumstances, we all have the possibility of being X, whatever X is. When one no longer believes the hallucination that there is something that one is *not*, then we understand our profound interconnectedness, and *that* is where there is only Love, Cosmic Love. Coming to love those parts of you that you would rather disavow, coming to find their gift, the key to healing, wakes us from the hallucination. And we have the free will to choose to come from the space of love. Wherever there is struggle in life is the first place to look for aspects of ourselves that need to be brought to consciousness in order to shine light on the shadow.

What does "bringing the shadow to consciousness" look like in "real life?" This happened recently. I gave a presentation and someone in the audience made a nasty comment. It was clear to me that the topic I was talking about threatened this person's worldview. I wasn't surprised and, at the time, didn't take it personally. I could tell that he was not attacking me personally but was attacking the ideas I was presenting. However, I later decided that the person who made the nasty comment was mean and that I didn't want to associate with mean people like him. The next time I saw him, I just ignored him. I wasn't unfriendly, but I wasn't friendly either. Eventually I realized that when I decided that he was "mean," I had become mean. I treated him meanly. My judgment of another showed me my own meanness, a shadow part of me that I hadn't fully owned.

It starts with small interactions like that, which add up culturally to where entire groups are projecting their shadow material on other groups. If I were to continue down that path of hallucinating a "me" and a "him," I might expand my judgments of meanness to others, perhaps others who looked like him, others of his gender. By then I would be too invested in making myself feel different in order to pretend to avoid the judgment I had heaped on myself. If we look at the situation from his perspective, we must ask what was I showing him about himself too? What was his shadow projected onto me that he felt the need to make such a comment? What part of himself needed to be integrated? When one realizes one's interconnectedness, what have seemed like one-way energy flows are seen to be two-way flows, that is, a recursive flow that goes out and comes back in, regardless of the perspective taken.

Tweaking Your Default Separateness Level

I love sailing and have raced many sailboats. You get an amazing feeling when the sails are trimmed right for the wind—that the boat and you and the world are in harmony. The boat practically sails herself. She just "feels good" (which, when you're racing, means that she feels *fast*). I like to trim the spinnaker downwind because there's a kind of "being one with" that happens with this type of sail. After you learn all the signs to look for when trimming the "spinny" (Is the luff curling? Is the pole at the right height? Are the clews even?), you just feel what needs to be done and do it without having to think about it. If you let your consciousness merge with the sail, you don't even have to analyze all those signs, your body just responds to what the sail needs. You become one with the spinnaker.

Why is it so easy, relatively speaking, to become one with inanimate objects, like spinnakers, and so difficult to become one with fellow human beings? Why is it more difficult to let my consciousness fade into another person's consciousness than to let it fade into the spinnaker? Perhaps simply because the spinnaker becomes an extension of my arm; I feel it through my own proprioception. Just as my hand knows where to go to scratch an itch, my arm via connection with my whole body knows how hard to pull on the spinnaker sheet. With people, I don't (necessarily) have that visceral connection. It is possible, however, to use various visceral ways to initiate a sense of being one with, for example, by looking deeply into each other's eyes for several minutes or by tone matching, where one person makes a tone and the other matches it and both intone together.

As infants, we remain connected with our mother through a state called *participation mystique*, a form of projective identification in which we do not feel separate from her. Eventually that sense of nonseparateness is disrupted, and we experience her as a different being with a separate center of agency. A boundary or border between us is created, and that boundary is necessary for our ego development and eventual individuation process. However, once that ego boundary is created, why does it become threatening to one's ego to again feel one with another person? Have we bought into a cultural hallucination of separateness?

Perhaps the depth of our own and the other's subjectivity is the source of the challenge. And when others challenge us, their otherness is amplified. When we emphasize our differences, we are less able to stay present to our already-always connectedness.

What conditions us to have a default mode of separateness rather than a default mode of connectedness? Our cultural assumptions? Our personal beliefs? The language used to express our assumptions and beliefs? All of the above? The correct answer is probably D, all of the above. And likely more.

If we stopped focusing on our separateness and focused instead on our already-always connectedness, how might we experience separateness differently? How might we understand our current intense social divisiveness differently? Is our cultural pulling apart a kind of mitosis before cell division—a necessary tension and separation required for growth? When a new being is forming, its cells go through a process of splitting into two identical daughter cells. Right before the cell splits, it is at maximum polarization. After it splits, each daughter cell is whole and distinct but still part of the same organism. Splitting is part of the organism's inherent development. If we can imagine that we are part of a being greater than us, then what we are experiencing in world life might be part of our collective growth and development.

I envision a time when we are present to both our unitedness and our uniqueness, similar to the way in which our own body's many different types of cells function together. However, because of the trauma that Earth and her inhabitants are experiencing currently—with all the wars, mining, drilling, underground and underwater nuclear testing, hurricanes, earthquakes, floods, genocides, and so on—it might be overwhelming or even paralyzing to feel the pain and discomfort of all the people, plants, animals, and minerals throughout the world. There is much suffering occurring on many different levels. And if we were so exquisitely present to our unitedness and our uniqueness, we would not be able to ignore all that suffering the way we currently do.

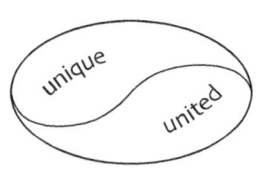

Indigenous cultures that share a kind of participation mystique with the land where they live do feel not only their own pain but also the deep pain of the land, especially when it is abused by mining; burned, flooded, or otherwise injured by climate change; or neglected even. Environmental philosopher Glenn Albrecht realized that we have few words to describe such experiences of deep emotional connection to the Earth, so he coined many neologisms to cover the array of positive and negative emotions we do feel or could feel.[26] "Coming to intimately know a place as home is at the same time a way of achieving heart's ease," he says to introduce the term "solastalgia," which refers to a kind homesickness for places that once provided that "heart's ease" but have since undergone negatively experienced environmental change. "The factors that cause solastalgia can be both natural and artificial. Drought, fire and flood can cause solastalgia, as can war, terrorism, land clearing, mining, rapid institutional change and the gentrification of older parts of cities." Although he coined several other words for other painful emotional states (e.g., tierratrauma, meteoranxiety [regarding weather], and terrafurie [anger about the injustice of human impacts on nature]), ultimately, his hope is to shift us out of the shock and depression resulting from human-induced Earth changes of the Anthropocene to a more hopeful state, what he calls the Symbiocene, based on the recognition that most inter-species relationships are symbiotic (see Chapter 7).

> The Symbiocene, as a period in the history of humanity on this Earth, will be characterized by human intelligence and praxis that replicate the symbiotic and mutually reinforcing life-reproducing forms and processes found in living systems. This period of human existence will be a positive affirmation of life, and it offers the possibility of the complete reintegration of the human body, psyche, and culture with the rest of life.[27]

In addition not only to feeling more deeply our connections with Gaia and being able to express such emotions, what other shifts in consciousness will alter our default way of being human? Specifically, how do we shift from seeing ourselves at the center of our existence to seeing ourselves as part of completely interconnected existence (Figure 4)? How do we step up to the challenge of bridging the apparent gulf between the depth of our own subjectivity and that of another? How do we sense what needs to happen and just do it as one unified *Gaianbody*? How do we become one with each other in such a way that we know our connectedness the way my body and your body each knows its own internal connectedness? How do we become a unified, global body-mind-spirit that preserves our uniqueness?

Figure 4. Default sense of being a separate human (left) and new sense of being human interconnected with the entire web of life (right).

There is no single answer; there is probably a different answer for every person. Many techniques exist, from meditation and prayer to extreme sports; there are many ways to enter *ecstasis*.[28] Such techniques alone might not be sufficient to elicit a global shift in consciousness, but if enough of us practice them, perhaps we could create a field or shift an existing field.

In addition to practicing ecstasis-inducing techniques, I believe that it is important to be able to hold a paradox in mind, or at least a set of polarities—for example, that one is both unique (distinct) and not-separate. Stem and flower are spatially contiguous parts of a plant and clearly not-separate even though they have distinct names. We can easily see the uniqueness and nonseparateness of such contiguous part-whole relationships, but we often fail to see the uniqueness *and* nonseparateness of beings on Earth because we seem spatially separate, noncontiguous. Although humans and Earth seem to be noncontiguous, perhaps we are contiguous in a way that we have not yet learned to perceive.

As trees are "rooted" to Earth and connected to each other through the mycelia on their roots, perhaps humans are rooted-connected through air

(Figure 5). Our lungs have a structure and function similar to that of roots. Both roots and lungs internalize elements from the environment that are necessary for life.

Perhaps tree : earth :: humans : air. Is one of the lessons the coronavirus taught us that we are connected to each other through air, through the very substance that seems to enable us to perceive our "separateness?" What irony.

Let's deepen this ability to hold paradox. Consider holding multiple physical and temporal layers in mind simultaneously—when you eat lunch, such as a spinach salad, consider the connectedness of you, the spinach you're eating, and the ground from which it grew. When you eat the spinach, it is no longer separate from you; its iron becomes your blood and muscles, and the spinach was not separate from Earth as it grew. If time and space seem to separate you from the spinach and Earth, try holding all those layers simultaneously while dropping out the time dimension; grok the simultaneity of the nonseparateness of Earth-spinach-yourself.

The separateness that Ardagh and Watts speak of refers not only to our sense of separateness from others but also from a higher power, however named. The poet John Dotson expresses oneness with a higher power succinctly:

the holy place
is secret because
it is
    so close[29]

Here is the catch that is the modern tragedy: find your connection with the divine, but don't talk about it in public.[30] "Connected with" does not mean "equal to." Satan's sin in *Paradise Lost* was to consider himself equal to God, and that is also why the folks at Babel had their language confused—they sought to equate the part with the whole, themselves with the divine. Just as there is a difference between being a facet and being the diamond, there is a difference between being the divine and being one with the divine. Finding your connection to the divine enables the power of the divine to flow through you. It is not your power.

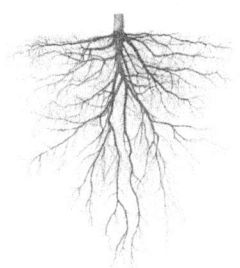

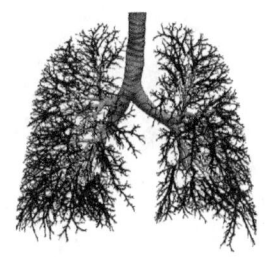

Figure 5. Top, the structure of tree roots. Wikimedia.org. Bottom, the structure of human lungs. Courtesy of Pacific Northwest National Laboratory.

Spaceisnotmadeofspace[31]

4

Hence it is clear that the space of physics is not, in the last analysis, anything given in nature or independent of human thought. It is a function of our conceptual scheme [mind]. Space as conceived by Newton proved to be an illusion, although for practical purposes a very fruitful illusion.[32]
—Albert Einstein

What is space? As a concept, it is knotted up with other concepts, including time and matter. Plato defined space metaphorically—as an unchanging receptacle in which being becomes (that in which things come to be). In answer to the ancient question "why is there something rather than nothing?" it was necessary to postulate a means by which something (visible, tangible) could exist. Plato first called it *hypodochē* (receptacle) and then later *chôra* (space). However, that was not sufficient for Aristotle, who wanted to better understand how space allows something to become. He focused not on *hypodochē* but on *hýlē*, which refers not to things with extension but to what is left when one has stripped away all the qualities of an existent. Yet, *hýlē* is not nothing; it is potency. This, for Aristotle, suggested that *hýlē* is one of the four causes, specifically the principle of individuation. The archetype (*eidos*) establishes the form an individual (thing) can take within its category, and *hýlē*, *as* material cause, provides its distinctness as a thing as well as a substrate for change.[33] Space and matter thus share an interesting entwining.

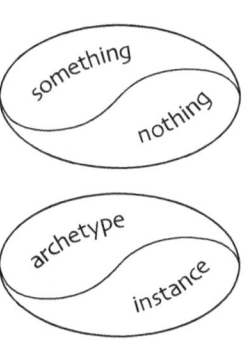

Plato's and Aristotle's attempts at definition could be seen as a transition from mythic consciousness into mental consciousness. Plato brings in the demiurge as the creator, then Aristotle de-personifies the creative doer as the prime mover at one level and as efficient cause at another level. As mental consciousness takes further hold, space is associated (through Latin and its derivatives) with an area (in which to do something) and with a period of time (interval). Its meaning as the emptiness between bodies, such as planets, didn't emerge until the 1700s.[34] Around that time, Kant abstracts space into simply a category. Since then, physicists have conceived and reconceived space in myriad ways (Euclidean and non-Euclidean, spacetime, etc.). Why is it important to reconceive space again? In this book, I focus on the non-separateness of subject and object, but because the old Greek assumptions still operate within our psyche, namely, that space is a container that holds or contains the (now unified) subject-objects, it is time to wonder whether space itself is not-separate from subject-objects.

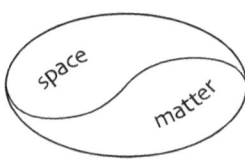

If the conception of space as a container is no longer adequate in a world where everything is interconnected, how might space be experienced by a being/someone interconnected with everything? And is the notion of space even necessary? If we want to be able to communicate *from* such connectedness, we will need to experience ourselves as spatial beings differently. Perhaps the following meditation will help you to become one with space. You can download it from https://untimelybooks.com/epel-meditations or record it on your phone and play it back so that the experience will be truly meditative. Just reading it to yourself might not give you that experience.

Meditation to Become One with Space

Sit comfortably.
Close your eyes.
Breathe. Again.
Each time breathe deeper.
As you exhale, sink into your body.
Move your consciousness around your body. Feel it in your butt, as you experience the hardness or softness of your chair.
Feel it in the bottoms of your feet touching your shoes, touching the floor.
Move it up to the center of your chest, around your heart and lungs.
With your consciousness, move into a cell of one of your organs, such as your heart. See your consciousness pop through a narrow channel which takes you through the cell wall into the gooey cytoplasm.

You swim through the cytoplasm, passing by the bulky organelles and hairy mitochondria, to arrive at the nucleus. Step through the nuclear membrane into an entirely different world. Here everything is orderly.

Watch your RNA making proteins to be sent to various parts of your body.

Marvel at the beautiful spiral structure your DNA has. It seems to be a living crystal, sparkling with light.

Now go into your DNA, into one of the bases—thymine, cytosine, guanine, or adenine.

Each base is made up of simpler elements, like carbon and oxygen. Go into one of them and see yet again how different it feels. Unlike the precise crystalline form of DNA, this space is cloudy. You feel a charge in the atmosphere. Indeed, the charges you feel might be electrons, but they are zipping around so fast that you can't really see them; you just feel their presence.

Notice that there really isn't any*thing* there, just a vague feeling of charge.

Feel into this charged emptiness.

Let your consciousness expand into it. Every atom in your body is this charged emptiness. Feel the spaciousness that your body is.

See it expanding beyond the skin. The skin is just as spacious.

Right now, space is configuring itself in this particular way at this particular time to form your body.

You are the way this space is configuring itself right here, right now.

Can you reconfigure space?

Imagine moving your arm up. You are the mover and you are the arm and you are the space. Your arm is simply space configured a certain way. As the unbounded subject choosing to move your arm, you are space reconfiguring yourself so that first "the arm" was down here and now it is up here.

Do this with your whole body. As you move your body, space simply reconfigures itself, from manifesting your body where it was to where it now is.

Now imagine that you could imbue space—the space that you are and will be—with a quality, like love or peacefulness or adventure. As space reconfigures itself, expand in a loving way, a peaceful way, or an adventurous way.

See space reconfiguring your arm as, for example, a space of love. See your whole body being reconfigured as space imbued with love.

See this space imbued with love expanding to the whole room, to the whole building, the whole city, and as far out into the universe as you can take it.

Just sit with that sense of being boundless, loving space. Let your mind take
you wherever it takes you.

Two years before I wrote that meditation I had a profound experience
of oneness. Although I am not sure that this description is "accurate" in any
objective sense, it conveys my experience. I felt like my soul lifted part way
out of my body. I didn't die and hover over my body on the operating table,
like people who have had near-death experiences, and no drugs were involved.
I felt myself expanding, like a pressurized gas that is released from a bottle.
I experienced such a vastness of my being that, during the experience, my
ego-mind thought, "How am I going to fit back into that tiny body?" When
I came out of the experience of expandedness and back into my body, I felt
truly one with everyone. It was a real experience of I-am-you-and-you-are-me.
When I hugged someone, there wasn't any sense of an "other." That was kind
of weird. When you hug someone, you feel a different body in your arms, but
after that experience, the sensation of difference went away. And yet it wasn't
like hugging myself either. As I said, it's hard to describe. These words, so rooted
in separateness, do not convey simply by stating the concept of nonseparateness
what the experience of it was like. It was orders of magnitude different and
more profound than any flow state I have experienced. I was simultaneously
"me" *and* dissolved back into the infinite energy of Source.

The glimmer of that experience led me to create that meditation. It
occurred to me that *as long as I feel separate from space itself, I am not experiencing oneness.* From what I know of basic physics, material things, including
human bodies, are mostly space anyway, with some positive and negative
charges zipping around somewhere. So I asked myself, what would happen
if I became one with space? I realized that everything, including me, is space
reconfiguring itself from moment to moment. Perhaps that is the *hýlē* aspect
of space described by Aristotle. The way we perceive movement (becoming)
might be similar to how a television screen reconfigures the pixels moment by
moment. It only seems as if the figures on the screen are moving; in reality,
the pixels are being rapidly reconfigured by different energy charges indicating

whether each pixel should be red, green, or blue. When I look around my yard, I'm not seeing the tree-in-itself. I'm seeing the photons that bounce off the surface of the tree as filtered through my perceptual organs and as made sense of by my conceptual structures. Photons are a 20th-century conception; in the future we might have a different way of explaining perception.

When I presented the preceding meditation at a conference, I did not yet know the term *spatiosubobjectivity*, which was later coined by Steven M. Rosen. *Spatiosubobjectivity* pertains to the commingling or fusion of subject, object, and space.[35] Rosen characterizes it as a dynamic process, or dialectical interplay, one evident even at microdimensions. It is not an amalgamated "thing." It is not like me or you in a box with some other people or things. Rather, it embodies the inherent paradoxical movement of Möbial and Kleinian surfaces. Since Plato, we have assumed a hard demarcation between space and objects and between objects and subjects. However, philosophers and mystics have been talking about unifying subject and object for some time now. Rosen suggests the further need to unify all three modes of being toward a fully integrated psychophysical reality.

Evolve, Co-create, Surrender

5

We are lived by powers we pretend to understand.
—W. H. Auden

Barbara Marx Hubbard's book *Conscious Evolution: Awakening the Power of Our Social Potential* gave me the courage to think that we don't have to leave language change to chance or to unconscious processes.[36] We could actively influence it. This idea is not hers alone; she stood on the shoulders of giants, including Pierre Teilhard de Chardin and James Mark Baldwin. Indeed, the Baldwin Effect suggests that learned behaviors that are adopted by a group (not simply an individual) can affect evolution's trajectory, since those who learn to adapt to changes in their environment live to pass on their genes.[37] By grounding the idea of influencing our evolutionary trajectory in the realm of human possibility rather than in the randomness of biological mutation, Hubbard made the possibility of evolving language real for me, with an urgency to *do something now.*[38] By further emphasizing human co-creation with nature, she and others[39] introduced a category shift to language that transformed the concept of evolution from biological randomness outside of our control to something within our locus of *responsibility*.

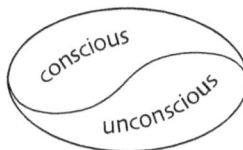

Time to Tell a Radically New Story

For Hubbard, the importance of language in evolving consciously consists of its role in enabling us to tell a new story about ourselves as humans. As part of that new story, I would add that a Möbial relationship between consciousness and language might help us live out a different type of relationship with Gaia, that is, with Earth as a living organism.

Over many centuries, our Western civilization–organizing stories have shifted from describing the exploits of gods and goddesses, to a story about a special man whose life was dedicated to transforming the world through the power of love (Jesus) or the power of compassion (Buddha), to the story of progress through knowledge of and control over how the "out there" works. In pursuing the latter story, we have created a culture of over-consuming, over-defense, starvation, violence, and polarization.

Many of us have forgotten other stories or, in some cases, the old stories have been actively suppressed by colonizers. The stories of indigenous cultures show how humans learned from divine animals, as in the story of Spider Woman, who gave the People language in one culture and Spider Grandmother, who gave the People weaving in another culture. It is not for me to tell the stories of those other cultures. If you want to connect with them, find the stories of the people who lived on the land where you now live. Learn the stories of that place—both the myths and the story that the place itself would tell (its history). By remembering the old stories, we can create a different vision of who we are and who we want to be, collectively.

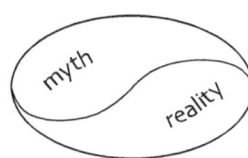

Unfortunately, we tend not to tell ourselves stories of positive visions of our future. Consider the dystopic and apocalyptic movies that Hollywood keeps making to prey on our fears of the future. What does that say about our values? To provide a counterexample, a story of a world that I would like to live in, I wrote a novel, *The One That Is Both*, that describes a place in which the inhabitants know their already-always interconnectedness and live in harmony with each other and their world. I invite you to imagine what such a world would be like. What kind of beings would we know ourselves to be? Would we still have money? Would people have to work in jobs they despised just to survive? And, of course, how would language itself be different?

Toward the end of his life, futurist Fred Polak looked not toward the future but back at the past, at what previous generations thought the future would be like. Today, we can go to Seattle and see some remnants of how people in 1962 envisioned the City of the Future.[40] My early visions of the future were shaped by the TV shows *The Jetsons* and *Star Trek*. Polak looked at how writers in the distant past imagined and described the future. He found that society's image of the future has largely been a self-fulfilling prophecy.[41] First we imagine it, then we communicate it, and eventually we bring it into existence—thought, word, deed. My generation developed the technology to bring into existence some of *The Jetsons*' and *Star Trek*'s technology, such as Skype/Zoom and 3D printing. Knowing that we create our future based on our image of it, and seeing the stories that movies and popular media are telling us about an apocalyptic, dystopian future, *what story do we want to have fulfilled by ourselves and our progeny?*

If we tell only a slightly new story, for example, by changing some of the players, such as whether the hero is an ancient Greek guy or a futuristic part-human/part-robot or whether the Sun rather than the Earth is at the center of the solar system (they are still both in orbital relationship), or whether God kills the nonbelievers or we annihilate ourselves, will we evolve much? Instead, what would be a *radically* new story?

> What kind of society derives from and supports the principles of co-creative participation in the unfoldment and evolution of a living, conscious, universe?[42]

Reread that quote. Put the book down and take a few minutes to imagine that kind of society. Imagine it in detail—how the beings in it would relate to each other and to their environment, what learning would be like, what transportation would be like, and so on. This is how we get to the "new model" that Buckminster Fuller called us to design.

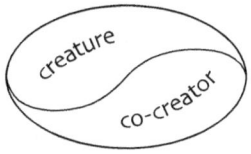

Now that you have imagined something, let me up the ante and ask more questions about telling a new story: is it possible to tell a radically new story using the language structures of the old story—not just the old language (the words or types of words themselves) but the old language structures (the way language is organized by culture, by logic, even by the rules of grammar)?

Consider that a radically new story also requires new types of language by which to tell it. In other words, to realize our evolutionary potential, we need new stories that also use new language structures.

Barbara Marx Hubbard said that "language is a design innovation, a way to pass on information exogenetically."[43] Language also does much more than that—it does things (such as bind parties in a contract); it hurts and heals; it conveys metamessages as well as messages.

Just as the wheel and other design innovations have been applied far beyond their initial uses, let's keep designing language, innovating it, finding ways to pass on more complex information, more simultaneous information, different types of information and connection, while taking care not to get stuck in the "more is better" mindset; indeed, "more is better" might be an important belief-story to revise.

In this era of hegemony of the mental consciousness structure (per Jean Gebser; see Figure 3 and note[44]), myths, fables, and other older forms of stories have been downgraded from epistemology to entertainment, while rational scientific stories/explanations have been elevated to "Truth." If you examine the science deeply, getting down to its essence, you see that such explanations are still a form of storytelling, albeit one that often disavows being a story. We say that explanations use logic rather than imagery and that they build up a structure called a knowledge base. They do, but scientific explanations still draw on imagery in the form of implicit and explicit metaphors (see Chapter 13). Stories, however, have a few perks that we might do well to re-engage: they can communicate multiple layers of meaning simultaneously; their stance is one of openness, of fostering curiosity and imagination rather than adversarial argument; and they can both show and say.

I am not suggesting that we return to using language that reflects a mythic form of consciousness, but because mythic consciousness is ever-present and already part of us, I am suggesting that we update our stories, our "explanations" *again*. We are continuously revising our stories. When we domesticated the ox to help plow fields, we did away with the pantheistic stories about the sacredness of all life, because yoking and whipping the ox did not conform to the values embedded in such stories. We replaced stories about gods and goddesses with stories about (accompanied by measurements of) entities such as protons and dark energy. Some people have replaced the story of a vengeful

46

god with one about a loving god. All forms of storytelling have their efficient—effective and useful—and deficient—ineffective or lacking—modes; perhaps we can better educate ourselves about the efficiencies of storytelling as well as the hazards of its deficient modes.[45]

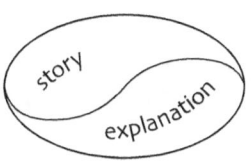

An indigenous Australian mode of exchanging stories for purposes of learning and growing is called *yarning*. "Yarning," says Tyson Yunkaporta, "is more than just a story or conversation in Aboriginal culture—it is a structured cultural activity that is recognized even in research circles as a valid and rigorous methodology for knowledge production, inquiry, and transmission. It is a ritual that incorporates elements such as story, humor, gesture, and mimicry for consensus-building, meaning-making, and innovation. … It has protocols of active listening, mutual respect, and building on what others have said rather than openly contradicting them or debating their ideas."[46] Yunkaporta's book, *Sand Talk: How Indigenous Thinking Can Save the World*, demonstrates the art of yarning. He simultaneously teaches readers what yarning is and shows how to do it. Although yarning might not get us to land a machine on Mars, its use of active listening and mutual respect definitely could help us to better live with each other without needing to stockpile nuclear weapons or engage in cyberattacks.

Yunkaporta introduces a set of glyphs representing different types of mind states, including kinship-mind, story-mind, dreaming-mind, ancestor-mind, and pattern-mind. These mind states are ways of knowing, being in the world, and interacting with life. What they represent are deeply engrained, profound cultural practices and beliefs. "Mastery of Indigenous epistemology (ways of knowing) demands being able to see beyond the object of study, to seek a viewpoint incorporating complex contextual information and group consensus about what is real."[47] Cultures with oral traditions, he says, are high-context cultures, whereas those that lost contextual reasoning and lost the use of dialogue to promote reasoning—low-context cultures—could more easily control a workforce and military. How might we reintegrate the practices of high-context cultures into those of low-context cultures?

Recall the Möbius strip and Klein bottle. Each requires a context of greater dimension than itself in order to exist. Perhaps by using such paradoxical and context-dependent structures as a novel way to evolve language, we could find ways to bring the importance of context into low-context methods of communication.

Co-creation

One of the foundation stones of Barbara Marx Hubbard's conception of conscious evolution is the notion of co-creation, namely, that we are partners with ((God, Source, the Divine, Great Mystery, whatever you want to call "the wellspring of creation"))[48] in creating our lives and our reality. Hubbard proposes a "new spirituality in which we shift our relationship with the creative process from creature to co-creator—from unconscious to conscious evolution."[49] Although she focuses on co-creating with ((God/Source/Great Mystery)), I believe that we must also learn to co-create with our fellow Earth dwellers and with Gaia herself.[50] One way to start co-creating is to ask "how would Nature do it?" We can look at how Nature has solved "problems" of all sorts. Nature has evolved over billions of years by adapting to change. Nature does not waste materials, for instance. Nature builds entities by additive processes, one molecule at a time, and recycles itself through processes of decay and reincorporation.

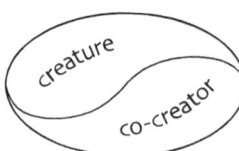

We would also need to be humble enough and open enough to listen to what animals and plants can show us and tell us. For example, *The New York Times* reported how a rancher had waged war against beavers by dynamiting hundreds of beaver dams. His son, who inherited the farm, instead realized their benefit. "Last year, when Nevada suffered one of the worst droughts on record, beaver pools kept his cattle with enough water. When rains came strangely hard and fast, the vast network of dams slowed a torrent of water raging down the mountain, protecting his hay crop. And with the beavers' help, creeks have widened into wetlands that run through the sagebrush desert, cleaning water, birthing new meadows and creating a buffer against wildfires."[51]

A shift is occurring among some segments of society toward respect for the innate intelligence not only of beavers but of all life forms. Fortunately, there are those among us—the horse whisperers, shamans, and animal and plant communicators—who can help teach us ways to communicate with nonhuman intelligences.[52]

Even before the pandemic, I noticed more wild animals approaching rather than hiding from humans—seals and otters jumping on kayaks; an octopus reaching out for a diver's camera in California and another befriending a diver in South Africa;[53] whales tangled in fishing lines approaching boaters and "asking" for help. Clearly, they are intelligent in ways beyond what we project onto them. With fewer humans clogging up the outdoors during the pandemic, wild animals found their way into cities and towns. I often see deer and wild turkeys negotiating downtown streets. Neighbors keep each other alerted when mountain lions roam through back yards making cameo appearances on security cameras. In my town, we let the mountain lions, bobcats, and coyotes be. We do not capture them or take them elsewhere because we understand that we are encroaching on their territory. Respecting their wildness also means that we keep our cats and dogs inside at night!

Surrender

Hubbard called for conscious evolution; hence, we must also look at the contrary—unconscious evolution—because, of course, they are interconnected. Something is "unconscious," in its shallow meaning, when it is inaccessible to awareness. One can become conscious of such psychic content; for example, you can become conscious of anger simmering below awareness if you pay attention to changes in breathing, constriction of muscles, and so on. The deeper meaning of "unconscious" takes us into the depths of psyche, of soul.

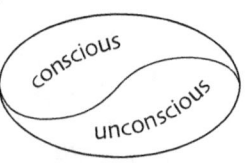

C. G. Jung reminds us that the unconscious is truly not conscious. It takes effort to discern *that* one is unconscious and *of what* one is unconscious. There are at least two layers of the unconscious—the personal and the collective. Jung believed that the collective unconscious is a deep wellspring all people can tap into and that humankind's ability to access the collective unconscious explains why certain symbols and images are found in multiple cultures spanning continents and temporalities. The collective unconscious can be accessed through instinct, the archetypes, and archetypal images that come to us in dreams, visions, and via creative endeavors. The power and importance of the unconscious in co-creating should not be underestimated.

I realized the reality of the collective unconscious shortly after I published my novel. In it, I describe a ritual that I called a Welcoming Ceremony. I went into great detail about how the main character was welcomed into a community that understood its interconnectedness. Indeed, they understood that this new guy needed to feel completely connected to them as well, or else he might ruin their stability if he felt separate, alone, or disconnected. After the book was out, I found myself listening to an interview of a Māori woman who described the Māori welcoming ceremony. Prior to that I knew almost nothing about the Māori, only that they lived in New Zealand. I was astounded by the similarities between what I had imagined in the novel and what the Māori actually did in their welcoming ceremonies. At that moment I realized that somehow I had tapped into the collective unconscious.

Jung also sees the unconscious as an active force in one's life that can push one to mature—specifically, to individuate, that is, to become who you really are by integrating the psychic parts of you that you would prefer to disown. Similarly, I think that one way to consciously evolve language is by surrendering to the unconscious. Perhaps it also pushes language to individuate.

Historically, intentional language change carries the baggage of coercion and colonizing. Invaders often forced the invaded to adopt the oppressor's language. The United States government, for example, forbade children taken to Indian boarding schools from speaking their native language. During the First Chinese Character Simplification Scheme in 1955, the Chinese government forced a new, simplified language on the populace.

Conscious evolution of language must instead emerge voluntarily. We must build, as Buckminster Fuller said, "a better model." A new form of language must be able to do things, express things, and convey relationships that our current language is unable to convey, so that people will *want* to use it. For example, many people have readily adopted emojis.

I am not the first to suggest that language has limitations. In 1962, *The Limits of Language* was published,[54] which included excerpted writings of scientists, philosophers, and literary figures. Physicists suggested that the paradoxes of quantum theory posed a problem for language. David Bohm recognized that problem and tried to find ways to deal with it. He wrote about forming a new mode of language called the "rheomode" (flowing mode)[55], and he participated in the inaugural dialogue with Native Americans and First Nations people[56] some of whose native languages were verb based and expressed process better than the noun-heavy English language. Such verb-based languages were more like the process-based rheomode that he envisioned. I participated in the offshoot of those dialogues, which deeply influenced the ideas developed here. Those dialogues are elegantly depicted in *Original Thinking: A Radical Revisioning of Time, Humanity, and Nature* by Glenn Aparicio Parry, who organized them for many years. That was my introduction to the Navajo language and the different set of ontological assumptions that underlies it (some of which are described in Chapter 19).

In addition to questioning the default state of being human and whether language can evolve with our conscious assistance, what other assumptions about language and consciousness might need to be questioned?

It Is Obsolete

6

Every some*thing* is really a some*one*.[57]
—David Spangler

Spangler's words hit me in a way that the usual psychospiritual talk hadn't. It forced me to face up to assumptions I have about the nature of life itself—specifically, what is sentient and what isn't. In my day-to-day life I certainly don't relate to most somethings as someones. For my conscience to let me put the coffee beans in the grinder, I would not casually say "I am making coffee." I would instead prepare sacred coffee-beings for ritual transmutation by water. Could I give away that shirt I haven't worn in five years if she (*la chemise*) was a someone? How quick we are to discard the somethings that stop working, no longer fit, or cease being desirable. Do we treat the someones in our life that way too?

To be clear, Spangler is not implying that our furniture and utensils can sing and dance, as in cartoons, but that it is possible to become aware of the sentient energy of the "things" around us. If we still lived in a mostly living environment (ever been camping?), it is easier to see the somethings as someones. When we live in a world of things made from dead trees and artificial substances like plastic, for example, it is not as easy. Perhaps artificially intelligent programs will either further confuse the issue or help bridge the gap; the results are yet to be seen. Spangler helps us imagine the subtle world that he sees by describing his sofa:

> The first thing I see when I look at my sofa is what anyone would see: its surface appearance. … If I shift my awareness to a deeper level, the sofa becomes something more. At the simplest level "inward," I am aware of an energy field surrounding it. All things are surrounded by this aura of energy. It's part of the subtle field of the incarnational realms. This field is "sticky" and can accumulate other forms of energy, such as those generated by our thoughts and emotions but also by our spiritual attunements. For example, if

I'm content and peaceful when I sit or lie upon the sofa, the vibration of that peace can enter its energy field and stick there, particularly if it's a consistent experience over time … To discover how the sofa itself is alive, I must go deeper. As I shift my awareness to do this, it's possible I may "overshoot" the mark and find myself slipping into a mystical state in which I become aware of a Presence and Life that is not just within the sofa but within all things. This is the primal Life from which all creation is emerging, and I think of it as the level of the Sacred. This Life is a universal condition. It's the Life we all share, the Life of the Cosmos, the Life of the One, however we understand that. At this level, the sofa is most definitely alive, but it's no longer a sofa. It's part of a universal oneness flowing through all things, underlying the manifestation of all things. … So as I examine my sofa with a deeper perception, I come to an energy phenomenon that is not a universal presence or force and not just an accumulation of characteristics and energies from outside itself but one that has its own particular unique, internally coherent and integrated organization. This is where I experience the sofa as something living, not in a biological way but in an energetic way.[58]

Spangler's statement is revolutionary. Although you have probably heard it before in different forms, such as "we are all one" or "the earth is a living being" or "I am because you are," to say "all somethings are someones" turns our typical conception of the world inside out and upside down, and dissolves but does not destroy the inside/outside boundary, like an exoskeleton becoming a cell wall. (I hope you are recalling Möbius strips and Klein bottles right now.)

In the Na'vi Language, Is Everything a Some*thing* or a Some*one*?

The movie *Avatar* told the story of some*things* being recognized as some*ones*. The first *Avatar* movie has essentially the same plot as *Dances with Wolves*, so let's review the basic structure that underlies both movies: a man encounters "others" (Indians or Pandorans) whose culture is different from his. His culture sees them as some*things*; he learns to see them as some*ones*. They befriend him and make him part of their culture. He must help them defeat his old friends (culture, identity) who don't believe that the "others" are some*ones* and who just want to exploit natural resources. This story is not just a movie plot, a myth, or a history lesson; it's archetypal. It happens in less extreme forms in many scientific fields. Those with a new theory, a different explanation, sometimes just a different perspective, are treated as the "other" and must face the same test of loyalty.

Both of those movies depict one culture living in harmony with the world and another culture exploiting the world for its material resources. Do we love these movies so much because they show us what our better selves already know—the path of greater heart? If so, why do we, particularly some politicians and corporations, keep choosing the lesser path, perpetuating cultures without compassion for our fellow someones and that deny our profound interconnectedness? Each of us must answer this for oneself. Nevertheless, even if we believe deeply that everything is connected, that all somethings are someones, that "I am that," our language constrains us to separate *I* from *you* and from *it*, first as a linguistic distinction but also implying an ontological one. A central question in our inquiry is this: how can we keep linguistic distinctions while recognizing ontological wholeness? Our response to this question calls for profound shifts in worldview and in our culture's fundamental organizing metaphors.

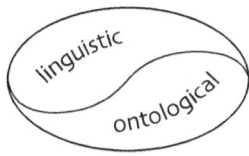

The world spirit, as manifested in the Tree of Souls, *Eywa*, the most sacred being on Pandora, spawns little jellyfish-like woodsprites that float in the air and seem to have their own consciousness and agency. Metaphorically, they seem to be points of consciousness that are simultaneously part of the greater consciousness. How is the attribution of consciousness conveyed when it pertains to nonhumanoids such as that? I ask these questions because I think it would behoove us to build similar types of assumptions into our own language, by way of our culture. Perhaps some creative Na'vi speakers might consider making up a new type of concept or new type of structure for existing natural languages that will make a difference in *our* world. Maybe if we think about these types of things for Na'vi, we can also think about them for English (and French and Polynesian and…). I hope that one of the sequels shows Jake Sully fulfilling his hero's journey by returning to Earth and bringing the Pandoran worldview to help stop us from continuing to plunder Earth.

I would enjoy learning more about how the language and the culture of Pandora intersect. What cultural assumptions underlie Na'vi itself, and how are they expressed in the language? If they can be expressed in Na'vi, then surely we can express them in English, right?

> The limits of your language are the limits of your world.
> —Ludwig Wittgenstein

I have been told that during an ayahuasca experience you see that everything is alive, conscious, vibrating. I have not had an experience with ayahuasca, but I get it. I have experienced William James's "blooming, buzzing confusion" during a vision quest. As we grow up, we lose the magic and mystique we knew in childhood. The world becomes "the real world" but dies to us; or is it we who die to the life of Life?

To conceive of the world not as filled with things—living or not—but as filled with points of consciousness, radically alters one's ways of being and doing. Essentially, we can think of every point as its own point of consciousness, like the jellyfish-in-air woodsprites. Many points make up a larger point, such as me or the chair I'm sitting in, the violet on the windowsill, and so on. Each of those points is a *holon*, that is, a part that is also a whole within a greater whole. We can imagine many different types of holons, from material ones (bodies composed of cells and/or microbes) to social ones ("We see that wherever human beings flock together—a phenomenon of collective consciousness is created."[59]) to frequency holons (a piece of music) to combinations thereof. Each person, for example, is both a physical holon and a social holon within the community. Each community is a holon. Each holon has its own sovereignty, and each is comprised of parts that have their own sovereignty as well. As the former cell biologist Bruce Lipton says, "you are in truth a cooperative community of approximately 50 trillion single-celled citizens."[60]

Indeed, if each of us is a universe, home to species who are home to species, then who is us and who is them? Maybe we need to come up with some new language structures that help us organize the worlds within worlds that we are and within which we exist. How do we switch between figure and ground, where what is "figure" at one level is "ground" at another—especially if meaning or truth changes when the switch between figure and ground is made?

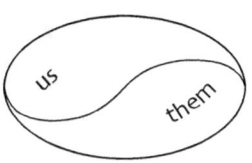

7

Being a Microbe on Gaia's Skin and Gaia for Trillions of Microbes

Glass artist Jon Kuhn makes sculptures from tiny pieces of crystal glued together to form a cube. Because of the way light refracts through each small piece individually and all of them together, the cube embodies for me a metaphor for our collective being, which I have been calling the *Humanbody* at one scale and *Gaianbody* at a more-than-human scale. The color pattern of light refracted through the pieces of the cube changes with the angle of the light or as you move your head. The beauty of the refracted colors is a metaphor for the way Spirit refracts differently through each of us individually and all of us together. Sometimes the cube looks almost entirely colorless, and other times it is a riot of rainbow hues. To me, his cubes illustrate how the integrity of the whole requires each piece, each one of us, to refract the light our own way. Spirit refracts through each of us uniquely—some can sing, others can paint, others design, build, bury, and even steal. Sometimes our colors align and sometimes they don't.

For those bits of crystal together forming a cube, it isn't the cube shape that matters, it's the way the light behaves as it refracts through the parts and the whole. Similarly, something miraculous occurs when a critical mass of unique-but-not-separate organisms forms a supraorganism, a new whole composed of existing wholes. That can occur intentionally or emerge spontaneously, depending on the situation and context. The supraorganism that forms, consciously or not, will constrain (not control) to a lesser or greater degree the behavior of the wholes that comprise it. Some supraorganisms allow for more self-expression than others: consider, for example, the difference

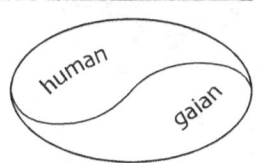

between a pond ecosystem and a gut microbiome. In a pond ecosystem, although the fish can't go far, the waterfowl can come and go freely. In the gut, the microbes stay within that domain. Gut microbes can wreak havoc on other microbial domains.

When I speak about an organism or a supraorganism as a whole or holon, it is a relative wholeness, a unity based on a pattern. Because active processes of decay and growth are always occurring, the "whole" we perceive is a wholeness of pattern, not simply a wholeness of stuff. We could shave off a molecule at a time and each time ask, "is it still whole?" and each time the answer would be yes, even down to the last molecule. That is the Sorites Paradox—when does something stop being itself if you remove one small piece at a time?

Similarly, how do we consider holons framed as social groups (family, tribe, community) compared with those framed as wholes of things? When psyche and matter are no longer split, those concerns will transmute themselves.

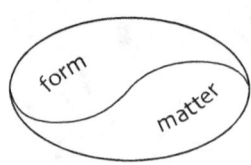

When I think about supraorganisms as holons, I prefer to think of them using the metaphor of a living system or body. As a medical editor, I learned that cells are complex microcosms that depend on the simultaneous functioning of holons, such as mitochondria that generate energy, proteins that start and stop cellular processes, and molecules that act as gates that let some substances into the cell and keep others out. A whole is not simply a collection of parts; it serves a purpose. A liver is more than a lump of liver cells; those cells work together to filter blood. Each of us is not a jumble of cells and microbes; we each have a purpose. And presumably, by extension, the larger wholes to which we belong also have their purpose(s).

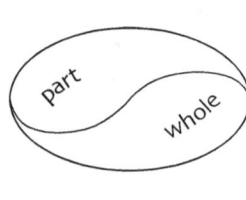

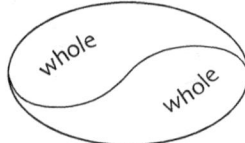

When a holon is part of multiple greater wholes, as humans are, conflicts can occur. Someone can be a person-holon within a family-holon as well as a within a corporate-holon as well as a community-holon as well as a water-shed-holon, and even Earth-holon...the list can be vast. One's function within a community, for example, might create strife (internal and/or external) in relation to one's function within the family. That can happen, for example, to first responders; the daily traumas that they are exposed to within the community-holon can traumatize them, making it difficult for them to not traumatize their family-holon.

Because the term "holon" is not specific to context or level of organization, it has not been particularly useful and hence has not been used much. How can we specify which context defines a particular whole? Such specificity might be important if something is true about a holon at one level but not true at another level or is true in one context but not in a different context.

Let's look at some holons that live in and on our bodies—our microbes. We are mostly unaware of them until they cause us some distress. Nevertheless, their essential importance for our ability to live has been recognized more clearly recently. Biologists have found that "inter-species associations, generally referred to as symbiotic relations, are equally (if not more) fundamental, and are also more pervasive [than non-symbiotic relations]. It is becoming increasingly apparent that symbiosis is the rule rather than the exception in the biological realm."[61]

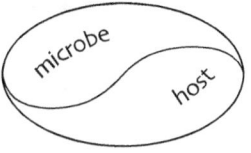

The term "symbiosis" is a neutral umbrella category that refers to one organism living in or on a living host and there being an interaction between species. Further subcategories distinguish the nature of the relationship: mutualism benefits both; commensalism benefits one but does not harm the other; and parasitism benefits one by exploiting but not killing the host. Often the exchange involves protection or food. Symbiosis occurs between species of different phyla, such as the Egyptian plover and the crocodile, the Colombian tarantula and the dotted humming frog, and the clownfish and the anemone, as in the movie *Finding Nemo*. By living among the poisonous arms of the anemone, clownfish not only receive protection but also get the leftovers of the anemone's meals. In return, they act as housekeeper, bodyguard, and chef. Clownfish also remove parasites from the anemone and scare away predators, and their excrement provides it with nutrients. Symbiosis also occurs with species living inside other species, as with Trichonympha, which is one of the gut microbes that enables termites to digest the wood they eat.[62]

As with Trichonympha and termites, some mutual relationships were so useful to both species that they made the collaboration permanent. In humans, parts of eukaryotic cells, such as mitochondria and chloroplasts, were originally independent bacteria that came together symbiotically millions of years ago. In other words, many organisms, including us—our cells—are made up of what used to be independent organisms—bacteria, in particular. How do we know this? Because those subcellular holons have their own DNA. The process by which those previously independent organisms came together to form new organisms is called *endosymbiosis*. The process of endosymbiosis was first postulated in the early 20th century but verified later by Lynn Margulis, who was also instrumental in developing the Gaia theory with chemist James Lovelock. The Gaia theory proposes that organisms interact with their environment in such a way that they form a planetary-scale self-regulating supraorganism. As her graduate student Greg Hinkle quipped, synthesizing the two theories, "Gaia is just symbiosis as seen from space."[63]

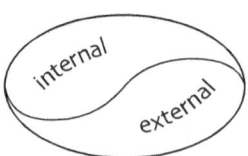

Other organisms live in symbiotic relation to us but have not undergone endosymbiosis to become part of our cellular structure. These organisms form our microbiome. The host organism together with its microbiome constitutes a *holobiont*. The human microbiome includes bacteria, viruses, fungi, Archaea, and other organisms that live on most epithelial (skin-like) surfaces throughout our bodies, in different communities depending on the characteristics of the region (e.g., moist/dry, warm/cool, exposed to oxygen or not, high/low pH). Microbes on the nasal, oral, skin, gastrointestinal, and urogenital areas have been studied the most, but microbes also exist in our eyelids, ears, and many other places.[64] There are more microbes with their own DNA in our body than there are human cells, and the amount of their DNA in us far exceeds the amount of our own DNA. Although humans generally share similar types of microbes, each person's microbiome is unique. One's own microbiome also differs at different times, depending on, for example, what one eats or what one has been exposed to in the environment.

Our microbes play important roles not just in digestion but in many of our other biological functions; for example, they influence cravings as well as help us fend off external pathogens. They also can influence mood, energy level, pain level, and many other biological phenomena.[65] They foster internal communication not only with one another but also with us, their host, by sending signals from the gut (or other regions) to the brain. They undoubtedly have functions that we have yet to discover. Thanks largely to the research impetus provided by the National Institutes of Health's Human Microbiome Project and the plethora of studies it spawned, we are beginning to learn about the vast ecosystems that our own bodies provide for many other organisms.

Just as we can manipulate our external environment, microbes can influence their external environment, including their host's internal environment. For example, when I have a craving for sugar and I eat sugary food, I feed a yeast called *Candida*. In fact, "gut microbes may manipulate host eating behavior in ways that promote their fitness at the expense of host fitness."[66] Similarly, in the oral microbiome, the periopathogen *Porphyromonas gingivalis* triggers disease not by inducing inflammation but by interfering with host immunity in a more subversive manner—preventing the host from detecting and clearing not just *P. gingivalis* but other oral microbes as well.[67] To illustrate the extraordinary complexity of microbe-host interdependence, here is a fascinating example of how microbes have evolved to manipulate their environment, including their host, to ensure the survival of their species:

> While *Toxoplasma gondii* can reproduce in one place only—the gastrointestinal tract of infected cats—the parasite can actually infiltrate the brain of any mammal (including humans), by outsmarting the blood-brain barrier, which functions as a firewall to isolate and protect the brain from any unwanted influences. Once cats are infected, they then dispel this microorganism in their excrement. ... In toxoplasma's ideal world, cats excrete the parasite, and rodents subsequently ingest it. The parasite then forms round cysts throughout the rodent's body, in particular, its brain. A cat in turn eats the infected rodent. The ingested cysts reproduce in the cat's gastrointestinal tract, the cat sheds newly hatched parasites in its feces, and the cycle of life continues. ... Under normal circumstances, a pathogen from an infected rat would be very unlikely to wind up back in a cat because rodents instinctively avoid cats. But toxoplasma-infected rodents not only lose their instinctive fear of cats—they also begin to prefer areas that smell like cat urine. ... The cysts also boost activity in nearby brain circuits that

control sexual attraction, causing toxoplasma-infected rats that smell cats to become sexually attracted to them.[68]

Such intricate coordination among so many organisms and their instincts is astounding—and that a microbe is, essentially, orchestrating it all is equally humbling. That same microbe, *T. gondii*, was also recently found to influence hyena and wolf behavior. Wolves in Yellowstone National Park in the U.S. share territory with a large cat, the mountain lion (cougar, puma), and are susceptible to infection by contact with an infected mountain lion or its feces. Researchers Connor Meyer and colleagues found that toxoplasmosis in wolves alters their behavior similarly to its effect on mice—increasing their risk taking/ foolhardiness—making them 11 times more likely to leave the pack (males especially) and 46 times more likely to become pack leader.[69]

Human-microbiome interactions are being clarified so rapidly that I encourage you, dear reader, to update yourself on the latest findings, which may expand on or even contradict the studies cited here. The important point is that our microbes are more than just "digesters of food" or "a line of defense." They are to us as we are to Earth. I am the environment for my microbes, as Earth is my environment. If my internal microbes get out of balance, they can ruin their environment (me); vice versa, I can ruin their environment, for example, by eating too much or not enough of certain foods. Additionally, environmental microbes can infect me and ruin my inner microbes' environment. All these interactions get complicated quickly! Just as my immune system can eradicate invading microbes, Gaia can likely eradicate her microbes, and recently she has been eradicating us, ironically, by means of microbes (coronavirus). What can we learn about our relationship to our environment by learning about the relationship of our microbes to us, and vice versa?

By realizing that the microbiome interacts with us, that there is mutual influence, we can better see ourselves, as humans, in a different light, at different scales, and as a qualitatively different kind of being. Gastroenterologist Emeran Mayer says, "According to the new science of the microbiome, we humans are truly supraorganisms, composed of closely interconnected human and microbial components, which are inseparable and dependent on each other for survival."[70] The micro-organisms that are in/on us have their own form of agency, albeit different from ours, and each species has evolved and together we have co-evolved not only to respond to but also to manipulate our local environments in order to survive. Because our bodies are our microbes' local environment, their influence on us can be slight or profound. On the slight hand, just the presence or absence of a particular microbe could, for example, predispose one to depression, to craving certain foods, or to being un/able to digest certain foods. On the profound hand, "as the microbial component is so closely connected through a shared biological communication system to all the other microbiomes in the soil, the air, the oceans, and the microbes living in symbiosis with almost all other living creatures, we are closely and inextricably tied into the Earth's web of life."[71]

When we do not realize our inextricable ties into the web of life, we are essentially cutting off the left hand with the right hand. By extracting so much from Earth, we are vampirically sucking dry our own blood. Can you imagine your own body not realizing that the foot is connected to the thigh? You couldn't walk. Can you imagine what would happen if your lungs decided to go on strike? Or if certain rogue cells decided to start a new body of their own and began reproducing at a faster rate than your immune system could eliminate them?

Awareness of our interconnectedness does not imply that there is no strife, conflict, or struggle, that there is always harmony and peace. There's nuance to this. The body has ways to keep things in order, from apoptosis (programmed cell death) to autophagy (killing and recycling damaged cells) to immune responses that sometimes overreact. If resources are scarce, the body will plunder parts of itself to try to keep the whole going. It has built-in redundancies, particularly among the genes. These redundancies, combined with checks and balances and feedback loops, enable us to be antifragile to environmental challenges.

Unless hijacked, our bodies innately know how to build themselves, how to fix themselves, even how to restructure themselves toward wholeness (of

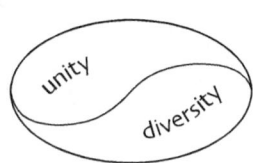

pattern). They produce exactly what is needed to grow an organ or to heal a wound; when healthy, they don't overproduce cells, although they might underproduce them if there are insufficient resources to build new cells.

When all the elements (parts and/or holons) are not functioning together smoothly, the whole organism doesn't function well. At the moment, the *Humanbody* does not seem to feel well—witness the levels of anxiety, depression, addiction, and chronic diseases. Perhaps Gaia herself doesn't feel well either—witness the extreme weather, loss of biodiversity (redundancy), loss of glaciers, and warming and acidification of the oceans.

In fact, a group of scientists recently published a report stating that very conclusion: "If planet Earth just got an annual checkup, similar to a person's physical, 'our doctor would say that the Earth is really quite sick right now and it is sick in terms of many different areas or systems and this sickness is also affecting the people living on Earth,' Earth Commission co-chair Joyeeta Gupta, a professor of environment at the University of Amsterdam, said at a press conference." The report says that we are exceeding seven of eight planetary boundaries (climate, natural ecosystem area, ecosystem functional integrity, surface water, groundwater, nitrogen, phosphorus, and aerosols); the only one within limits is air pollution. Unlike previous scientific reports, this one also included consideration of environmental justice, which includes fairness between generations, between nations, and between species.[72]

Try to imagine the *Humanbody*, or better yet, a *Gaianbody* that functions as a whole, completely interconnected being, the way your body does. For the fun of this thought experiment, add another level to it: self/consciousness.

To explain the disconnection within the *Humanbody*, it could be argued that there has always been strife, war, humans killing other humans—our version of predator-prey power relations. That may or may not be true. Marija Gimbutas argues convincingly that a pre-patriarchal Old European indigenous society lived in relative peace until they were invaded by the more aggressive Kurgans (Proto-Indo-Europeans).[73]

Regardless of whether our ancestors were peaceful, the current situation has gone far beyond one tribe warring with another. It has even gone far beyond the world wars. We will always face challenges and death due to the randomness and chaos in our environment from natural disasters. However, the local fragilities of our ecosystems will continue to create long-term anti-fragility unless we push ourselves to the breaking point beyond which our already fragile systems cannot recover. That defines the metacrisis I mentioned at the beginning of this book, the perfect storm of crises that we continue to help create. This is where we have gotten to by failing to recognize and honor our symbiotic nature, our connectedness with each other and with all else on this third planet from our local sun.

In contrast, human communities that do live in conscious connection with their environment readily perceive the symbiotic interdependencies among their cohabitants. In Australia, where the disconnected simply see wild nature, local Aborigines see how the ecosystem is out of balance. Tyson Yunkaporta explains, for example, how he "sees the termite mounds, oversized now because the place is out of balance and sick, although to tourists taking photos it looks like untouched wilderness. The parrots that used to lay their eggs in the mounds are gone now, because the moths that used to lay their eggs in the same nest are gone as well. They used to hatch at the same time, and the larvae would eat the waste of the baby parrots. After the moths were wiped out by cane toads, all the newly hatched parrots drowned in their own shit."[74] Such interdependent ecosystems are collapsing all over, not just in Australia.

A web with more strands will withstand more stress; one with fewer strands, or a network with fewer connections, is more fragile. Although our ecosystems are losing species, thus our webs are losing strands and connections, it is not known whether this fragility will lead to global civilizational collapse or whether it is part of a transformative process, as when the caterpillar in its chrysalis turns into a sticky mess of imaginal cells that reform themselves into a butterfly. It is my intention to help us accomplish the latter, to transform ourselves from separate beings, separate species living on a cooling rock orbiting through spacetime into a self-aware planetary being that is up to something in the universe. I'm not sure what we might be up to, but it'll probably be grander than my imagination can currently conjure.

Human/Gaian Communication

Suppose that endosymbiosis does occur and the *Humanbody* becomes a commensal or even a mutualist with the *Gaianbody*. Might we discover how to communicate directly with our own microbes and, similarly, with our host, Gaia? If we humans function as a type of higher-complexity microbe on the surface of Earth, then by revising our activities from being a user and exploiter of Earth and other life forms to being a symbiont, what might be possible? Might that upgrade our level of consciousness, enabling us to connect directly to Gaia's consciousness such that, like the microbes that affect our choices, we could influence the accomplishments of Gaia?[75] By understanding ourselves and our interrelationships this way, we might be able to end the Anthropocene and initiate the Symbiocene, the idea of ecophilosopher Glenn A. Albrecht. In the Symbiocene Albrecht imagines "human action, culture and enterprise will be exemplified by those cumulative types of relationships and attributes nurtured by humans that enhance mutual interdependence and mutual benefit for all living beings (desirable), all species (essential) and the health of all ecosystems (mandatory). Human development will consist of creative actions that use the very best of biomimicry together with other eco-industrial, eco-technological, eco-agricultural and eco-cultural innovation."[76]

Stop for a moment and breathe. That previous paragraph requires some rewiring of our assumptions. It requires us to consider that Earth is not a rock (with a thin layer of "life" on its "skin") hurtling through empty space. As microbes live on all our epithelial surfaces, we are like microbes or lice on the skin of Earth.[77] If Earth is an organism, then how many greater forms of organisms might there be? Is our solar system an organism? Our galaxy? The universe? Its biotic structure suggests that it might be.[78]

If each of us is a self-conscious symbiont of a supraconscious organism, what, if anything, would happen to personal agency? Might I become aware not only of my own will but of a will that is beyond mine, into which mine can flow (or not, assuming that there is still free will)? What would that be like? Perhaps like being a cell in a finger getting the signal (from the supra-conscious organism of which you are a part) that the skin on the nose itches. A response is coordinated automatically through the hand and the arm to get you and your other finger-cell buddies, with the help of arm cells, over to the nose to scratch it. And it all happens seemingly effortlessly, through different communication systems (e.g., the nervous and endocrine systems, perhaps even electrical or field dynamics[79]). Is something like this happening, for example, in our responses to natural disasters? Are we being called, individually and together, to respond to Gaia's itches, to the *Gaianbody's* infections?

What can this *Humanbody* co-creating with the *Gaianbody* accomplish by you accomplishing your part and everybody else, all the other cells or microbes, accomplishing theirs? To be clear, the *Gaianbody* needs each of us in our exquisite uniqueness to be who we are. The unity is in the diversity.[80]

If we want to participate with Gaia in her grand adventure, then we might need to be able to communicate with the trees and the birds and the microbes and the rest of Gaia's symbionts.[81] Although some indigenous cultures never lost the ability to communicate with other aspects of Nature, we Westerners are beginning to understand, in a limited, scientific way, how trees communicate with each other—through mycelial networks among their roots, through chemicals released into the air, and perhaps other ways.[82] We are still trying to understand the communication of dolphins, whales, cephalopods, and other highly intelligent species. Perhaps if we could communicate, we could work together to heal, so as to unite endosymbiotically. Before we can get to this place of integration, we need to expand our ways of being in "communication" with one another. I put the word "communication" in quotes because it is so much more than the external type of linguistic smoke signals that we currently send to each other through writing and speaking. It is more like a communication that involves *co-feeling from the inside*.

Sometimes that kind of co-feeling communication happens when you're in love and in such resonance with your beloved that you can sense her/his/

their thoughts and feelings. Have you felt those moments of oneness with another? Do we ALL need to be in that state of profound being-in-love-with in order to attain the kind of internal communication that my body's cells and microbiome have with one another? This type of love isn't necessarily personal, nor is it the feeling state caused by a rush of oxytocin; rather, it is *the place you come from.*

Let's try it and see what happens.

Interlude
A Comparison of Stories—Ancient and Modern

In Chapter 5, I asked "is it possible to tell a radically new story using the language structures of the old story—not just the old language (the words or types of words themselves) but the old language structures (the way language is organized by culture, by logic, even by the rules of grammar)?" You probably intuited that I think the answer to that is "no." Since we have not yet devised new language structures, let's look at how new stories can be told using new words and new types of words. The following stories also illustrate a shift from mythic to mental consciousness structures. Someone operating from a mythic consciousness structure might indeed say that the second story is radically new. Similarly, what would constitute a radically new type of story to someone operating within the mental structure of consciousness?

First, let's look at a very old Arabic story, a myth from perhaps the 8th or 9th century, called the Vision of Arisleus.[83]

> There is a king who lives at the bottom of the sea. His kingdom is not prospering; that is, nothing new is being created, only the same old things, because like only mates with like. The king calls on the philosopher Arisleus to help him. Arisleus descends to the bottom of the sea and sizes up the situation. He tells the king that for his kingdom to prosper, like needs to mate with unlike. Specifically, Arisleus tells the king that his children, his son Gabricus and daughter Beya, who were borne of the king's brain, need to be mated. They comply, and in the act of mating, Beya's immense love for her brother engulfs him completely into herself, which dissolves him. The king punishes Arisleus for killing his son by imprisoning Arisleus in a

triple glass house (an alchemical retort) where he is tortured and subjected to intense heat. In a dream, his teacher, Pythagoras, sends a disciple of his to bring Gabricus back to life with miraculous food of life from the tree of immortality.

This story uses characters, plot, and symbolism to convey ideas that extend beyond the seemingly simple action of the story. As a myth, everything in the story stands for something else. Children borne of the brain clearly represent ideas. But what kind of ideas? Their names give us a clue. "Gabricus" sounds like the Arabic word for sulfur, and "Beya" means white. In an alchemical interpretation of this myth, Gabricus and Beya represent sulfur and mercury, respectively. Thus, Gabricus/sulfur mating with Beya/mercury tells us that we must bring our pure passion and intention together with heat to create something new, namely, a new way of understanding within oneself by uniting our own (psychological) opposites.

The historian Thomas Willard puts that story into a larger alchemical context: "Beya and Gabricus disappear after they are united in the alchemical vessel, or rather they are assimilated into the larger pair of Sol and Luna, Sun and Moon."[84] The transformation that they undergo is integrated into the processes of life and death. Willard shows us a fractal pattern or synecdoche wherein what happens on one scale (micro) blends into and also happens on a larger scale (macro).

Beya engulfs Gabricus, seemingly killing him. However, he is merely "dissolved." This corresponds to the alchemical transformation *solutio*. Think of what happens when you dissolve salt or sugar in water. It seems to disappear, but it has transformed the taste and properties of the water. Thus, it turns out that Gabricus is not dead but transformed. His old boundaries have dissolved. He is within Beya, and he is brought back to life by food from the tree of immortality. He dissolved but has been reconstituted as part of a greater whole that enables him to be reborn and renewed. Does that sound familiar?

In Chapter 7, the story of Gabricus and Beya was told using scientific language ("endosymbiosis") rather than mythic language ("mating" and "engulfed"). It is the same story of one being becoming part of another and hence (symbolically) dying in the process but simultaneously continuing the expansion of life, of creativity, within ever-more-encompassing beings or structures in the universe. In the 9th century, the story was told using allegorical images of personal transformation. Were the alchemists attempting to bring about in themselves a similar uniting of opposites resulting in subsuming themselves within Mercurius/Beya, who represents the unconscious engulfed by Cosmic Love, in order to be reborn within a greater being?

In the 21st century we tell a similar story using scientific explanations for why mitochondria are within our cells and other microbes are within our bodies, and perhaps even why we are here on Earth and why Earth is in this solar system, in this "arm" of the galaxy, and in the universe. What might our stories be like in another thousand years or after another structure of consciousness has emerged? Will we tell this story using new language, perhaps a more integral vocabulary? Or will we have developed a new structure for language so that we can tell a radically new story? More important, will our love for our brothers and sisters, the cohabitants of Gaia, be equal to Beya's?

8

If Only the Ouroboros Had Spoken to Eve

Similarly, he [David Bohm] believes that dividing the universe up into living and nonliving things also has no meaning. Animate and inanimate matter are inseparately woven, and life, too, is enfolded throughout the totality of the universe. Even a rock is in some way alive, says Bohm, for life and intelligence are present not only in all of matter, but in "energy," "space," "time," "the fabric of the entire universe," and everything else we abstract out of the holomovement and mistakenly view as separate things. The idea that consciousness and life (and indeed all things) are ensembles enfolded throughout the universe has an equally dazzling flip side. Just as every portion of a hologram contains the image of the whole, every portion of the universe enfolds the whole.[85]
—Michael Talbot

The ancient worldwide symbol of the ouroboros depicts many notions of wholeness: primordial unity, the end flowing into the beginning, the alpha meeting the omega, cycles that start over again and again. From its early symbolism of the oneness of Allness, it later acquired, for alchemists especially, a more paradoxical nuance: the snake, by eating its own tail, kills itself to survive. The psychological implications of doing that are distressing, from burying memories of trauma to splitting off parts of yourself as ways that we "kill" ourselves to survive what, at the time, feels like unbearable pain. I have seen such self-annihilation in the faces of people riding the subway to work. They looked dead inside, like zombies, on their way to a job that enables them to pay for their food and shelter but gives them no joy. It took one to know one.

Collectively, we are eating our own tail in the numerous ways we enact the Tragedy of the Commons,[86] for example, when we consume more resources than we can replenish thereby living out an ouroboric tale that ends with civilizational collapse.[87] In the past, only specific civilizations in localized areas, such as Mesoamerica and ancient Rome, collapsed completely. Since then, we have weakened redundancies in our ecosystems not only by reducing their size but also by reducing the diversity of species. And given our economic, ecological, and political interdependencies, which span multiple scales and levels, the next civilizational collapse will likely be global. The supply-chain issues resulting from the coronavirus pandemic gave us a small taste of what could come.

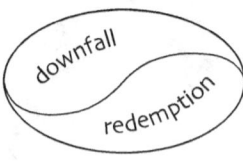

In true ouroboric fashion, our global connectedness could be our downfall and/or our redemption. For global connectedness to be our downfall, we would need to continue to believe in our separateness while simultaneously creating a material infrastructure that binds us together for the supply of goods and services. If we retain such a materialist worldview, we could easily collapse modern civilization, especially if we do not ensure that it is sufficiently anti-fragile, a concept introduced by Nassim Nicholas Taleb. *Antifragility* refers to the ability of a system to improve or get stronger as a result of environmental volatility.[88] If our global systems are fragile, one rogue player could literally or metaphorically blow up the whole Earth. Conversely, our inherent inter-connectedness at all levels and scales from the quantum to the microbial to the economic to the spiritual could redeem us by fostering the emergence of a new type of supraorganism.

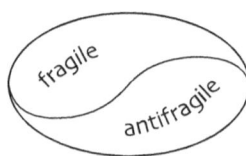

Centuries ago, when scientists realized that Earth was indeed round rather than flat, people's lives did not change much. Even today, when I walk to the store or ride my bike, I operate in such a confined space on the surface of the globe that, apart from the hills, it seems flat. I don't have to account for Earth's curvature when I plan my daily activities.

What did our awareness of the roundness of Earth open up for us? I think that our ability to see the whole darn thing in the famous Earthrise photo taken from the Moon woke us from going further down the rabbit hole of greater fragmentation. It returned those of us who had gotten lost in the funhouse of "separateness" back to remembering our interconnectedness. We could no longer conveniently forget where the polluted water that we dump into the rivers goes. It doesn't magically go away—out of sight, out of mind.

It all stays here in Gaia's circulatory system. To keep her, and us, healthy, we *do* need to bother with it. The atmosphere that encircles and protects Earth isn't demarcated by national borders; pollution from one place travels around the globe. In addition to our planetary consciousness, what will our awareness of our oneness as a being-in-becoming open up for us?

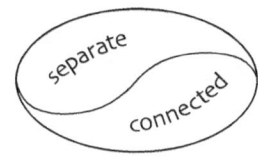

Many teachers over many centuries have incarnated to show us how to develop mindfulness practices, intuition, flow states, and other ways of inter-being. Those practices can help one develop ways to become aware of wholeness. My small contribution (recall the crystal cube) involves language, or more specifically, the language–consciousness relationship. Usually an experience of oneness is considered beyond language, because language distinguishes and categorizes. My question is how can a new form of language foster a more-whole expression of wholeness?

To find a way to speak *from* wholeness (not just *about* wholeness), we can entertain different metaphors for wholeness. Previously, I used the metaphor of a body, as in a human body or the body of Gaia. Now, let's use the metaphor of a diamond. Consider the shape of a cut diamond with its many facets, each edge of a facet a boundary between two adjacent facets. Let each facet represent a "separate" consciousness (in the old paradigm). If I imagine myself as one facet and you as another facet, we might be connected along an edge or two, for example, by being neighbors, relatives, friends, or colleagues. Given our proximity or similarity, I am often able to "see things from your perspective." However, if I get stuck in my own perspective and can't see the perspectives of others, that is a state I call "facet consciousness." On the other side of the diamond there are facets that I am not connected to by any edge. They seem completely separate from me—that is, if I stay in facet consciousness. However, the diamond is not simply a collection of facets; it is that (material) by which the facets can and do exist. The diamond is whole, and the facets are not and cannot be separate from the diamond. If I switch from facet consciousness to "diamond consciousness," that is, by knowing myself as the diamond rather than as a mere facet, then I can see that facet consciousness is simply a limited way to perceive. By knowing myself to be the diamond, I can choose to

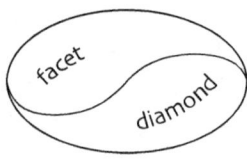

perceive through a particular facet or another, if I want to. I can also choose to ware myself as the whole diamond.[89] Knowing oneself as the diamond can't be achieved intellectually; it occurs as an "aha moment" of realization. It is not mental, it is experiential.

The psychoanalyst Antonino Ferro described the following dream of a client of his. It shows a transition from facet consciousness to diamond consciousness, albeit using different language:

> There followed a dream in which the patient [Stefano] had three enormous baskets of plants; he had a place for two of them, but not for the third, which was different. It was easy to put it to him that he might be thinking of aspects of himself as things that could be integrated even if there was not a space for them all.
>
> Next day he needed to communicate something to me urgently: for the first time he had discovered—in an underground railway carriage—that depth, height and thickness existed. Having previously lived in a totally flat world, he was now bowled over by this discovery, whereby he now saw the whole world differently, with a space, depth and three-dimensionality he had not known existed. I immediately thought of Edwin Abbott's *Flatland* (1899), a fine tale of a two-dimensional world, and told him that he seemed to have moved on from plane geometry to its three-dimensional, or "solid," counterpart. Stefano went on to say that the many surfaces of himself could now link up with each other and acquire the dimension of thickness; previously he had always thought of himself in either one way or another or yet in another. I told him that, now, thickness and depth belonged to him too and to his internal world—so he could think of himself as a boarding-house that could "accommodate" the various parts of himself, including those he feared and despised most.[90]

The image in the dream is holographic, as Talbot described in the opening quote for this chapter. There are facets of oneself as well as oneself as facet that can be integrated via diamondness.

Ferro perhaps did not recognize the full significance of the underground railway carriage: in addition to its obvious symbolism of the unconscious, which the dreamer has integrated with consciousness, the underground railway is how slaves in the United States were conveyed from the South to the free states of the North. I interpret that to mean that integration of facets and of consciousness with the unconscious into wholeness/diamond consciousness also brings with it a kind of freedom. If you know yourself to be whole and to be able to direct your consciousness to any seeming "part" of the whole, then you would be able to bring to consciousness different, even opposing, perspectives. You might not polarize yourself against another person or another group, because you, via diamond consciousness of your implicit connectedness, know that you are not separate from them.

By seeing through facet consciousness to diamond consciousness, we are better able to question our assumptions. By seeing the world through a different perspective, we are better able to understand the different ways in which different cultures and individuals perceive "reality." By seeing from a different point of view, in reality or through the imagination, we enter a multidimensional reality that can contain all our limited perspectives.

Consider Earth as the diamond, for instance. What are her facets? We could define Earth's facets in many different ways—for example, according to geographic "boundaries" such as biomes or watersheds, cultural "boundaries" by which people of one place differentiate themselves from people of another place, but I would caution against using artificial boundaries, such as those of nation-states. They are not intrinsically of Earth. Earth, as an embodiment of diamond-consciousness, connects us through her depth. She holds consciousness of her wholeness. Each of us, through our being Of Gaia, has access to Gaian diamond consciousness—if we connect through that form of consciousness rather than through facet-consciousness. A diamond can be seen through. We must cultivate an ability to see through Gaia, as we can see through a glass cube to the faces facing away from us. On a sphere, too, there are arcs arcing away from us, rivers running up and mountain peaks pointing down in the southern hemisphere, relative to my facet-perspective in the northern hemisphere. From Gaia's perspective, all mountains everywhere reach out from her center.

Let's also consider different scales of interconnectedness (Figure 6). As there are cycles of the seasons, there are also cycles of interconnectedness that one can traverse on the journey of becoming more whole. There is much to integrate at different scales and levels of organization. There is neither a single path nor a correct path, as long as the intent is to continue integrating more of what you consider not-you into who you are.

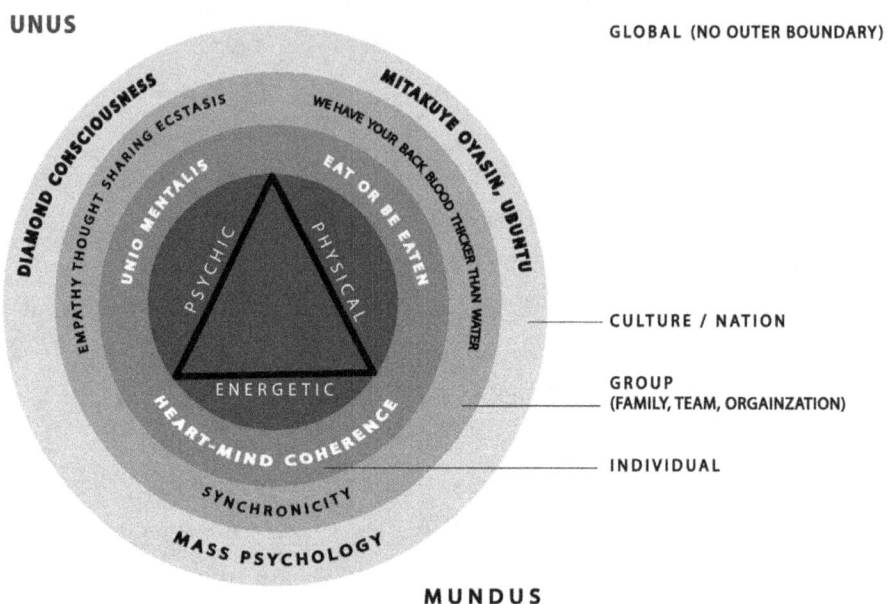

Figure 6. At different scales (individual, small group, and culture), physical, psychic, and energetic experiences manifest differently. The journey toward wholeness involves integrating them within oneself at all scales. The corresponding conjunctions (*unio mentalis*, *coniunctio oppositorum*, and *unus mundus*) are covered in more detail in Chapter 19.

Figure 6 shows, in a nonholographic way, the holographic replications of physical, energetic, and psychic experience that occur at different levels, from the individual to the all-encompassing. At the individual level, the physical manifestation of the first level of integration can be summarized as "eat or be eaten," and the energetic integration is heart-mind coherence. At the small-group level (relationship between oneself and at least one other), the physical manifestation of integration can be expressed as "blood is thicker than water" or "we have your back." At this level, the individual contributes to the group, and the group protects the individual. The energetic manifestation at this level occurs in the form of synchronicity, that is, meaningful coincidence through an acausal connecting principle. At the level of culture or nation, the physical manifestation of integration can be expressed as the African concept (Zulu, Xhola, and other languages) *Ubuntu* (I am because we are) or the Lakota concept *mitakuye oyasin* (all my relations). Energetically, we see evidence of mass psychology at this level, whether in positive forms, such as patriotic unity, or negative forms, such as fear-based warmongering. Fourth is the level of the *unus mundus*, the ground of possibility from which the actuality of all the previous levels spring. At this level, physical, energetic, and psychic manifestations merge, so it is not possible to say anything specific about each.

How do we speak *from* the perspective of ongoingly integrating (at whatever level), that is, from the perspective of the inherently paradoxical beings that we are?

Let's imagine ways to do that.

If I Am You and You Are Me, Then Who Are We?

9

I first became interested in language through the exploration of questions. I was fascinated by how we could know enough about what we don't know to ask a question about it. Then, if someone answers the question, how do we know that they answered it sufficiently? Do we have epistemic itches that go away when scratched by accurate answers? I was also curious about why some people ask a lot of questions (ahem) and why some people do not.

Next, my curiosity about language shifted to dualities, such as the curious nature of light as both a wave and a particle. Seeing the unity inherent in duality was like acquiring a new set of glasses through which to see the world. I started seeing both/and everywhere—nature and nurture, heart and mind, spirit and matter, and so on. I had an aha! moment in which I saw everything profoundly connected to everything—but that such oneness unfortunately could not be expressed using language. Nevertheless, I began to wonder how we could better express relationships of interdependent co-arising, like yin and yang, and how we could speak from the perspective of being all one while respecting our uniqueness and differences.

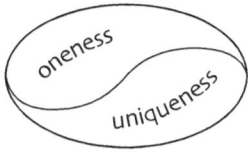

How can we formulate answers to questions about our assumptions if we use the same assumptions to ask the questions?

I began to see that I had a bias in my worldview: I had been trained to see the world through lenses of "either/or." As a result of my aha moment, I was starting to see through lenses of "both/and." For a while, though, I did not see how deeply engrained either/or thinking was for me, because I was still opposing "either/or" and "both/and" in an either/or manner, like this:

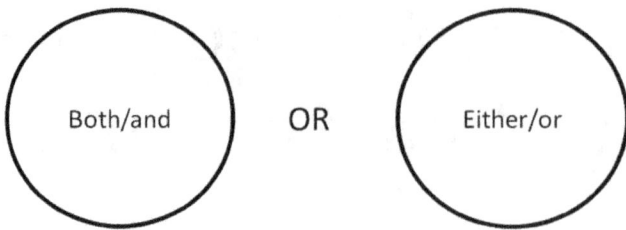

Not until I saw that either/or is actually a subset of both/and did I really understand the power of both/and thinking and how it could honor difference and distinction while also joining together, like this[91]

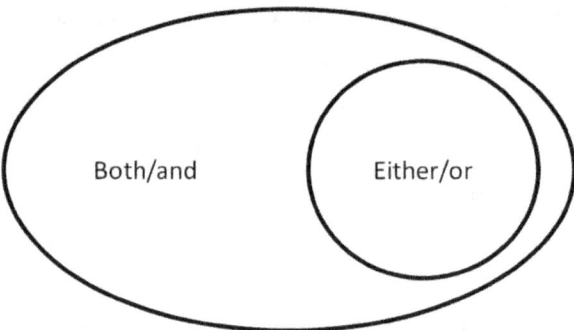

There are circumstances in which "either/or" is appropriate (e.g., I will buy this car or that car, but not both of them) but others where it leads to false dilemmas. For example: I have to stay in this job or get another one; you're either with us or against us; politician X criticized capitalism, so s/he must be a socialist. Especially with regard to people, the boundaries between such polarities can be rather murky. Given the complexities of intention, motivation, level of consciousness, and so on, from a both/and perspective, it seems impossible to ask an oversimplified question such as, "Is that person good or bad?" Rather, as Alexander Solzhenitsyn said, "The battleline between good and evil runs through the heart of every [hu]man."

If you are rightly wondering where neither/nor fits into that schema, to me, neither/nor represents the void, the absence of anything from which something can emerge. Hence it is the ground, the context, the potentiality from which all/and and both/and spring and from which either/or then differentiates what has sprung. Perhaps it is like David Bohm's notion of the implicate order—a source of all possibilities before they have become actualities. Of course, absence and presence are also interdependent and latent in neither/nor.

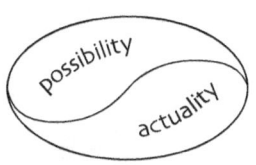

Like the beams of a house that hold it up but are hidden behind walls or under shingles, logic is an invisible architecture. Because very few of us are taught logic explicitly, we "see" the words we use more clearly than we "see" the logic we use. Logic is, however, a key structural element of language, and because I suggest that language structure needs to change, logic is an area ripe for innovation. Although our logic, from Aristotle through the modern era, has concentrated on "either/or," Indian logic acknowledges all four possibilities: something is the case, something is not the case, something both is and is not the case, and something neither is nor is not the case. Although logician Graham Priest has shown how Western logic has indeed acknowledged more than just "either/or,"[92] those ideas have not yet become prominent in our culture. Priest writes about the cutting edge of new forms of logic that allow for more expansive thoughtforms.[93] Bringing into being a new form or structure for language would involve bringing new logic(s) to fruition.

How, though, do we teach both/and thinking to young children? That's when the principles of logic get conveyed, albeit indirectly—in those early games and exercises. In order to teach children to think using both/and, we first need to recognize all the ways in which each of us embodies both/and. Barry Johnson, in his recent book *And: Making a Difference by Leveraging Polarity, Paradox or Dilemma*, describes the extent to which we live within such polarities and they live in us.[94] For example, we must breathe in and breathe out; we must be active and we must rest. Too much of one without the other will lead to ill health or death. Many aspects of life operate within interconnected polarities. From the physiological level (inhaling and exhaling) to the ego level (balancing caring for self and caring for others) to the cultural level (balancing spiritual issues and material issues), humans and the organizations we have created function within polarities. Johnson not only shows us the many layers of both/and within which we live, he also provides a great way to manage them by elaborating the upsides and the downsides;

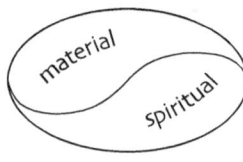

assessing how a given polarity is functioning in your life, in your business, and in society; and developing pathways to shift from the downside of one pole to the upside of its opposite, then manage both appropriately to prevent them from becoming overly imbalanced in the future. There is no stasis in managing polarities; it is always a dynamic balancing act.

Although we are both material and spiritual beings, in typical either/or fashion our scientific culture has tended for the past few centuries to emphasize the material part, separating that from the spiritual part. Although turf wars between science and religion are not as fraught as they have been in the past, the prevailing paradigm in science still mostly considers humans to be first and foremost a body that operates as machines do (although that is changing in some quarters). In many fields, discussion of soul, spirit, or psyche immediately discredits you. Hence, you can imagine my shock when I started reading physicists who claimed that matter might not be most primary[95] but that consciousness might be more primary. Regardless of the implicit prohibitions against such ideas, I realized that such scientists were having difficulty advancing that notion because of how the English language is structured based on assumptions of either/or. Combined with ingrained beliefs that matter is primary, scientists and ordinary people struggle to speak from the perspective that consciousness interpenetrates or is both/and with matter. One way that the English language "assumes" that matter is primary is its noun heaviness. Compared with some indigenous languages, English emphasizes the "thingness" of the world rather than its "processes" and consequently turns many ontological processes and even abstractions into linguistic things.[96]

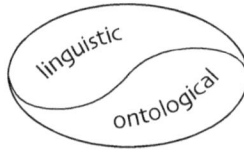

Within language itself there is a polarity of separateness and connectedness. On one hand, language separates by drawing distinctions, while at the same time meaning is created by connecting strings of words. Connecting consciousness and matter by saying "consciousness interpenetrates matter" still keeps them separate while joining them through a bridge word. What if we had a direct way to express their interpenetration?

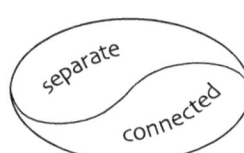

To that end, how might we take Barry Johnson's work a step further and build such polarities into a *new type of concept*, so that we can automatically activate such interdependencies in our minds as distinct-but-not-separate ideas? Specifically, how could we use the Klein bottle to help us think about different types of "linguistic containers" that can hold both/and and all/and? First, thinking of words as linguistic containers activates a prevailing metaphor that WORDS ARE VESSELS, containers for meaning, that enable the speaker to convey ideas to others (there's another metaphor—LANGUAGE IS A CONDUIT; see Chapter 13 for more about the metaphoric aspects of language and thought). I suggest new types of concepts because simply adding neologisms, new alphabetic words, to convey our profound interconnectedness is like pouring new wine into old bottles. New words for radically new types of concepts will fail to do justice to the new concepts, because we will fit them into the old structures of language (discussed in more detail in Chapter 16). I am suggesting instead that we develop new types of "containers" for these new types of paradoxical concepts. How will they look and function? Could we develop new types of graphically based glyphs that activate right brain or pattern-recognition activities? We will need to think about this topic more thoroughly, so we will return to these questions in Chapter 19.

Table 1 shows the metaphoric differences between the either/or mindset on the left and the both/and mindset on the right, which can be extended to an all/and mindset.

Table 1. Linguistic Containers: Wine Bottles vs. Klein Bottles

Wine bottle	Klein bottle
Either/or mindset	Both/and mindset
Inside vs. outside	Inside and outside are a continuum; one merges into the other
Holds and contains something	Embodies the notions of contained and uncontained
Static unity	Dynamic, interpenetrating unity
Words used to convey separateness and distinctions	Glyphs/graphics used to convey interconnectedness, process, paradox, and unity

I am proposing that we develop ways to shift current structures of language (left column) to structures that embody the right column. Such a project will not happen overnight, maybe not in my lifetime. This is not like inventing a new conlang. It will not be plug-and-play or a variant of emojis. Inventing a new type of language—one with a new structure—will involve altering some very deeply held beliefs and assumptions about the world and about language and logic.

When medieval cathedrals were designed, the architects, masons, and stone carvers had to trust that their vision would be realized, eventually, by generations not yet born. Unfortunately, I'm not sure we have hundreds of years to realize this vision for language.

Applying Language to a Both-All/And Mindset

As you probably noticed in the discussion of the microbiome at one scale and Gaia as a supraorganism at another scale in Chapter 7, the language for discussing the relationships among wholes within wholes within wholes is not well developed in English. What might have seemed like simple either/or distinctions between separate objects turn out to be not so simple. Although microbiome researchers are actively looking at microbiomes from a wholistic, ecological, and dynamic perspective,[97] many still do so from within a paradigm that largely prioritizes either/or, linearly causal, mechanistic thinking. When considering the microbiome or Gaia, what is inside and what is outside, what is self and what is other, no longer seem so cut and dried. To those in the old paradigm, our microbes (except, of course, those on the skin) are little Others "in there," and to our microbes, perhaps we are "out there," their environment or their place, locally as well as like a distant galaxy or even another dimension. Are they aware of or even tuned in to our consciousness field?

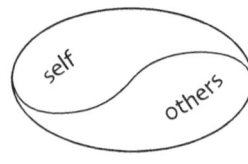

We humans became who we are through a long process by which some of those bacteria and viruses and spirochetes were symbiotically incorporated by many iterations of beings over billions of years. The result is that my microbiome is as much me as my cells are. Who am I, then, if I consist of millions of other beings? And who am I among gazillions of other beings in, on, and surrounding Gaia who are part of that holobiont known as the Milky Way, and so on, perhaps ad infinitum?

Just as our environment contains a multitude of organisms—plants, animals, insects, microbes, and so on—that exist in specific ecological balance, the multitude of organisms in our *in-vironment* also exists in specific ecological relation to us, their host, as well as to each other. Our microbiota have a complex system of predator-prey relations, food-chain hierarchies, governing bodies, opportunistic invaders, and defenders.[98] Thus, to me the microbiome-self-Gaia-space relationships seem Kleinian.

The Klein bottle gives us a way of thinking about the various combinations of inside and outside that comprise the holobiont. Just as the Klein bottle is a unified and dynamic example of inside-being/becoming-outside, the host-microbiome relations reflect a range of inside-outside combinations. There are some relationships that remain outside-outside (such as microbes in the sand when I walk on the beach), some that span outside-inside (as when I am infected by a bacterium or virus), some that traverse from inside to outside (as with sneezing or in excrement), and some that remain inside-inside (such as our mitochondria). The Klein bottle provides a way to envision holobionts that encompasses more than simplistic notions of Inside and Outside. Indeed, nested or otherwise interconnected Klein bottles, such as the HyperKlein bottle noted by polymath Diego Lucio Rapoport and modeled by artist Alan Bennett, exemplify such relations.[99]

A challenge to languaging the interactions of environment-host-microbe systems is that the microbes, the host, and the host's environment are at different scales and levels, and they are not part-whole perspectives (as in a cell-organism system) but thoroughly integrated whole-whole perspectives. Systems biologist Denis Noble differentiates scale and level this way: "Scale is a matter only of extension, i.e., how large a part of nature is considered. Level is a matter of organization, which could be a cell, an organ, an organism, a population and so on."[100] Microbes are whole organisms that can also comprise a part of a larger whole organism, which is part of an even larger whole (Gaia).

As such, they are inseparable. For some microbes, such as those in the gut, the human body constitutes their entire environment (with our environment going through a process of metabolism before it becomes their environment). For others, such as those in the mouth or on the skin, the body is only part of their environment, because our environment, such as our air and water and the microbes in them, is also theirs. It is also necessary therefore to consider how the physiology of the host or the pollutants in the host's environment influence whether a particular microbe is beneficial, pathogenic, or neutral. When this entire picture is accounted for, such fundamental distinctions between pathogen and commensal might have fuzzier boundaries than previously assumed.

Consider the complexity that could ensue: a particular species of microbe in a healthy host might be a commensal, but it might become pathogenic in an unhealthy host or in a local environment lacking its usual community of other microbes. That is one form of dysbiosis. Consider also this type of complexity: a microbe could be pathogenic on initial exposure but initiate an immune response that protects the host against other microbes. It is both harmful and beneficial, albeit not simultaneously.[101]

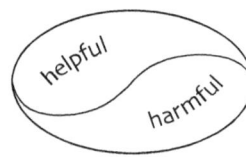

If we look at the microbiome only from a narrow perspective—as microbe and host and not as holobiont—then we run the risk of ignoring their animacy, even if it is a different, collective, instinctual form of animacy for which we have few words in English. Hence, it is important to be able to take the microbes' and/or Gaia's perspective, just as we can take our neighbor's perspective or our boss's perspective. If we can look at the system in question—such as our human body or the body of another life form—from the microbes' perspective, we will see an evolved organism fulfilling a role in/for a larger organism, exerting agency to survive, just as we do on the organism called Gaia. To do that effectively, Stephan Harding suggests that it might be necessary to personify the microbes,[102] that is, treat them as some*ones* rather than some*things*. Unlike anthropomorphizing, whereby we project human characteristics onto other species, personification would essentially give them their own *type* of personhood (while fully knowing that they are not human persons), which could engender a greater level of relatedness between humans and nonhuman lifeforms.[103] They would no longer be seen as strictly "other" or as "it." Such personification has been anathema in science. However, it might enable us to do biological science from a radically different paradigm. Harding suggests that "we must keep alive and nurture a sense of the 'otherness' of whatever phenomenon we might be considering, allowing a strange kind of intimacy to develop in which the urge to control is replaced by a quickening awe at the astonishing intelligence that lies at the heart of all beings. We must oppose the tendency of conventional science to de-personalise the world and hence to control it."[104]

Thanks to the research on the microbiome, we can see that human beings (as well as other organisms) are "one that is many" or "a me that's a we." A type of binocular vision is required, in which the one (or self) can be seen clearly and the many (such as the microbiome) can simultaneously be seen clearly. This gives us a new kind of "depth perception"—the perception of the depth of reality—allowing us to see that there are more levels contained within any given level, as in a fractal. The "others" (microbes) within one's self both enable the self to be and are "selves" in their own right. To put this binocular perspective into language in a way that is widely communicable will be a major advance.

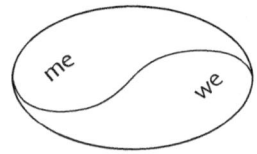

Figure 7 shows **pluritatis**, a glyph I invented that could mean "the one that is many/the many that are one" or a process by which one becomes many which then become one. This could be interpreted literally or metaphorically and can occur at macro or micro levels. At a macro level, for example, the biological process of seeding involves one plant creating many potential replicas of itself, each of which becomes one plant that creates many more replicas, and so on. At the micro level, in the suprachiasmatic nucleus, the main biologic clock that regulates circadian rhythms in the brain, as well as in cells in peripheral tissues, various genes (e.g., *Period, Clock, Cryptochrome,* and others) orchestrate the production of proteins that are released into the cell's cytoplasm, where they clump together to form complexes. Perhaps when a saturation point is reached or when a light-intensity signal from the eye reaches the cell, the protein complexes move into the cell nucleus and there

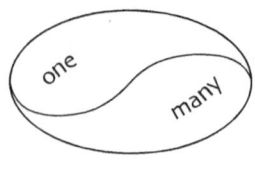

inhibit (turn off) the gene(s) that created them (the reason they translocate to the nucleus is not known yet). The proteins are cleared from the cell, and the process starts over, with 24-hour regularity.[105]

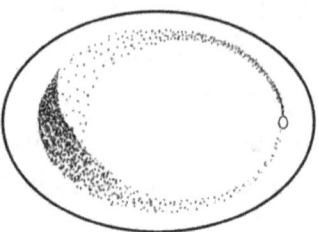

Figure 7. Glyph for **pluritatis**, indicating the paradox that many are/become one and one is/becomes many. It shows the many congealing into a point of emptiness, and the point expanding into multiplicity (as a representation of allness). This glyph could be marked somehow to indicate, for example, that an individual is a vessel for soul, and soul is a vessel for individuals. This kind of representation of all/and combines levels (individual, soul) and categories (physical beings, nonphysical being).

As I mentioned earlier, pluritatis and the other glyphs presented here are proposed as examples of new types of elements of language that we could begin to tinker with. They are not intended to be a fully realized conlang, just initial forays into showing new structures for language, particularly structures that embody paradox. This one shows a way to embody both polarities or a way to show dynamism between polarities by combining both levels and categories. Such glyphs obviously would not function in the syntax of a sentence as ordinary words do, and they even require a different kind of logic, one that can handle the simultaneity of opposites.[106] Because this type of glyph combines both levels and categories, it could be useful for signifying human/microbiome, human/Gaian, and microbial/Gaian relationships, among others.

One of my key reasons for proposing such glyphs is so that both poles of a polarity are held in mind. Hence, it becomes impossible to think of one without regard to the other, thereby fostering not only binocular vision but also the perception and expression of the depth of reality. Instead of bridging separate concepts with connecting words, this is a way to integrate the concepts.

Humans have shed much blood fighting one another about whether to live with emphasis on individuals or on the collective. That is a false dichotomy.

Individual rights and responsibilities must be balanced with collective rights and responsibilities. And that balance must be dynamic, responsive to the immediate context as well as long-term contexts. It is time to stop arguing "either/or" for one idea or the other, as in capitalism or socialism. It is time to recognize the validity and necessity of balancing all the polarities we live within and that live within us. To that end, we need new linguistic structures that enable us to express such interdependencies and new cultural practices and structures that remind us of them. The three interrelated polarities in this paragraph can be visualized like this:

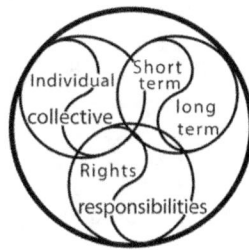

Figure 8. Example of a set of interconnected concepts.
Imagine them as interconnecting Klein bottles.

One culture that remembers its relationship with all life is the Kogi (or Kogui or Kagaba). I first heard about this culture in the late 1990s, in a documentary made by Alan Ereira for the BBC. I never forgot that documentary, and in 2017, I had the opportunity to travel with a group to Colombia to meet with some Kogi people. Rather, they wanted to meet with us, to convey that humanity's destructive ways—not living in harmony with Gaia—are causing dysbiosis in all of Gaia. We were not anthropologists, and we were there for only a few days, but the ways in which the Kogi still live in balance, not only with Gaia but also with one another, made a deep impression on me. We have much to learn from them. Let me give you a taste.

Wanted: Language Architect to Design Paradoxical Linguistic Spaces for Human Cogitation

10

> Architecture, when understood in the broadest sense, refers to structured spaces in which we evolve individually and collectively. These spaces can be easily accessible to our senses (building architecture, space occupation) or partially perceived (language, money, social conventions, time…). In the first case we will refer to visible architectures, in the second case we will refer to invisible architectures.[107]
> —Jean-François Noubel

Photo: Theresa Gasper

Architecture is one of the arts that structures our world by defining and delineating physical spaces for us. The architecture of buildings is intended to have specific effects on us. Cathedrals are designed to make us look up, sometimes to make us feel small and/or experience awe. Opera houses are designed so that you can hear voices even from far away (in the cheap seats). Imagine yourself inside each of the buildings in the pictures to the right—a Kogi hut in Colombia on the top and Schönbrunn Palace in Vienna on the bottom. How do you feel in each structure? What kind of "world" is created inside each building? Does it feel different to be within a circle compared to within a rectangle? I juxtaposed these two structures because the simplicity of the round mud-and-palm-leaf Kogi hut and the gilded exuberance of the palace do not, respectively, reflect simplicity and complexity of meaning imbued in each space. On the contrary, there is much symbolism and meaning built into the Kogi dwelling, with the roof structure representing their nine-level cosmology. Being in that womblike space reminded me of my place in the world, and, having a dirt floor, it put me in direct connection with Earth.

The Kogi people of Colombia were until recently one of the few cultures of South America that the European invaders had not conquered. They lived the last 500 years or so with little influence from the West. Consequently, they retained their ways of communicating with Earth, as well as their ability to see beyond mere vision and to keep Earth in balance through their rituals. That is, until recently. Earth is so out of balance that the Kogi have come out of their isolation to tell the rest of us that we need to stop destroying the ecological systems that sustain not only their lives but also all our lives.[108] They were warning us not to be the snake eating its own tail.

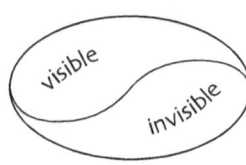

On the other hand, Schönbrunn, the summer residence of the head of the former Hapsburg Empire, was transformed from a hunting lodge into a palatial residence by Empress Maria Theresa. When I visited Schönbrunn, it felt designed not to remind us of our connectedness to Earth and divinity but to showcase the power of the Hapsburg Empire.[109] When you walk in the main gate, you are enclosed within a rectangular world. There are modest buildings to the left and right, where the servants used to live, and the main building (pictured) in front of you. In its many rectangular rooms, each decorated differently, ornamentation and façade seem to be what the designers thought was important.

An alchemical dilemma involves how to combine the circle and the square. We still confront this dilemma, albeit in different ways now. How do we live within circular and square worlds—symbolically speaking? I don't just mean the indigenous and the modern as represented by these examples, but also the emotional and the logical, the cyclical and the linear, the sensing and the intuiting, the secular and the sacred, and so on. How do we integrate seemingly incompatible worldviews?

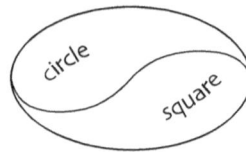

Environments are invisible. Their ground rules, pervasive structure, and overall patterns elude easy perception.
—Marshall McLuhan

The architecture of a building defines the space inside of which the inhabitants or users operate. The design of space can channel movement through narrow hallways or leave movement unrestricted in large open rooms and can encourage certain activities or discourage them. Obviously, walls serve as boundaries, but so can patterns on the floor. Windows can encourage or discourage interaction with the outside world. The visible architecture can influence you to feel many different ways—free or oppressed, comfortable or uncomfortable, pious or raucous.

If you attend a workshop and the chairs are arranged in neat rows and there is a podium in front, what expectations do you automatically have? If the chairs are arranged in a circle, with no podium, how do your expectations differ? What if you arrived at an event where the chairs are scattered haphazardly, facing all different directions? Would you feel and behave differently in those visible architectural contexts?

Invisible architectures, on the other hand, consist of ways that our world is structured for us and by us, except that the structure itself is not immediately visible in the way that walls and ceilings are. For example, you use money—whether bills and coins or electronic bits—but when you pay the store clerk you do not see the entire banking system that enables your transaction to occur. It is vast and global now. An invisible architecture might or might not be intentionally obscured. Social conventions, for example, structure our interactions and might initially have been created intentionally, but after generations of being repeated unquestioningly they have become unintentional invisible architecture.

As the arrangement of chairs in a room illustrates how visible architecture can influence our expectations and behavior, let us consider how language, at different levels, functions as an invisible architecture. A classroom set-up might influence the teacher to lecture at students who are "empty vessels to be filled" or to ask questions and allow students to grope through the darkness of unknowing into the light of knowing. Similarly, how does the structure of language affect the "space" in which we communicate? The structure of the discourse can, for example, affect the power dynamics involved in a linguistic exchange. Such invisible architectures reveal the power dynamics—who can and cannot speak at what times and what they can and cannot say. A Catholic mass is more highly structured than a Quaker meeting, which is more highly structured than a discussion with friends at a pub.

Another type of invisible architecture can be discerned in the structure of the language being used, regardless of the previous architectures—visible and invisible (and yet the visible and invisible architectures can be aligned or misaligned, promoting additive or canceling effects). Benjamin Lee Whorf proposed that "the structure of a human being's language influences the manner in which he understands reality and behaves with respect to it."[110] The structure of language, that is, its architecture, is not learned explicitly; rather, we learn the invisible architecture of language implicitly when we are taught which words can be used together, what can be or cannot be predicated to what. As children, our parents and teachers are quick to correct us when we make a mistake, e.g., by drawing a purple dog. Even though drawing might not necessarily involve language directly, we are still learning the categories and conventions by which language applies to the world—what can and cannot be said.

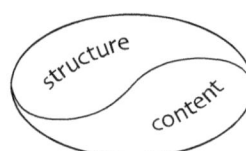

> Principles of predication are at the same time ontological principles.[111]
> —Ashok Gangadean

One way that language functions as an invisible architecture is through the principles of predication, i.e., which words can be put together to make sense, reflect the speaker's worldview, and provide a way to communicate that worldview. Except for the Introduction, almost everything I have written so far has conformed to ordinary principles of predication. However, if I started writing frothy sentences that wildly pulled red meanings from a blatant countryside, you might not understand me and might even question my sanity. I clearly did not obey the principles of predication in that prior sentence, and the result was nonsense—in this context of expository prose. However, the poet Dylan Thomas writes:

> Always when He, in country heaven
> (whom my heart hears),
> Crosses the breast of the praising east and kneels,
> Humble in all his planets,
> And weeps on the abasing crest, …[112]

He has stretched the structure of the language far beyond ordinary predication (hearts don't hear; the east does not have a breast). In doing so, he has made language's invisible architecture visible in order to eff about the ineffable.

Similarly, in science, sometimes great discoveries are made when one is willing to think beyond those same principles of predication. For example, the mathematician Georg Riemann and then Einstein made it possible for us to speak of space as curved. Until they showed how the idea of curved space made sense, it would have been nonsense to say that space was curved. Hence, "language is a paradigm generator—guiding us toward a particular world view, an epistemological framework—determining what and how we can learn [about] and know our world, an ontological map—it proscribes what we see as meaningful and significant to pursue as humans."[113]

Thus there can be vastly different worldviews not just between languages but also within a culture that speaks the same language. For example, George Lakoff in *The Political Mind* describes how different notions of family and the political worldviews that follow from them result in radical differences between conservatives and liberals.[114] In short, he says that conservatives have a Strict Father conceptual frame of the family and liberals have a Nurturing Parent conceptual frame. Those frames are composed of interconnected webs of beliefs, such as, for conservatives, the man is the head of the household, other family members must defer to him, and in return he keeps them safe. Others must obey his rules while also developing their own self-discipline and self-reliance and modeling themselves in his (or his wife's) image (daughters

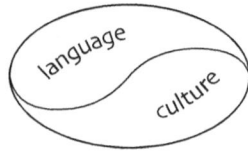

only). For liberals, the key value is empathy, and the web of beliefs consists of the following: the parents' role is to nurture their children and help them become responsible, caring, and equal to others. Those functioning in the liberal conceptual framework have a wider concept of family, which can include the whole world as brothers and sisters. This is how conservatives and liberals can use the same words pertaining to family and/or politics but have vastly different understandings of the meaning and implications of the words.

Even syntax can be considered an invisible structure of language. We can learn much from cultures that have languages with syntax rules different from those of English. In the United States, it is not a common phenomenon for native English-speaking people to inhabit different "language spaces." Learning a foreign language is no longer a requirement in many schools. Even when it was, the foreign language was often taught as if English were the model language and students must simply learn the other language's word for the English concept. Hence, in learning French or German, it wasn't necessary to get into the way German or French people structured their world based on the invisible architecture of *their* language. For example, it didn't dawn on me that the French understood the world differently than I did until I learned about reflexive verbs, where the direct object is the same as the subject of the sentence. For example, *s'enneuyer* means to be bored, but the reflexive part, the *se* contraction at the beginning, means that the verb is something you do to yourself (or something s/he does to her/himself, and so on); hence, *s'enneuyer* means to be boring to oneself. This syntax implies that you are responsible for your state of being bored! I find the French way of understanding boredom to be much less nihilistic than the English way. (English has a different way of conveying meaning similar to reflexivity, as in "she threw her*self* into a new hobby.") Reflexive verbs in many languages are not all as explicitly self-referential. Some reflexive verbs (in Spanish, for example, *caerse*, to fall down; *enfermarse*, to fall sick; and *morirse*, to die—note the "se" at the end of the verb) do not imply the same degree of personal agency. Reflexive verbs can serve many different functions, which perhaps have evolved differently in different languages.

In a German language space, the verb at the end of the sentence comes. One German-speaking friend of mine said this about how this structure differs from English: "English's subject-verb-object order results in sentences about who is doing what to whom, while German's subject-object-verb order is more concerned with who to whom is doing what. This syntactic difference is one reason why English-language natives tend to expect a sentence to express itself immediately, to state from the start what it's all about, whereas German-language natives are more conditioned to uncertainty, given that their full comprehension of a sentence must be suspended until its end. Because an English-language sentence usually announces its basic purpose at the beginning, it almost always can only amplify or modify that purpose and never, or rarely, upend it." Perhaps that is also why Wittgenstein suggested that "A serious and good philosophical work could be written consisting entirely of *jokes*." The punchline is at the end of the sentence, which is where the punch of a German sentence is found.

If No *Other,* Only Reflexive Verbs

11

In Chapter 3, I quoted Arjuna Ardagh and Alan Watts, both of whom proposed a radical shift in the nature of relationship—that there is and isn't an "other." What you perceive to be other than you, or not-I, actually is still you. Hence, a radical boundary redefinition is required. The boundaries that you think define and delimit where you are located, compared with where supposedly otherness (other things, other people, other places) is located, are permeable, fractal, fuzzy. We have seen too that the invisible structures of language help to keep boundaries in place.

Yet, when we look more deeply and consider the webs of connections at all scales from micro to macro, we see that there's more interdependence among beings at all levels than our language structures allow us to express. Perhaps new forms of expression are needed to convey the paradox of being distinct (you and Other) but not separate.

I'm writing this in downtown Chicago near "The Bean" (more precisely, *Cloud Gate,* pictured above), a kidney bean–shaped sculpture in Millennium Park. It's made of highly polished stainless steel so that it reflects like a mirror. Because it is shaped like a kidney bean, and the inside of it is funnel shaped, its reflections can be highly distorted. When people move toward it and away from it at certain spots, their reflection splits into two images; at other places, the two images combine into one. Given that space can be curved, this experience serves as an interesting model for perceptions of our own reality. How might our perceptions be distorted in ways we aren't aware of because we can't see the bigger "space" or the curvature (or some other quality) of the space we're made of? Perhaps meditating to become one with space will reveal such distortions (see Chapter 4 "Spaceisnotmadeofspace" for that meditation). Will we realize, for instance, that our opacity is a distortion or that what seem to be boundaries are not boundaries at all, just different configurations of space? In the way that squares on a chess board demarcate different spaces and define where one's chess piece can or cannot move, do we have ways of demarcating space—with color, with names, with other types of boundaries—that artificially limit our possibilities?

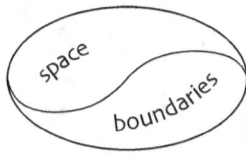

Might Ardagh and Watts be pointing to one such distortion, namely, our perception of ourselves as separate? If there is no Other, i.e., no you or it "out there," then that alters the whole nature of relationship, as there is only "me" (for each of us) and hence nothing "else" to be related to externally. Interesting paradox—if there is only "me" for me and only "me" (from your perspective) for you too. It reminds me of the quote that has been attributed to various thinkers: "God is a circle whose center is everywhere and circumference is nowhere."

If there is no you, no it, no them, then it makes no sense to say "I love you" or "I hate you." In those moments, the only reality is the loving or the hating that I am experiencing *of myself* (*as the illusion of both of us*). In this, we see that relationships are central to the way we've been communicating but not necessarily to the way communication might happen in a world where we understand the perception of separateness to be illusory. With no separation between the subject and object there is only the (reflexive) verb.

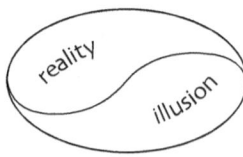

How does the experience of loving and hating compare to, say, murder? Does this argument for "no other" hold if someone kills another? In the world of mental explanation, one person ceases to exist. If we shift from self-other facet consciousness to diamond consciousness, and I kill you, I have just killed myself. Consider the level of self-destructiveness that is necessary for one person to kill another, that is, for one to kill oneself. If diamond consciousness includes all of Gaia, then we are killing ourselves when we destroy Gaia's rainforests, wetlands, and oceans. This is not to say that there should never be death. As we saw in the passage from Heraclitus, in a paradoxical way there must be death in order for life to continue renewing itself. Honoring death as transformation of life, as recycling of materials (from a different perspective), is necessary to continue playing the infinite game.

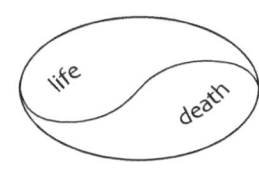

This kind of reflexivity in syntax, in the context of there being no separation between us, as Watts and Ardagh suggest, would imply, essentially, that all verbs should be reflexive. Whatever is happening "out there" is not separate from "me" and so is happening to me-who-is-all-of-it—diamond consciousness experiencing everything.

With no differentiation between perceiver and perceived, there is only the happening.

In the Hopi language, Frank Waters explains: if you want to say "the light flashed," because there is no difference between the light and the flash, you need only say *rehpi* or "flashing" for the entire phenomenon. The experience of the flashing is not separate from the experience of the light. Even without knowing many specifics about Hopi culture you can glean a significant difference in worldview from this simple (perhaps oversimplified) difference in how a basic phenomenon would be described, for what is it but the light and the flash combined, synonymous subject and verb?[115]

As I sit writing near The Bean (distinguishing my boundaries from those of Others), I watch people taking pictures, relaxing at tables, texting (always texting!), and I even watch people watching me watching them. I consciously try to shift from observer of all these activities to being a co-participant in them. All of what I see (and don't see) is me walking, talking, taking pictures, pushing a stroller, flying, watching. It's like an anti-magic trick. Instead of physical sleight-of-hand, it requires mental shift-of-mind, in which the Other shows me my own reflection albeit somewhat distorted, as are the reflections in The Bean.

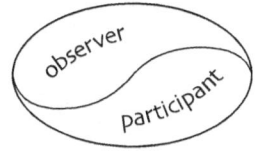

I seem to be able to do it piecemeal right now. I can put my imagination over there and become the Other, for example, by seeing through the eyes of a seagull or imagining myself-as-seagull eating myself-as-peanut. However, I haven't yet developed the capacity to simultaneously experience what the seagull and the man taking a video of his family and the girl in the pink shorts playing with her dolls and the businessman sitting on a bench texting and the 17 people all taking pictures of The Bean from different angles are all experiencing. If I could do that, perhaps Ardagh's and Watts's words would no longer make sense to me.

If there is no Other, then how I treat you is how I treat myself. If I cheat you, I am cheating myself. Someone else already said this better than I could: "Whatsoever you do to the least of my brethren, that you do unto me." Jesus recognized our human tendency to treat those of lower social status worse than we treat those of higher social status. This understanding of non-otherness changes the way we might think of ethics. No longer would behaving ethically be based on an external set of principles, like the Ten Commandments, the law, or social codes such as taboos; it would be about how you treat yourself based on all the various forms "yourselves" take. To the extent that legal codes—as written in language—assume a hard distinction between self and other, they support an ethics based on separateness. They help to keep us entrenched in that mindset. What kind of ethics could emerge from an integral mindset and a new form of language?

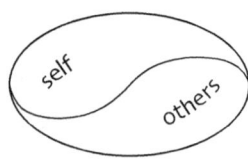

Imagining Language 2.0 on the Way to Language ∞

12

Like jellyfish in water, we're immersed in language. As water is "space" for jellyfish and other aquatic beings, language forms a linguistic space or environment within which humans operate. However, we tend to be unaware of the linguistic spaces in which we swim and of how we use language itself to create and alter our linguistic environments. Indeed, that is a Kleinian loop in which figure and ground morph into one another. Figure creates the ground for its own being just as language creates the space in which we can create it.

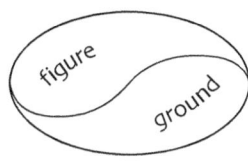

Jellyfish also need water for their physical structure and function, to enable locomotion, and to provide sustenance. If jellyfish could alter the viscosity of the water in which they lived simply by moving within it differently, that would be akin to us altering our linguistic space by using language differently. In fact, we do this naturally, without having to think about it most of the time. For example, lawyers write legal briefs by using language in a particular way, but if you are a lawyer I hope you do not come home from work and talk to your children using your "legal brief" language. Although we use many of the same words, the way we use language at home compared with other contexts creates different linguistic spaces.

We often unconsciously make linguistic environments in which we then live, and sometimes we act like we don't know that we made our environment. Those environments condition us to think and behave in certain ways, to make certain assumptions, and to have certain ethical standards. Once we become conscious of the linguistic environments (ecosystems) we create simply by using language a certain way, then, if these environments become toxic to us, we can ask ourselves how we can create new ones, starting with language and then translating language into action in the world.

Using the Klein bottle now as a model for our *relationship* with language, we can say that language interpenetrates our being. Language structures both our environment (*Umwelt*) and our in-vironment (*Innenwelt*). Language shapes us psychologically and socially, and we generate it creatively. Our linguistic creations, including this book, then become part of and thereby shape our linguistic *en*vironment and *in*vironment. Internally generated, creative use of language becomes externalized and part of the world, part of the environment of others.

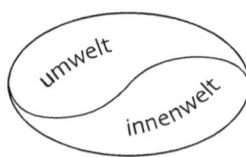

Although anyone can use language creatively, different languages and cultures make it more difficult or less difficult to create new language. Etymological dictionaries attest to creative shifts in language use, including how old words take on different hues, flavors, or tones at different times or in different circumstances. To avert the metacrisis, however, new words and new meanings for old words are little more than the equivalent of rearranging the deck chairs on the *Titanic*. Will neologisms be sufficient for the changes to the structure of language that I have been suggesting? No.

> We can't solve problems by using the same kind of thinking we used when
> we created them.
> —attributed to Albert Einstein

Why not? Earlier I quoted Arjuna Ardagh, who said that our social problems, such as child abuse, domestic violence, people lying to and cheating one another, environmental degradation, and war, arise from our sense of separateness, a sense of a "me" and a "not me." Those types of problems will need to be solved by coming from a different mindset, perhaps diamond consciousness in addition to facet consciousness, or a mindset that sees uniqueness-but-non-separateness. And yet the structure of our language itself assumes separation. Consequently, any time we talk about such problems, even as we try to solve them, we're stuck in the same separatist mindset in which they were created.

Although the mindset is beginning to change in society—I hear it echoed in statements like "we are all one" and "everything is connected to everything"—such a mindset is hindered from widespread uptake by a lack of reinforcement from language that conveys the underlying and perhaps unrecognized paradox of those statements, namely, that our *individualness coexists with our connectedness.* An either/or mindset needs to be expanded to include all/and AND neither/nor.

That is today's "problem that has no name." Like the problem that had no name until Betty Friedan[116] recognized and named it, which catalyzed the women's movement, and the problem that Martin Luther King addressed for Black people, which catalyzed the civil rights movement, our problem with no name involves not only our culture but also our language.

Our generation's problem with no name is harder to recognize because it does not involve an easily identifiable subgroup or minority. It lurks in the structure of language, and because everyone uses language, it affects everyone. Who is disempowered by this problem that has no name?

We all are.

Because there is no contrast between an empowered subgroup and a disempowered one, no us-against-them, no basis for struggle, the language problem with no name is harder to see and thus to address. Unlike the previous problems with no name—the naming of which helped to empower women and minorities, respectively—this liberation movement is for everyone, regardless of race, creed, culture, gender orientation, political persuasion, or language spoken. This liberation movement, although it involves language, is ultimately about liberation from the limits of our separate-mindedness. A conscious evolution of language that alters the fundamental assumption of separateness embedded in the structure of language could enable us to better express our knowing/being/experiencing of whole-within-wholeness and becomingness.

Whereas the women's movement and the civil rights movement brought awareness of and changes to discriminatory social codes, the language problem requires us to go much deeper than social codes. I don't know if there is even a word for the kind of code that our language gives us—an ur-code? Language underlies social codes, moral codes, legal codes—most codes, because the social, moral, and legal codes themselves (even so-called unwritten rules) are rooted in language.

It will and will not be easy to identify the kind of thinking that we used to create our problems. Doing so forces us to look at ugly truths, blind spots, the best intentions that ignored their unintended consequences, and our motives for thinking the way we think. It is not easy to look back at human history and how we thought through issues such as slavery, environmental exploitation, war, debt, and education, to name a few. It is even harder to look at oneself and how one has thought through relationship issues, career issues, child-raising issues, and so on. How might you have solved some of your previous problems if you had been able think and communicate in terms of both/and at the time?

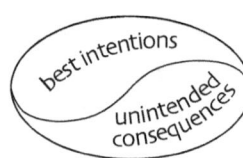

If our current ways of thinking have led us to an increasing sense of fragmentation and to the breakdown of old structures, such as the nuclear family, the corporation, community, marriage, and even democracy, then what will a new way of thinking provide?

What seems to be missing from our current worldview, which a new way of perceiving/thinking could provide, is awaring of and living from wholeness. Although no one can perceive an ultimate picture of wholeness, one can at least seek glimpses by attempting to expand one's point of view to include the perspectives of others. A way to live from wholeness is to keep connecting dots so that you can see the connections all the way around, that is, to the point of enantiodromia where your perspective changes and you see that you are really the one opposing what you thought was opposing you. It's like walking all the way along a Möbius strip—at some point you might realize (because the view is different) that, although you didn't switch sides, you're on the opposite side (of course, now you know that there is only one side although it seems like there are two). The ouroboros circles around and in doing so shows us how to shed our ego-identified perspectives, to seek the perspectives of others, or take a perspective that is vaster than that of one's own ego, perhaps even the perspective of something larger than human.

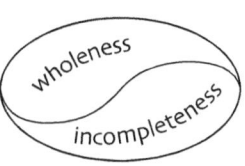

From there, how do we take our first steps toward a wholistic and integrated way of communicating? What is our first baby step? Many years ago, when I switched from dial-up internet service to broadband cable service, the speed of downloads increased tremendously. I was thrilled. It was easier to watch videos. The sound and images flowed and were synchronized. Broadband meant more bits per second, which translated into sound, images, and words simultaneously, like having a full information orchestra playing, not just a pennywhistle.

What are some of the ways that we already get more linguistic "bits per second?" When talking with someone who is physically present, we get their words, tone, and gestures, the verbal and the nonverbal language, the message and the metamessage. In some tonal languages, additional layers of meaning or different meanings entirely are conveyed by the tonal patterns with which the words are spoken. Although English does not yet have a formal lexicon for tone, the meaning that tone conveys has been studied extensively (e.g., higher pitch can convey uncertainty ["Are you *sure*?"] or it could indicate irony ["How *could* you do that?"]. Thus, the meaning of word-plus-tone (in context, of course) is left in part to subjective interpretation.

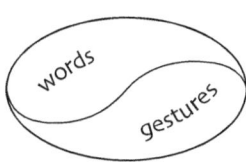

In what other ways could we expand the ability of language to convey not just more information but also different types of information? Gregory Bateson pointed out a language trap he called the double bind, in which a message, *M*, is negated or contradicted by a metamessage.[117] "A function, an effect, of the metamessage is in fact to classify the messages that occur within its context."[118] A simple example is the signaling of humor or play, so that your interlocutors do not assume that you mean literally what you say. Even your dog signals paralinguistically that his growling while tugging at the toy is not actual warning-growling before an attack but simply playful growling. A more serious contradiction between message and metamessage, however, can leave you feeling damned if you do and damned if you don't. This type of metamessage can take the form of explicitly saying "Even if you do X, I will still love you," but conveying by tone or gesture that "if you do X, I will *not* love you." Children are often put in such a bind by their parents, who are likely not conscious that they are putting the child in such a bind. And many a text or tweet has been misconstrued because the metamessage was not conveyed adequately, for example, not accompanied by a winky-face emoji.

> Syntax is too slow.
> —John Dotson

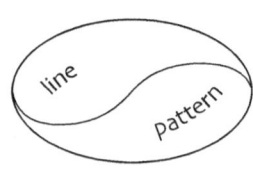

To convey those and other types of metamessage classifications, perhaps we could expand language to draw more equally on both modes of our neural processing capacities—the linear, temporal mode and the pattern-based gestalt mode. The text that you are currently reading is primarily activating parts of your brain that process information in a linear fashion (pattern recognition of letters and words, contextualizing, and other cognitive processes are also occurring). To innovate the structure of language, we might need to adopt elements, such as glyphs, that activate our pattern-recognition and gestalt-processing capabilities. Pattern-based signs might better express that we live in a both/and world where nature and nurture, individual and collective, freedom and responsibility, for example, all need to be integrated. Our current alphabetic language (and current logic) pits such concepts against each other, implying an artificial finite game in which one side will or should win. Thus, power struggles emerge between those who believe it is one way and those who believe it is the other. And they're both right, AND they're both wrong, because the absolute separation of such polarities is artificial and inaccurate. Both are necessary for wholeness.

With computers and cellular telephones becoming more graphics based, it would not be difficult to add more graphic elements to writing. Images can convey more types of information simultaneously by means of structural relationships. The glyph to the left could be used to convey, for example, six interrelated structures, perspectives, or processes, such as key stakeholders, departments of a corporation, key species of an ecosystem, and so on, within their immediate context (the inner space that is lighter in color), as well as a wider context (the outer membrane that also seems to be pointing beyond itself). If we add color to that graphic, we could represent even more types of relationships.

Color could be used, for example, to convey context—one color signifying the ego lens, another signifying the nondual lens, and a third signifying an integration of those two lenses, based on color theory, intensity, saturation levels, and so on. Alternatively, color could be used to distinguish several perspectives being discussed simultaneously, showing where perspectives overlap by blending the colors.

Why might we want to do this? Is it *really* necessary? To answer those questions, we must look not just at where we are but where we are going or, more pointedly, where we want to go as a *Humanbody* or *Gaianbody*. Time seems to be speeding up. The world is becoming more integrated and global. All this is leading to a shift: from understanding ourselves to be separate beings to understanding ourselves to be an interconnected human-planetary organism. In the latter conception, each of us is like a cell in or microbe of a much larger organism (see Chapter 7). When the tuned-in-ness of the whole occurs, we will be flooded with information about what the billions of us are up to. That's a lot of information to sort through each millisecond. Although we're learning how to process a lot of information externally—through social media, 24/7 news, and the incessant bombardment of advertising—the information will not be external; it will be both internal/external in a Kleinian both/and paradoxical way. The information flow will become so integrated that it will seem instantaneous.

Currently, our communication system is based on the metaphor of transmitting to and receiving from other someones "out there." However, when we become a fully integrated supra-human-Gaian organism, we will know that there is no other "someone" or "something" "out there." (I used scare quotes to show how ironic this sentence would seem from that future perspective.) The convergence of space-subject-object into a unified whole (spatiosubobjectivity, as Steven Rosen calls it) will be complete. But we are not there yet. I hope that this book and the activities it inspires will help us get there.

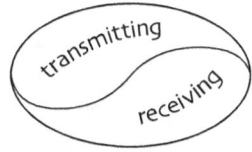

The role of language in this coming-to-wholeness is important because I think we are heading toward a way of being that won't require spoken language. Instead, we will all be tuned into each other (Language 2.0 is a small step toward Language ∞) so that when the foot itches, the hand knows where to scratch. The cells in my body, be they as different as muscle cells and nerve cells and skin cells, function as a whole and can communicate with one another seamlessly (when not injured or diseased in some way). Imagine our world and even the universe being like that! Likely it is, and we are still coming to understand that it is so.

From where we are now, that kind of near-instantaneous communication is a huge leap to make. The shifts in language that we are exploring here are mere stepping stones. I learned to ride a bike by starting with a tricycle, to practice the pedaling motion. Next, I had a bicycle with training wheels, to get the basics of balance. After bicycles are mastered, we humans can master the operation of cars, boats, airplanes, and helicopters. We will have to master increasingly complex linguistic forms in a similar way, by building up new skills gradually. To go from a mindset of radical separation to one that integrates more information (without it freaking us out), we must first find a way to speak from wholeness rather than from separation. We need to build assumptions about our connectedness into our everyday ways of thinking and communicating. We need to build paradoxes into the infrastructure, the invisible architecture, of language. Then we might truly be able to act (and speak) from that place of wholeness. Since our thinking/being/awaring is so interwoven with our language, it is clear that they mutually influence one another.

What Might Language 2.0 Look Like?

Do you think the images in Figure 9 are language?[119] Why or why not? Does the column/row structure of the top one, like Chinese and Japanese, suggest that to you? Or the angular shape of each glyph?

What about the bottom image? Is computer code a language? Are flowers presented to another person a language, as they were in my grandmother's day? If you had not watched *Game of Thrones*, would you recognize Dothraki as a language, simply because the people were speaking it? Is Christopher Alexander's *A Pattern Language*[120] really a language, or is it more of a game in which the puzzle pieces consist of archetypal architectural building blocks? Underlying those questions are two more-fundamental questions—what is language, and how does it work? Almost any introductory linguistics text could tell you how to recognize language, but I am looking beyond that kind of answer. I am asking it because if we consciously evolve language, how do we do it in such a way that the end result is recognizable as language, particularly, as language that people would find useful?

The early mobile phones were not as useful as our current cell phones are. They were large and heavy; they did not have a screen; Siri was not yet born. However, enough people recognized the usefulness of mobile telephony that tech companies kept revising the design, making it smaller, lighter, and eventually more than just a telephone. Similarly, how will we see the usefulness of novel language structures, even if they are initially rather clunky and inelegant? If we put as much effort into innovating language structures as we did into innovating telephones, we could get to Language 10.0, then Language ∞, before full endosymbiotic inclusion.

How, then, might we invent new types of structural elements, akin to function words, with the difference that the function they serve is to convey the new types of relationships discussed here? The standard function words express how two things are related in space (*on, in, above, over, under, between*), related in time (*before, after, with*), or related in other ways (*for, except, by*). So, I decided to invent a new type of structural element to express a Möbial/Kleinian relationship. Let me know if you find it useful.

It looks like this

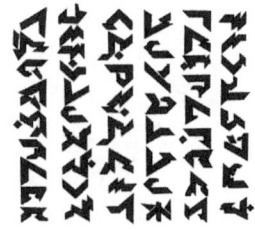

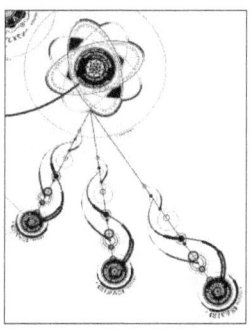

Figure 9. Top, Ithkuil language created by John Quijada. Middle, purported alien language. Bottom, glyph from *The One That Is Both*.

113

and connects two concepts that are "distinct but not separate (from)." The internal loop distinguishes a separate space from the external oval, but it is still within it. It is spelled **mobi** and pronounced moe-bee (after Möbius). It would be used like this:

We are ∾ Earth.

I am ∾ my microbiome.

All living things, and perhaps even nonliving ones, can be considered ∾ each other. How? Let's compare it with the Möbius strip and derivatives of it—the lemniscate and sublemniscate (Figure 10). Seeing the two sides as two versus seeing that they are really just one continuous side requires that we span only one spatial dimension. The difference in scale is not that great. However, the difference in scale between you and Earth or you and your microbiome is much greater. For objects in 3D, the difference is not dimensional, it is in levels of hierarchy or levels of inclusiveness. We are ∾ Earth through levels and scales down to the quantum and up to the cosmic. Gebser spoke about transparency and *seeing through*; it takes the ability to see through multiple levels to grok the connectedness that ∾ refers to. That might require familiarizing oneself with the different disciplines that pertain to different levels, for example, microbiology, molecular biology, and biophysics at one end and psychology, sociology, ecology, and cosmology at the other end.

Although ∾ still seems to keep subject and object separate even while declaring their nonseparateness, it is a step toward a new type of integral interrelationality, a way for us to tell a new story about ourselves. However, it is not yet a new *structure* for language to take. It's simply a bigger tweak of the old structure than a neologism would be. But we have to start somewhere…

Outside the context of this book, would you have recognized such a glyph as a new form of language? Does it seem useful? In other words, does it enable us to express something beyond what the words used to define it convey? By *showing* "distinct but not separate from," does it convey more than the words alone do?

Figure 10. Top, lemniscate, which is made by cutting a Möbius strip in half down its center. You don't get two Möbius strips, you get a single lemniscate that has two twists. Bottom, sublemniscate. If you cut a lemniscate down the center, something different happens. You get two intertwined lemniscates. They are ∾ in a way that differs from the way the sides of a Möbius strip are ∾. For a more in-depth discussion of these fascinating topological figures, see *Topologies of the Flesh* (Rosen 2006). Used with permission.

Perhaps this example is simply a type of shorthand. What could convey more than words alone and still be recognizable as language?

Let's put our collective creativity together for the evolution of both the *Humanbody* and *Gaianbody*.

Hall of Metaphors

13

> One of the problems of the way in which twentieth-century biology was frequently presented to the public was to mistake the metaphors of up and down—and many other metaphors—for reality.[121]
> —Denis Noble

I used to give presentations to Rotary groups about the need to invent new metaphors to replace the many war metaphors (MARRIAGE IS WAR, HEALTHCARE IS WAR, SPORTS IS WAR, POLITICS IS WAR, WEATHER IS WAR, and so on) that *bomb*ard us daily (see?). I argued that one of the reasons we can't seem to live in peace is that we keep reinforcing the importance of war by using such metaphors in many areas of life, even those seemingly unrelated to war. How, I wondered, could we ever create peace if we understand and describe so much of our world in terms of war imagery? I implored people to create new metaphors. I implore you now. Metaphors aren't just for poetry; they are at the heart of how we speak, how we reason, how we live, and what we consider true.

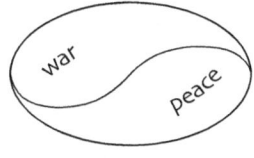

Looking at language through the lens of metaphors can be like trying to find your way in a hall of mirrors.

When we use language, we use metaphors at multiple levels of depth, from obvious to obscure, surface to subterranean, conscious to unconscious. Different fields of study—from literary analysis to cognitive linguistics and philosophy to anthropology—each seem to focus on a different level of metaphor. First, I describe four levels of metaphor—explicit, implicit, culture-organizing, and root metaphors—then describe how implicit metaphors affect our reasoning and behavior, culture-organizing and root metaphors affect our context and what we consider real, and lastly suggest that if we want to alter the structure of language we must consider all four levels of metaphor and be aware of the metaphors we use to describe and think about language itself.

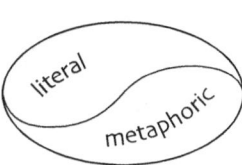

Aristotle defined metaphor thus: "Metaphor consists in giving the thing a name that belongs to something else; the transference being either from genus to species, or from species to genus, or from species to species, or on grounds of analogy" [Poetics 1457b], for example, by calling Achilles a lion. By "genus" and "species" he means part and whole or category and instance. More recently George Lakoff and Mark Johnson, in their classic book *Metaphors We Live By*, simplified the definition to "understanding and experiencing one kind of thing in terms of another." They named these two parts the *source* and the *target*. More importantly, they showed how ordinary language (that is, when we think we are being literal, not poetic) is based on conceptual metaphors that underlie the actual words. For example, when I say "I would like to spend time with you" or "that was a waste of time," I am employing the conceptual metaphor TIME IS MONEY.

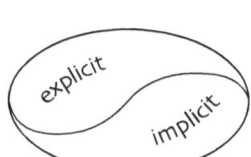

Because Lakoff and Johnson showed how some metaphors are used consciously (as in poetry) while others (conceptual metaphors) are used relatively unconsciously, I chose to distinguish Aristotle's poetic metaphors as *explicit metaphors*, which include those in which all parties are conscious of the metaphoric nature of the comparison, from Lakoff and Johnson's conceptual metaphors, which are implicit and might be used without consciousness that the comparison is metaphoric. This distinction enables us to see other instances in which metaphors are explicit or implicit, not just in the ways those authors describe. For example, scientific models can be considered explicit metaphors, while scientific terminology makes extensive use of implicit metaphors. Similarly, the metaphors that structure cultural belief systems can fall along a continuum from explicit to implicit.

Explicit Metaphors

The explicit metaphors of poetry are used deliberately, often self-consciously. Aristotle points out that only certain characteristics of the source apply to the target: "by describing Achilles metaphorically as a lion, the speaker intends to focus on the Greek hero being brave (also possible: fierce, savage). Achilles, however, does not resemble the lion in walking on four legs or having huge canines or a mane."[122] Because much has already been written about this type of metaphor, I will not go into detail. Instead, I offer you a little Shakespeare, a master of metaphor who, in this poem, pokes fun at the metaphors poets use to describe their lovers:

> My mistress' eyes are nothing like the sun;
> Coral is far more red, than her lips red.
> If snow be white, why then her breasts are dun;
> If hairs be wires, black wires grow on her head.
> I have seen roses damasked, red and white,
> But no such roses see I in her cheeks;
> And in some perfumes is there more delight
> Than in the breath that from my mistress reeks.
> I love to hear her speak, yet well I know
> That music hath a far more pleasing sound:
> I grant I never saw a goddess go,
> My mistress, when she walks, treads on the ground:
> And yet by heaven, I think my love as rare,
> As any she belied with false compare. (Sonnet 130)

We find another type of explicit metaphor in scientific models, such as the solar system model of the atom, the computer program model of the gene, and the factory model of the cell. These metaphors are used primarily for building theories because they give the scientist a way to organize information so that the simplified model can be used to ask and answer questions about the complex system being modeled. Models are not meant to be true, as they do not claim identity between source and target (e.g., that a gene really is a "blueprint" or "program"). Models allow one to map characteristics of one thing onto another, with the reduction of characteristics making it easier to explore relationships or dynamics for a specific purpose. The model of "genes as text," for example, spawned a rich set of associated functions, such as gene editing, transcription, translation, and proof-reading polymerases.

Philosopher of science Andrew Reynolds explores the history of biology through its metaphors in a book that reveals not just the use of metaphor in science but also how metaphors then catalyzed scientific innovation. The cell, for example, was initially a metaphor for structures of dead cork viewed under the newly invented microscope. The shape and pattern reminded Robert Hooke of the chambers of a honeycomb. In contrast, Antonie van Leeuwenhoek was observing living microscopic organisms for the first time and called those protozoa, bacteria, and spermatozoa "animalcules." Other terms for what was being observed included bladders, boxes, bubbles, caverns, chambers, and pores, as well as cavity, globule, and vesicle. The German term *Zelle* was used to refer to plant cells that are "living organisms and individuals in their own right, but also capable of leading a second kind of communal and dependent life as parts of a larger multicellular plant individual."[123] Modern biologists no longer consider the term "cell" to be metaphoric. It no longer conjures mental images of monks' cells. It has become a dead metaphor, now a literal term for the fundamental unit of life. Metaphors that were once explicit, when they die, shift to being implicit and hence harder to recognize as metaphoric. However, the CELL IS A FACTORY metaphor was so influential that it sparked an innovative approach using genetic engineering to "splice the gene for human insulin into yeast and bacteria so that these cells produced the hormone." The metaphor actually inspired researchers to turn cells into actual hormone-producing factories.[124]

> All models are false, but some are useful.[125]
> —George Box

Models have their utility but also their inherent limitations. For example, medical researchers sought to develop drugs that would function as a metaphorical "silver bullet," whereby the drug would alter a specific target that would initiate a cascade of downstream events that would promote healing. When that proved difficult, the trend turned toward mixtures of drugs called drug cocktails (another metaphor), because healing requires simultaneous alteration of many different interconnected processes.

Another metaphoric model—to conceive of airflow as a fluid—provided a highly useful way to predict weather. When this new way of weather forecasting was invented, it required new metaphors to make the complex mathematical concepts easy for everyone to understand. Unfortunately, a war metaphor was adopted, so we now speak of warm and cold *fronts* (after the front lines of World War I). Imagine, instead, if we had focused on the coming together of opposite types of air (cold, dry air spiraling clockwise and warm, moist air spiraling counterclockwise) with the implicit metaphor WEATHER IS SEX. The TV weather reporter might instead say things like "the icy air from the north will only flirt briefly with the voluptuous southern air, so the chance of precipitation is low."

Just as metaphors can reveal similarities between source and target concepts, they can also hide information. Lakoff and Johnson illustrate this point with the metaphor LABOR IS A RESOURCE. This metaphor has been used in nearly all economic theories—from capitalist to socialist. By treating labor as a commodity or like a natural resource, with various costs and supply dynamics, this metaphor hides or fails to articulate a distinction between meaningful labor and dehumanizing labor. Hence, "cheap labor" is seen as a good thing in all those economic theories, while they ignore the consequences on the humans providing that cheap labor. As a result, we don't collect data on meaningful labor versus dehumanizing labor (and gradations in between) nor do we construct our economic systems based on such a distinction. During the pandemic, public reporting on conditions in meat-packing plants, for example, shone a spotlight, albeit briefly, on dehumanizing labor under dangerous conditions. The "great resignation" also happened then, as people became unwilling to tolerate being dehumanized. In industries where LABOR IS A RESOURCE, you also frequently find this metaphor "at work": WORKERS ARE REPLACEABLE PARTS OF A MACHINE.

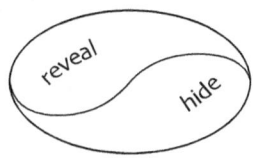

Implicit Metaphors

Scientific language also uses many implicit metaphors both in peer-to-peer communication and, especially, in communicating complex ideas to nonscientists.[126] Doctors are taught to use metaphors to explain technical concepts to patients.[127] As expected, the war metaphor has been *drafted* to help *fight* against cancer, drug addiction, even microbes.[128] For example, antibiotic-resistant bacteria have been described as powerful adversaries and "a new killer," when many of them live on us without doing any harm most of the time. Concomitantly, solutions and even treatments have been framed as weapons, including "silver bullet" and "sledgehammer."[129]

Lakoff and Johnson's book *Metaphors We Live By* opened new fields of inquiry into the linguistic underpinnings of metaphorical thinking that occurs mostly unconsciously. Their ideas have been confirmed many times with empirical studies.[130] Although we use implicit metaphors in ordinary language mostly unconsciously, they nevertheless have a profound impact on how we frame problems and seek solutions.

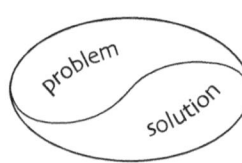

To determine how profound an influence metaphors have on our reasoning, Paul Thibodeau and Lera Boroditsky conducted a now well-known study about metaphors used to frame the topic of crime. They found that implicit metaphors influenced people's attitudes about how to deal with criminals.[131] For example, if crime was described as a beast preying on one's city, people suggested ways to catch and jail supposed criminals. If crime was described as a virus infecting the city, people suggested ways to determine the root causes and treat the problem through social reform. Even when the experimental scenarios differed by only one word—beast or virus—subjects still proposed those different solutions to the problem of crime.

What happens if you're the type of person who generally thinks of crime using the virus metaphor, but all around you are people who want to deal with crime as if it were a beast? Does it feel like you are talking about the same thing? Next time you watch the news, pay attention to the metaphors being used to frame the stories. How do those metaphors influence the way you feel about what happened? What effect might a different metaphor have had?

In light of the power of metaphor to affect not only how one characterizes the world but also how one reasons about it, the U.S. military funded a program to understand the metaphoric bases of other languages, most likely languages of people we spy on, as that might help us better understand intelligence intercepts.[132] Other cultures might use metaphors that are radically different from ours, which would need to be taken into consideration by the translators. Fortunately, the military's study also helps us better understand our own language and its implicit metaphors and assumptions. Indeed, their research resulted in the creation of the MetaNet Wiki,[133] which lists main metaphors and their subcases or variants. For example, NATION IS A VEHICLE is listed as a main metaphor, and NATION IS A CAR is a variant; another variant could be NATION IS A SHIP, as in "the ship of state," which goes back to the poetry of ancient Greece. Indeed, the list includes LEADING A NATION IS STEERING A BOAT.

Because the MetaNet Wiki documents hundreds of common metaphors, it can be used as a database for inventing new metaphors: scroll through the list and think of alternatives. For example, it lists ADVOCACY IS PHYSICAL COMBAT. When you click on it, you learn that this metaphor is a variant of ARGUMENT IS PHYSICAL COMBAT. If I were an advocate for, say, the rights of Nature, perhaps I do not want to describe my efforts as combative or warlike (e.g., *fighting* for Nature), because I don't want to activate an associated assumption that someone (or even Nature) must lose. Instead, what kind of new metaphor might I invent? I would prefer metaphors such as ADVOCACY IS PHYSICAL EMBRACE ("Let us wrap our hearts around protecting the sovereignty of forests, oceans, the Arctic National Wildlife Refuge…"; "We tree-huggers want to rain support on the state's efforts to reduce the number of uncontrolled forest fires") or ADVOCACY IS NOURISHMENT ("Feed the Earth, feed your soul").

When All of Life Is Either War or Game

When something is characterized using the metaphor X IS WAR or X IS A GAME, an associated assumption is that there will be a winner and a loser. Must all games be won though? The philosopher James Carse wrote about the difference between finite games and infinite games. "A finite game is played for the purpose of winning, an infinite game for the purpose of continuing the play."[134] What happens when we mistake infinite games for finite ones, when

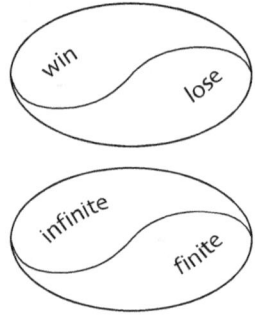

we assume that there must be a winner and loser when actually we want the game to continue?

Democracy, for example, is intended to be an infinite game with finite games (such as elections) embedded within it. (Recall Heraclitus: some things stay the same only by constant change; the ongoing turnover of elected leaders enables the infinite game of democracy to continue.) Recently, however, Americans seem to be playing the democracy game as if it were entirely and only a finite game. In the short term, there are winners and losers of elections, but overall, politics, especially democracy, must be played so that we can continue playing the game. In contrast, monarchies ensure an infinite game by specifying that the head of state will continue to be chosen through a family blood line. I'm not suggesting that America become a monarchy, only that we refocus on the long-term (infinite) game and the ways it must be played differently than a finite game.

When one player/party decides that it must win always and at any cost, then the game of democracy has been hijacked and will, ironically, end in authoritarianism. In such situations, history shows us that the players who must always lose, in that formulation, inevitably rebel. Humans want the opportunity to try to win. When they see that they cannot, that the game is rigged, there are insurgencies. When one player/group rigs the game and simultaneously cries foul that the game is rigged, does that help, hinder, and/ or explode the ongoing playing of the infinite game?

> A war fought to end all wars, in the strategy of finite play, only breeds universal warfare.
> —James Carse

Similarly, a war against an abstraction, such as a war on terror, is not meant to end said war, to be "won" by "the good guys." It is meant to establish a context by which to create a permanent military-based economy. The war on "terror" constitutes a pseudo-infinite game that is, paradoxically, "won" (economically, by a few wealthy business owners) by "losing" (that is, by not eliminating every terrorist, given that a war on terror breeds new terrorists).

Thus, there are different winners and losers depending on whether you consider a war on terror from a local context (military versus "terrorists") or a global context (owners of the corporations that make up the military-industrial-academic complex).

When I searched "game" in the MetaNet Wiki, I expected to get a long list of metaphors in the form of "x IS A GAME," but there were just a few, including ELECTION IS A GAME and CONSIDERING THE IMPORTANCE OF RIGHTS IS PLAYING A GAME, as well as related metaphors like BUSINESS COMPETITION IS COMPETITIVE SPORTS and the variant ELECTIONS ARE COMPETITIVE SPORTS EVENTS. Perhaps because the MetaNet Wiki was funded by the military, it didn't focus on general metaphors such as LIFE IS A GAME. Or maybe because life is an infinite game, it didn't fit with the usual types of finite games.

As I write this in 2022, the political situation in the United States embodies the metaphor "CONSIDERING THE IMPORTANCE OF RIGHTS IS PLAYING A GAME." It does indeed feel like our politicians are playing with our rights—our right to vote and our right to appropriate maternal health care, for example. Essential rights should not be a game with winners and losers. If the distinction between elections as finite games but politics itself as an infinite game made its way into the mainstream, perhaps we would restructure political games to be played differently than they are now. We might ask, "What are the goals of this game?" If the goal is not to win but to keep playing or to keep ensuring life, liberty, and the pursuit of happiness, then what becomes possible? It seems to me that we humans, as seemingly finite players whose strutting and fretting upon the stage does inevitably have a final scene (LIFE IS THEATER), would do well to ponder the open-endedness of our being—and then to develop our metaphoric language to reflect our paradoxical finitude and infinitude.

Culture-organizing Metaphors

Culture-organizing metaphors are further removed from consciousness than implicit metaphors. Culture-organizing metaphors not only express comparisons between ideas, but they also structure core beliefs and values within a culture. Such beliefs are usually taught as "the way it is" and are rarely questioned. Money or Exchange, for example, has become a fundamental metaphor organizing much of Western culture (in contrast to Gift in other cultures/ economies, for example). Given that the metaphor LABOR IS A RESOURCE is an unquestioned belief that structures American society, it gives both workers and owners a sense of value. An unintended consequence of that culture-organizing metaphor is that relationships become transactional, and not just employer-employee relationships but many kinds of relationships. For example, LABOR IS A RESOURCE has been expanded to education, where there have been proposals to pay students to study or do their homework. Doing that would turn what should be an intrinsically motivated activity (the pleasure of learning) into an extrinsic, transactional one.

Another Western culture–organizing metaphor might be expressed as PROGRESS IS MARCHING FORWARD. It codifies time as linear and implies that despite seeming hardship things tend to get better. It implies that the future lies in front of us (whereas in some cultures, the future, because we cannot see it, lies behind us), and we can get there in an orderly manner (by marching, another military metaphor). What if, instead, progress was characterized by increasing levels of integration of opposites? In support of such integration Reynolds (discussing metaphors of evolution) says:

> Michael Ruse argues that if not for the cultural tradition of viewing the plant and animal kingdoms as creations designed for some purpose, Darwin would not have asked the types of questions he did, and would not have eventually arrived at the answers he did. The metaphors, Ruse insists, are constitutive of and integral to the science. But what, then, does that suggest about its objectivity? He writes: One has to transcend dichotomies of objective/subjective, discovered/created, description of reality/social construction. Science, Darwinism in particular, falls on both sides of the divides.[135]

Different cultures use different metaphors to organize communal life. For the Kogi of Columbia, weaving is a culture-organizing metaphor.[136] Women spin the fibers into thread, and men weave the cloth, all the while focusing on their simultaneous participation in weaving the world together. The loom itself represents the four directions. Weaving even structures how they plant their fields, with the women planting in a warp direction and men in a weft direction.

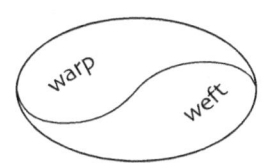

On the other side of the world, the Abelam of Papua New Guinea use the yam as a culture-organizing metaphor.[137] As the focus of a male initiation ceremony, the yam cycle functions to structure time in an episodic and cyclic way.[138] Also serving as a way to recognize linear and historic time, the yam ceremony keeps ancestral lineages going, as one's yams are passed on from generation to generation. Anthropologist Richard Scaglion describes how "yam beliefs and the yam cycle indicate the overwhelming social importance of yams, suggesting how their cultivation and displays help structure Abelam behaviors and temporal patterns."[139] The yams are grown by the men and often reach lengths of nine feet or more. One community competes with another community, and at the conclusion of the cycle, there is an enormous feast provided by the women.

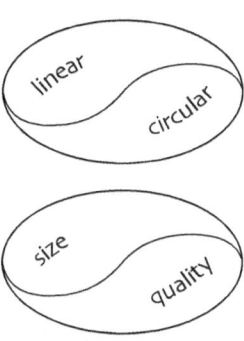

> After the displays, tubers are given to male ritual exchange partners (*sambura*) as part of a competitive exchange process in which recipients are obliged to grow similar specimens in subsequent years and give them in return. Thus ceremonial yams have an important political function: to a large extent, male status, prestige, and power are dependent on the size and quality of ceremonial yams grown. In addition to their importance in the political arena, "long yams" have considerable expressive content. They are imbued with complex, multivalent symbolism, the levels of which interact in a mutually reinforcing manner. Since all yams are propagated vegetatively, yams also form a link between living Abelam and their ancestors, who planted genetically identical yams. Abelam often invoke their *gwaandlu* (clan ancestral spirits) when growing and tending yams. The link between a man, his ceremonial yams, and his gwaandlu is very close. Yams are of paramount social, symbolic, and religious importance to the Samukundi.[140]

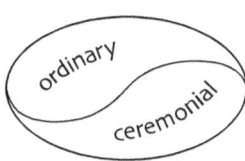

Because yams are thought to be sentient and to be disturbed by social discord and "hot" things, there are many taboos governing behavior during the yam-growing cycle, including sexual abstinence and avoiding certain foods (e.g., wild game). Conflicts during the yam-growing season occur less often and are settled more quickly and peacefully than those that occur during ceremony season. Thus, yam-growing and yam-celebrating seasons organize a yin-like period and a yang-like period, respectively, in the life of the Abelam.

Houses are another common culture-organizing metaphor, as related people live in, come from, the same House. Houses house kinfolk. From the "houses of Congress" to the idea of "social structure," buildings organize not only the physical spaces we inhabit but also our communal and mental spaces. *A house divided against itself will not stand.* That goes for a country, warring cousins, and even one's own heart and mind (housed together in one's body). Is language, as an invisible architecture of culture, also a house divided against itself?

As we ponder these questions, we should be careful to heed Roger Keesing's advice not to mistake implicit metaphors for metaphysical understanding of other cultures.[141] For example, he describes how "taboo" has been interpreted to mean both sacred and forbidden. *Taboo* comes from the Polynesian *ta*, "marked off," and *pu*, an adverb of intensity. "The compound word *tapu*, therefore, means no more than 'marked thoroughly' and only came to signify 'sacred' or 'prohibited' in a secondary sense because sacred things and places were commonly marked in a peculiar manner in order that everyone might know that they were sacred."[142] English dictionary compilers cite the meanings of *tapu* as "prohibited" and "sacred," but

> Something is off limits, tapu, only given a perspective. What is off limits to one person or category of persons may be "permissible" or even enjoined for another person or category of persons. A menstrual hut may be tapu from the vantage point of men; from the vantage point of a menstruating woman, it would be tapu to be anywhere else.[143]

The inherent contextuality of "taboo" was lost when it was given—by Westerners—an aura of absoluteness. That type of slippage between the linguistic and the metaphysical is not limited to anthropological studies. In our own culture, for example, we still speak of the sun rising and setting when we know that the sun is not pulled across the sky by a god but that Earth orbits the Sun and that day and night are determined by whether our current geographic position is facing or revolved away from the sun. Although we have changed our beliefs, we have kept the old metaphor. In what other ways have we allowed ourselves to be lazy with language and not change it to reflect new understandings?

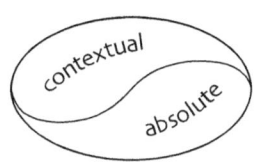

Root Metaphors

In contrast to explicit and implicit metaphors and culture-organizing metaphors, which have been characterized as having greater or lesser linguistic power and are used with more or less self-awareness that one is using a metaphor, the final type of metaphor that we will examine here is qualitatively different yet organizes one's experience just as powerfully and unconsciously. The philosopher Stephen C. Pepper identified world hypotheses based on different root metaphors (even "root" is metaphoric, suggesting something underground and hence not seen).[144] He identified four world hypotheses and their corresponding root metaphors by which we fundamentally organize information and knowledge. In other words, "world hypotheses influence what we count as facts."[145] Pepper identified the most adequate world hypotheses as *formism*, *mechanism*, *contextualism*, and *organicism*.[146] Before we dive into the details of each one, let's look at the category of "world hypothesis." Pepper made it clear that a theory of world hypotheses is a set that contains itself as a member. Those four world hypotheses are mutually independent; and each has its own root metaphor, categories, and statements/laws that render it relatively incommensurable with the others: "what are pure facts for one theory are highly interpreted evidence for another." Pepper thinks that attempts at synthesis (eclecticism) limit the scope of each world hypothesis and thereby produce confusion. Perhaps, like Gebser's structures of consciousness (see Figure 3), these world hypotheses are all ever present. Consider each world hypothesis as a holon, a paradoxical whole that is part of another whole.[147]

Pepper's world hypotheses function at both individual and collective levels. As mentioned earlier, they are even less available to our awareness than implicit metaphors: "We all have and use world hypotheses … it's just because world hypotheses are so intimate and pervasive that we do not easily look at them from a distance, so to speak, or as if we saw them in a mirror."[148] We see others' world hypotheses more easily than we see our own. Unlike the implicit metaphors of language, which are used to understand the world, "each hypothesis gives a reading of what is in the world (ontology) and how evidence is marshaled to support claims about that world (epistemology). Thus, they can be taken as orientations that govern our knowledge claims and value claims, as well as actions we take based on such beliefs."[149]

Here, I want to focus on the root metaphors of these hypotheses, rather than on the world hypotheses themselves. Unlike the culture-organizing metaphors in the previous section, in which the organizing image was something ubiquitous in that society (woven cloth or loom, yam growing, house), root metaphors are more abstract, which also makes them harder to "see."

The root metaphor of the world hypothesis that Pepper calls formism is *similarity*. There are two types of formism, depending on whether your perspective focuses on immanent form or transcendent form. In immanent formism, one looks through the similarities among different manifestations in substance in order to see the pattern. You learn concepts this way as a child; for example, to teach you to discern the form of a triangle, you are shown several three-sided things. Conversely, transcendent formism is a perspective by which you look through a pre-existing pattern to see its different manifestations in substance. Archetypes are such patterns. You can never "see" an archetype directly; rather, you only see its manifestations. In both cases of formism, you are looking for similarities either among existents or between the form and the existent. Essentially, this root metaphor suggests that looking for similarities is a fundamental way of being in the world and understanding it. It influenced Western philosophy particularly from Plato and Aristotle onward. Metaphors themselves, by bringing together similar aspects of different concepts, participate in this root metaphor.

In the mechanism world hypothesis, the root metaphor is *machine*. Again, Pepper proposes a bifurcation—between discrete and consolidated forms of

immanent

transcendent

130

mechanism. Physical machines or tools (discrete form of mechanism, as in the most basic tool, the lever) have been overshadowed recently by electromagnetism (a field phenomenon, or consolidated form of mechanism). Indeed, field and matter are complementary concepts, so he includes the electromagnetic field as a representative "machine" in that it extends the human capability to have an effect on the world, even at a distance. Pepper slides nearly effortlessly from showing how a machine is a configuration of parts that have specific location in relation to one another to showing how "the determination of any one location whatever depends upon *all* the dimensions of the field." He essentially describes them as distinct but not separate [as in ☯].[150] Mechanism, to be useful, requires matter and laws that describe the actions of matter. Laws, however, resemble forms in that they are not of matter or fields but describe regularities (similarities) operative in matter/fields. Mechanism straddles formism and the next world hypothesis, contextualism.

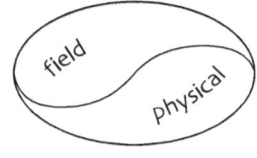

In contrast to formism and mechanism, which are analytic world hypotheses, contextualism and organicism are synthetic, and their root metaphors are not common-sense concepts. For contextualism, the root metaphor is the *historic event*, but not a past event, rather the past up to the present that makes the now what it is—an occurring, not a thing but a doing, a *changing*. Although Pepper did not use the term "order-disorder paradox," he described a categorial feature of contextualism as, essentially, the order-disorder paradox, wherein as you create order you simultaneously engender inherent disorder (you don't have one without the other). Contextualism presupposes change and novelty. Contextualism also seems to require a kind of internal space+time (to differentiate it from physical spacetime), which is arrived at intuitively. In other words, a whole (pattern, meaning, event, etc.) is intuited before the details comprising that whole are delineated. Think of putting the first bite of lasagna in your mouth. You taste the whole of it. In the second bite, you might discern the hints of basil or oregano in the sauce, the tang of parmesan cheese amidst the creaminess of the mozzarella.

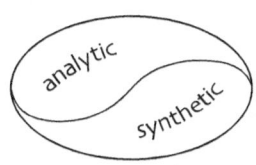

The fourth adequate world hypothesis, organicism, also lacks a concrete root metaphor. Although "organism" seems a natural choice of root metaphor,

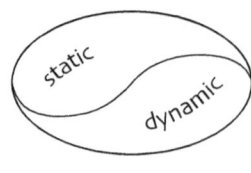

Pepper dislikes its static, biological implications; he offers "integration" as an only slightly better root metaphor. The Gaia theory discussed earlier draws on this root metaphor, offering Earth as the integrating organism.

As with contextualism, in organicism there is an emphasis on the event, even though organicism "takes time lightly." The difference between contextualism and organicism is the insistence in organicism on the integration process rather than the duration of the event. Consequently, Pepper believes that organicism suffers from the weakness of internal contradiction: it both presupposes wholeness and strives toward it. I do not see that as a weakness, rather as an epistemological triumph over the other world hypotheses. The fragments to be integrated by an organicist depend on successive prior integrations. Organicism, then, involves an iterative process of integrating fragments into more complete (more whole?) systems. Such a process is not smooth; it involves encountering and working through contradictions. (Jung's process of individuation involves a similar iterative process of working through contradictions as a striving toward wholeness, which is, paradoxically, already presupposed as the archetype of the Self. See Chapter 19.) Furthermore, complexity compounds: nothing has a single opposite. Indeed, that is exactly what we are encountering here with language and how it hinders our ability to further integrate. By the end of the chapter on organicism, Pepper is pointing out how ubiquitous contradictions, self-contradictions, and paradox are in the various categories of organicism. Pepper, however, does not seem to integrate Gödel's incompleteness theorems into the organicism world hypothesis: wholeness of a system implies contradiction; without it, the system would be only partial. There is a tendency in organicism toward transcendence, but Pepper says that transcendence isn't the elimination of contradiction; it is the ability to see the apparent contradiction within its new context, wherein new boundaries are drawn such that, for example, it is impossible to conceive of yin without yang and vice versa; where yin includes yang and yang includes yin—they are not just integrated externally, they are also integrated internally. Such a redrawing of conceptual boundaries, along with novel ways to express those new boundaries, is the core idea of this book. Paradoxical structures, such as the Möbius strip and Klein bottle, could help us do that.

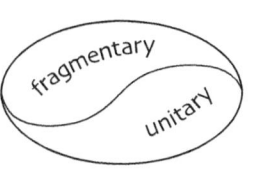

Pepper observes that "psychology also has its history of successive integrations pointing, just as astronomy does, to the ultimate integration of the absolute. The system of psychology has not, however, as yet attained to an integration with the astronomical system...So we can predict that intrinsically the psychological system is integrated with the physico-astronomical system."[151] When Pepper published *World Hypotheses* in 1942, Carl Jung was still working out that integration, which he later published in *Psychology and Alchemy* (1953) and *Mysterium Coniunctionis* (1963). It is not without irony that science, still in the thrall of the mechanism world hypothesis, pushed away early attempts at such integration: it had pushed away Aristarchus's heliocentric system long before Copernicus "revived" it, and it dismissed alchemy's attempts to integrate the external and the internal worlds, which Jung rediscovered and Richard Tarnas and Carl Johan Calleman elaborated in great detail by showing astrological correspondences (Western and Mayan, respectively) with collective/cultural trends.[152]

That Was a Deep Dive. What For?

Why has it been important to excavate these layers of metaphors? In this book, I'm calling for a redrawing of boundaries, hence a re-structuring of language. Let's put those two metaphors—excavating and building—together: excavating pertains to digging deeper; structure pertains to building something up. When you want to build a structure, the size and type of structure requires that you dig to different depths in order to secure it against external forces that could destroy it. We have looked at metaphors that operate at increasingly deeper levels of consciousness, starting with explicit (poetic) metaphors, through implicit linguistic and cultural metaphors, to implicit root metaphors of our epistemology and ontology. If we use a metaphoric model equating depth of soil and depth of our metaphors, the shallower metaphors (explicit ones) are like securing a tent in topsoil. It will hold under nonextreme conditions, but

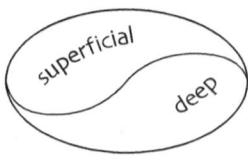

lots of wind or rain (analysis, critique, or change of context) could dislodge it. If we want a more permanent structure, like a house, we have to dig down six feet or so to put in footings that will give the house a solid foundation. To build an even bigger structure, like a skyscraper, we must dig deeper, to bedrock, in order to give it a secure foundation.

With regard to restructuring language, I am suggesting that we examine all levels, but especially the deepest levels of structure, as they have the greatest impact on our un/consciousness. The root metaphors influence the culture-organizing metaphors as well as implicit and explicit cognitive-linguistic metaphors. For example, in several of his books, George Lakoff characterized the differences between conservatives and liberals as being rooted in different conceptions of "family," with conservatives having a more hierarchical conception and liberals having a more egalitarian conception. From a formist worldview, the conservative conception of "family" could be symbolized by a triangle, the liberal conception by a circle. Perhaps, though, the differences run even deeper. The current conservative worldview might be grounded in mechanism, whereas the liberal worldview is more organicist. Here we see how different ways of talking about politics are rooted in different implicit linguistic metaphors, which are in turn grounded in different root metaphors. Those different "bedrocks" result in different cultural metaphors and different implicit conceptual metaphors.

Metaphors About Language and Consciousness

If we look through the layers of metaphors about the topic of this book—a Möbial relationship between language and consciousness—what do we see? To use an explicit metaphor, I would say that metaphors are a coin of the realm. Implicit metaphors about language include LINGUISTIC EXPRESSIONS ARE CONTAINERS, LANGUAGE IS A CONDUIT, LANGUAGE/TEXT IS A BUILDING (in the sense of being/having a structure), LANGUAGE IS WEAVING, ARGUMENT IS WAR, WORDS ARE VESSELS, WRITING IS A JOURNEY, A CONVERSATION IS A JOURNEY, and COMMUNICATION IS SENDING AND RECEIVING (MESSAGES, CODES, etc.).

Implicit metaphors about consciousness include CONSCIOUS IS ABOVE GROUND (UP)/ UNCONSCIOUS IS BELOW GROUND (DOWN), CONSCIOUSNESS IS SEEING, CONSCIOUS IS FINITE/UNCONSCIOUS IS INFINITE. Metaphors themselves have their basis in similarity, the root metaphor of formism. Consciousness, I would venture to suggest, feels at home in organicism.

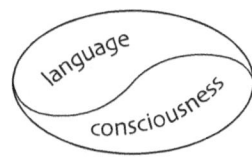

Now we must ask how bringing paradox into the workings of language—into our concepts, logic, and metaphoric structures—will alter all those types of metaphors. The form of metaphor, X IS Y, would have to expand such that X and/or Y use paradoxical concepts, as in X is A and not-A. The most relevant implicit metaphor is LINGUISTIC EXPRESSIONS ARE CONTAINERS. Words, sentences, even paralinguistic phenomena (intonation, gestures) contain or hold meaning. The containers we usually associate with such containing are static entities such as bottles or bowls (see Table 1 on page 85). I am suggesting that we also consider the Klein "bottle" (more accurately, the Klein surface) as a metaphor for how language paradoxically contains and uncontains (i.e., leaves open) meaning. This paradoxical structure could help us find better ways to convey the paradoxical wholeness of organicism. How might new glyphs integrate the root metaphors of the world hypotheses?

Bewußtsein-*what?*

14

Innumerable confusions and a profound feeling of despair invariably emerge in periods of great technological and cultural transitions. Our "Age of Anxiety" is, in great part, the result of trying to do today's job with yesterday's tools—with yesterday's concepts.[153]
—Marshall McLuhan

In 2012 I left Chicago after living there for 25 years, and in 2013 I returned to visit friends. That trip resulted in a plethora of conflicting thoughts and feelings, or cognitive dissonance. It felt like I had never really left Chicago. I negotiated my way through O'Hare Airport as if I was returning home. Indeed, the feelings of arriving back home were quite strong, although I was there only for a short vacation—I would leave in a few days to return to my new home in California. As the week progressed, I visited my old neighborhood and walked familiar streets. The pleasant and comforting familiarity collided with sadness from knowing that I would be leaving, as well as certainty that I had made the right decision to move. It felt so good to be back in Chicago and so good to be returning home soon.

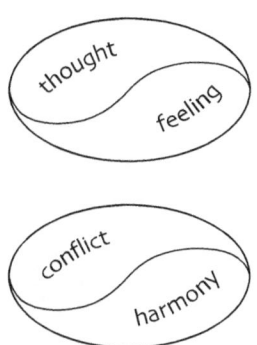

I felt like I was both there and not there, like a ghost from the past wandering the streets of the present. I have such fondness for those streets, and yet I wore them out from over two decades of circumambulation. It would have been so easy to slip back into my old routines, but I did not want to be drawn into their gravitational pull.

These tensions in which consciousness is pulled in many directions are not rare. Some have greater consequences than others. Whether to move house, quit a job, leave a partner, confront your accuser, do something you know is wrong even if it is just—all these situations put us into an uncomfortable inner tension. When there is no clear or obvious resolution available, we can find ourselves pulled apart by our own thoughts or feelings. If the outer world reflects the inner world, I would guess that many of us are feeling so torn right now.

137

What tools do we have to deal with our personal and collective cognitive dissonance? Such dissonances can be rooted in the language used to describe them, and therefore language might be a key to resolving the tension—if we can embrace the paradox(es) in our lives and integrate paradox into our language. Whether the tension of opposites is from the clash of local and global contexts, of left- and right-hemispheric processing, or of understanding and feeling, it confronts us in many ways and on many days. Just as fear and excitement are two different experiences of the release of adrenaline into the bloodstream, cognitive dissonance can be a pleasant or an unpleasant sensation, depending on the meaning you give to the instigating experience. It can feel wonderfully creative, like being on the verge of a breakthrough, or painfully demoralizing, as when facing a divorce. Because paradox has mostly been abhorred by our culture, cognitive dissonance carries with it an unpleasant connotation. But that need not be so.

To fully embrace paradox, we will need to feel the excitement aspect of the emotional dissonance reaction that paradox frequently causes.

As we alter our mindset to embrace paradox, it might feel strange and uncomfortable at first, until we get used to—and eventually even feel energized by—the *Bewußtsein spannung* (tension of consciousness) of living within the context of all/and.

A few years ago, I attended an event at one of the California missions founded by Junípero Serra. The event was part protest, part remembrance ceremony. Local indigenous groups were protesting the impending sainthood of Father Serra. They gathered in the graveyard outside the mission to draw attention to the fact that Serra had used their ancestors to build his Catholic empire and, in attempting to do what was right by his own ideology, imposed conversion to Catholicism on them. Some of those native people are buried there in unnamed graves, marked only by abalone shells or a weathered wooden cross. This event was a quiet affair, with some elders speaking, a drum beating, bowed heads. And in the middle of this protest, the parishioners of the church concluded their own ceremony with the singing of Easter hymns. The pipe organ, with its deep wood bass tones, nearly drowned out the drumbeats. The people inside were singing about the risen Lord. The people outside were mourning their ancestral dead. The hymn's energy rose up, up, up. And the silent screams of the dead arose from the Earth and joined in paradoxical tension. Tears streamed down my cheeks.

Unlike the tension between the truth and a lie, the *Bewußtsein spannung* of paradox occurs when you are facing contradictory truths. If you try to hold the tension of such opposites equally, it can feel like you are going mad, being split down the middle, or becoming bipolar. To be in the uncertainty of both/and feels particularly uncomfortable if you are waiting for something or someone in the external world to resolve your own inner tension. That is why I think that the warm fuzzy comfort of cold hard reason has made paradox taboo in Western cultures.

In Indian logic, however, there is a term for the multiple truth values that can be applied. The term is *catuskoti*, meaning "four corners." Any statement can be judged according to the following four possibilities: it could be only true, only false, both true and false, or neither true nor false.[154] The latter two possibilities introduce an interesting wrinkle, but a wrinkle that I think is important to our quest to consciously evolve language. Logical conundrums such as the famous example "This sentence is false"—in which it's true if it's false and false if it's true—are not the kind of paradoxical wordplay that interests me. However, when you examine such paradoxes, you sometimes see that their irresolvability involves conflating two different levels, two different contexts. To see the two contexts more clearly, consider instead the sentence "This sentence is red," printed, as it is here, in black ink. We must evaluate the meaning of "this sentence is red" by looking beyond the meanings of the words to the color of the printed words. That takes us into a different context. Similarly, with "this sentence is false," we have to do a meta-evaluation of its meaning that takes us into a different context, not of its color but instead to a context of truth-value evaluation.

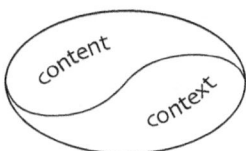

When something is stated that applies differently in different contexts, then I'm interested. As we saw with the Möbius strip, we can say that it is both two sided and one sided. Here is where context is key: at the local context (if we were small beings walking around on the surface of the Möbius strip), it does indeed seem two sided, like an ordinary piece of paper. However, if we are outside the Möbius strip, that is, in a different context, we can also see that there is only one side. Each claim seems true within its context.

How does such a conundrum show up in real life? Most days it is sunny, cloudy, rainy, or snowy. Sometimes it is 60 degrees in February when you would expect it to be snowing. Such anomalies are not uncommon. When I lived in the Midwest, it seemed like we often got a reprieve from winter for a few days in February. At this time scale, I do not "see" climate change happening. So how can the weather seem normal while climate change is pushing us toward a dangerous precipice? The context for climate change is larger (both spatially and temporally) than the context of the weather each day. I'm sure you have already heard this argument.

Where else in life does context make a difference in how we perceive something? Is your child's context different from yours? How about your boss's context? When one is embroiled in dysfunctional family dynamics, it can be difficult to see the whole drama playing out, as an outside observer might. Similarly, using those "local" examples to expand your thinking could help you see how the *context* of someone whose political views are opposite yours might differ from your own context. People who have different world hypotheses are coming from different contexts. What about people who have different ways of learning and knowing, such as those of indigenous cultures? Instead of invalidating the truths of people whose context differs from one's own, how can we evolve language to be able to "contain" seemingly contradictory truths from radically different contexts?

Such a project requires many people with many different skills and sensibilities—social wisdom. It needs to be done with all available information about possible downstream effects or consequences. In movies like *The Social Dilemma*, we see the unintended consequences of technology design that was not thoroughly thought through. Linguistic innovation is not in the same class as technology. Language is sacred. It mediates our relationships with one another, the world, and the transcendent. We should co-create novel structures for language with each other, the world, and the unknown.

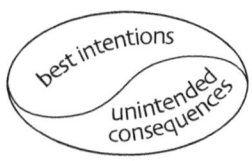

Heraclitus's emphasis on flux and change might hold a key to dealing with *Bewußtsein spannung*. If we assume that nothing is static, then we can hold the tension of opposites by dancing with them, first this way, then that. Many of my tango teachers have characterized that intricate dance as simply walking, first on one foot, then the other. Organizational consultant Barry Johnson gives us a method by which to dance with any polarities.[155] The key is determining both the upsides and the downsides of each pole of a polarity. Sometimes a good thing can flip into its opposite. For example, an abundance of unstructured time can lead to a lack of focus, and too much structured time can leave you feeling constrained, so you escape by daydreaming. By knowing when a good thing is slipping into being not so good, you can keep things from spiraling into a truly bad situation by injecting a bit of the opposite pole. When you feel yourself losing focus on a project, for example, you can quickly regain it by scheduling an activity that will either give you a real break or put you back on track. I like to take a brisk walk, then come back to the project refreshed and able to focus. Such a practice requires greater-than-usual self-awareness as well as knowledge of the boundary between the positive and negative aspects of a pair of opposites that you know you are holding in dynamic tension.

Recently, the topic of sensemaking[156]—how we make sense of the information that we are exposed to—has become prominent, particularly in light of the many disinformation campaigns that political parties, corporations, and others have been running. In the past, visible and invisible structures have helped us make sense of our world. Various authorities, from governments to religions to news commentators, have done so in a way akin to the podium-and-seats-in-rows metaphor. Similarly, in indigenous talk circles or ceremonies, sensemaking occurred via the seats-in-a-circle mode. Recently, it seems, we are facing haphazard-seats-with-no-apparent-order. No longer can we trust the old authorities or the media companies to tell us the truth. (When could we trust anyone, really? Even though we come into this world wanting to trust, even our parents betray our trust sooner than later. After all, you don't believe in Santa Claus anymore, do you?) Although we have been lied to systematically since the dawn of advertising, the new phenomenon of social media as assistant sensemaker has emerged at the heart of the conundrum because of how their artificial intelligence algorithms curate what we see on a given platform. Most often they simply tell us what they think we want to hear, based on our prior choices (the videos we watched, the links we clicked on). The resulting information bubbles reduce our ability to think critically and to question the information we take in, because they activate confirmation bias.

Thus, the question of how to make sense of conflicting or confusing information takes us into realms of interpretation that go beyond the most basic level of what a text means at face value, based on dictionary definitions. Context must be accounted for; the values, motivations, and subtexts of the speaker must be teased out; and, most importantly, one's own epistemic biases must be factored into the sense of others' words. How does one take stock of one's epistemic biases? You might be doing so unconsciously while reading this book, as many of the things I have said are likely to trigger those biases. Did you chafe, for example, at the idea that all some*things* are some*ones*? Conversely, did you chafe at the notion that Earth is a living organism, with systems and structures akin to our own bodies? If you did chafe at those ideas, did you simply dismiss them, or did you pursue a deeper understanding to try to make sense of them? If you dismissed them but are still reading, then kudos to you! Keep going. The ride will continue to be fun and challenging.

How Do We Speak *from* Wholeness?

15

People are addicted to their beliefs. When you try to change someone's belief they will act like an addict.[157]
—Bernie Siegel

What does Siegel mean by "addicted to their beliefs?" Perhaps it means that, similar to the way addicts won't give up their addiction until it ruins their lives, people won't give up their beliefs until they see how those beliefs are ruining their lives. Alternatively, it could mean that we will abandon our ethics just to get reinforcement for what we believe. Such social approval (likes, retweets, etc.) gives one a dopamine hit, which is a neurophysiological basis of addiction.

How much do we have to ruin life on Earth before we change our beliefs and their concomitant behaviors? How many species must die, how many rivers must dry up, how many towns must flood before we choose to stop believing that we're all separate beings in a fight to the death for scarce resources? Admittedly, such beliefs are extraordinarily hard to change because they, too, are entrenched in many facets of life. Such beliefs have been firmly embraced by the culture through our laws and institutions. They are also invisibly reinforced by language, so that now we just take it as an unquestioned and almost unquestionable fact that being separate is what is real.

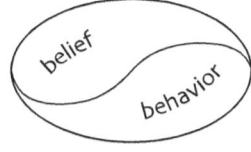

Language has served as a way to bridge a perceived gap between consciousnesses who believe themselves to be separate. By another reckoning, language has served as a crutch to help us hobble through the woundedness of feeling separate. We have been living with the language crutch for so many thousands of years that we consider it the defining characteristic that makes us human—supposedly the capability we have that other animals do not. We now know that animals and plants have a variety of ways of communicating with one another. How difficult will it be to transform and eventually relinquish our current form of language-crutch as we integrate into a new level of wholeness as a *Gaianbody*—without losing the uniqueness of one's own differentiated identity?

Individually and collectively, we need to be the whole being(s) that we are, *in addition to* the separate being(s) that we think we are. How do we speak from those paradoxical places of wholeness within greater wholeness?

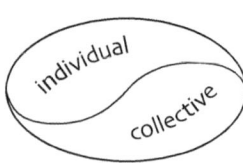

Let's look more closely at what it means to speak *about* and what it means to speak *from*. To speak *about* something, one stands outside it, separate from it, and describes it as an observer. When speaking about something, attributes are applied to it, perhaps even projected onto it. Even if the something is a someone, linguistically it doesn't matter. When we speak *about* someone, the someone becomes objectified.

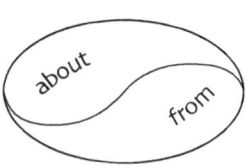

Conversely, to speak *from* a given perspective, one participates in it. To speak *about* being a parent, one could generalize about the trials and tribulations involved in raising a child (e.g., "It's difficult, rewarding, frustrating, and has caused me to lose sleep six days out of seven.") To speak *from* being a parent, you would say entirely different types of things (e.g., "clean up your room" or "do your homework first, then you can watch TV"). You probably would not speak *from* being a parent to your boss, but you might slip into that mode with employees. It feels weird, though, to consider speaking *from* someone else, or even from someone else's perspective. However, by imagining another's perspective (what it is like to be in their context), it might be possible to approximate it.

To speak about the concept of *speaking from wholeness*, it is necessary to address the paradoxes of being whole. First, it is not possible to speak *about* wholeness *wholly*. Ultimate wholeness is greater than we could ever put words to, so silence can be appropriate when speaking about or from wholeness (!).

**Wholeness defies objective description because
it includes the hole in the whole.**

The philosopher Henri Bortoft expresses the paradox of wholeness and partness eloquently:

> Just as there are no independently separate masses on the large scale, then, there are also no independent elementary particles on the small scale. At both levels, the whole is reflected in the parts, which in turn contribute to the whole. The whole, therefore, cannot simply be the sum of the parts—i.e., the totality—because there are no parts which are independent of the whole. For the same reason, we cannot perceive the whole by "standing back to get an overview." On the contrary, because the whole is in some way reflected in the parts, it is to be encountered by going further into the parts instead of by standing back from them.[158]

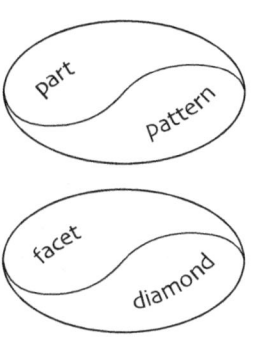

Although wholeness cannot be cut into parts, aspects can be distinguished. Any such aspects are intrinsic, not "outside of one another." To that, one might (inaccurately) say, "I am only a small part of the whole. How can I possibly speak from wholeness?" Bortoft's point is that wholeness is not an object with parts, so you are not part of wholeness in the way the keyboard is part of a computer. Hence, speaking *from* wholeness begins in the imagination and requires a shift of perspective akin to the shift from facet-consciousness to diamond-consciousness (see Chapter 8). Wholeness has no singular perspective. As Gebser suggests, it is aperspectival.

Perhaps it is easier to grok this idea if we expand the term "speaking" to include any form of expression. Picasso, later in life, was attempting to paint from wholeness. In our attempts to come from a place of wholeness, the change in perspective that is required to get out of facetness or partness or brokenness serves us well.

> If you could say it in words, there would be no reason to paint.
> —Edward Hopper

The neuroscientist Iain McGilchrist shows how our brains are structured to be able to attend to and process both whole, patterned information and linear, segmented information—presenced and re-presented experience, respectively.[159] Western culture has overvalued the latter information in recent

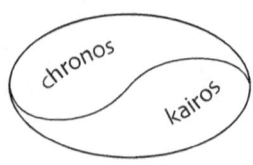

centuries—from reading letters strung together into words and sentences to digitizing Chronos time at the expense of Kairos time, to measuring everything and devaluing what cannot be measured. Speaking and listening from wholeness will engage our innate pattern-seeking tendencies.

Listening from Wholeness

Speaking and listening define two poles of communication—production and reception. Although I have focused mainly on the language-production side (speaking/writing), the language-reception side is equally important. Much has been debated about the reception of language (especially from a "speaking about" perspective; e.g., hermeneutics and deconstructionism). I have nothing to add to those debates. Instead, let's consider what it means to listen from wholeness by first examining what it is not. Listening from a part of you that seeks agreement, reinforcement of your beliefs, or a certain outcome is not listening from wholeness. While talking to someone, have you ever felt that the person was not paying attention to you or was reacting with silent disdain, disagreement, or boredom? You can sense when others are not listening from wholeness, and others can sense when you're not. Thus, how you listen to someone affects the space into which your interlocutor can speak. When someone is not listening from wholeness, how free to speak your mind do you feel? When that happens to me, I get tongue-tied. I can't even talk about topics that I really love to discuss. It's as if the other person's listening style has put up an unspoken barricade—"no, I won't let your ideas in."

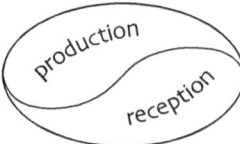

If you listen from wholeness, as if the other person is your best friend or your favorite role model, or even as if they are you (at your best, of course), the space into which others can speak feels light and expansive. Because listening from wholeness, also called active listening, contributes as much to the conversation as speaking does, the interchange feels productive. However, if you listen judgmentally or only pretend to listen, you limit what can be said in that space. If you intentionally try to shut someone up by not listening, that tactic might backfire on you; it might make your interlocutor angry, louder, or more insistent. Not listening well is a double-edged sword.

Listening from wholeness allows whatever needs saying to be said. Regardless of how painful the message might be to hear, wholeness allows for all of it. Does that mean tolerating lies, hate speech, or other acts of verbal violence? Again, yes and no. It does not mean tolerating in the sense of "putting up with"; rather, coming from wholeness would enable you to see that pain-inducing speech often comes from a context of pain, and if you look deeply into yourself, you will likely find such pain there too. Our individual and collective pain needs to be acknowledged or dealt with by bringing those contexts to consciousness.

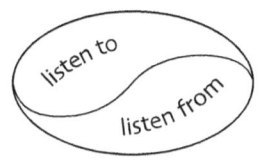

An Emergent Language of Paradox[160]

16

As someone interested in transforming language to better express the complexities of both/and thinking and paradox, I greatly appreciate that Steven M. Rosen suggested a novel way to signify the paradoxical nature of Being.[161] While pondering whether and how his suggestions for signifying Being could be applied more broadly, I realized that much more than his semiotic innovation would be required. Here, I explore how other linguistic infrastructures and exostructures[162] will require equally innovative changes in order for language to embrace paradox more systematically.

Rosen argues that phenomenology currently refers to Being by using a sign, namely, the word "Being," that does not adequately convey the richness of the discourse about Being. Essentially, its form cannot sufficiently express its content or meaning. The word "Being" lacks the fullness of that which it signifies, in particular, the paradoxical quality by which Being itself encompasses and transcends the seeming division into subject and object. Rosen says that "Being can be elucidated effectively only by surpassing the division of subject and object long prevalent in mainstream philosophy" but that "the underlying semiotic structure of such discourse [on Being] has been tacitly geared toward maintaining the split [between subject and object]."

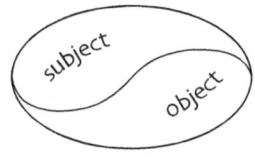

To address that deficiency, Rosen proposes the use of signifiers that radically embody paradox, such as the Necker cube and the Möbius band; he concludes that neither is sufficient. Ultimately, he arrives at the Klein bottle or Klein surface, a fully paradoxical entity in which inside flows continuously into outside. Indeed, the Klein bottle is an apt structure for representing Being, as it requires four dimensions, not the usual three, to exist in itself (i.e., not as a projection, such as the drawing of it on page 10). The Klein bottle is not a conventional object in space. Topologically, the fourth dimension is necessary so that the Klein bottle can flow back into itself without cutting through itself, just as the two-dimensional Möbius strip requires the third dimension for its twist. Phenomenologically, Rosen emphasizes that the fourth dimension is not another spatial dimension but rather is Merleau-Ponty's depth dimension, which is a psychophysical dimension that integrates psychic and physical "spaces." Rosen describes the depth dimension, quoting Merleau-Ponty, as "the experience of the reversibility of dimensions, of a global 'locality'—everything in the same place at the same time, a locality from which height, width, and depth [the classical dimensions] are abstracted." Rosen further clarifies that the depth dimension is "a self-containing dimension, not merely a container for contents that are taken as separate from it; and it is a dimension that blends subject and object concretely, rather than serving as a static staging platform for objectifications carried out by a detached subject."

As many creation stories tell it, after Being has been distinguished from Non-Being (the Void), Being splits into further dichotomies, including subject/object. From that split, other dichotomies derive—living/nonliving, body/mind, matter/spirit, sentient/nonsentient, and so on. Consequently, finding a way to transcend and hold such dichotomies in tension in language, being able to express the unity-in-duality (or multiplicity) of such splits, could have far-reaching implications for "understanding reality and *behaving with respect to it* [emphasis mine]."[163] Rosen draws upon the discourses in phenomenology about Being as a unity-that-encompasses-duality. However, the linguistic gymnastics that are required to express such paradoxical notions (such as that multiply hyphenated phrase) fail to embody, and thus convey, the fullness and richness, particularly the complete experience, of Being.

In seeking a clearer way to represent and express such nondual dualisms, Rosen advances some topics that deserve to be investigated in greater depth, topics that are implicit and deserve to be made explicit. Specifically, in addition to the semiotic limitations that Rosen raises regarding the split between subject and object, I will illuminate other linguistic infrastructural and cultural exostructural aspects of language that enforce the split between subject and object in ways that generally go unnoticed. The two separate words, *subject* and *object*, imply that they are two separate "things"; however, their use also requires a complexly intertwined set of infra/exostructures. As most of an iceberg is below the surface, the tacit infrastructures of language generally operate below the level of conscious linguistic processing; hence, they constrain what can and cannot be said and what must be said, in ways that the everyday user of language does not question. I enumerate some of those structures and focus on how they maintain the split between subject and object—so that we may question them.

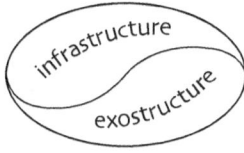

My intention is to hold up a prism to language to reveal a spectrum of assumptions operating as tacit infra/exostructures when we use language. "Spectrum," however, is not quite an adequate metaphor, because in a spectrum each color is separated out linearly from the others. Rather, the tacit infra/exostructures are differentiated only for purposes of identification. As trees, air, water, and organisms function together in an ecosystem, the infra/exostructures function collectively as integrated systems within and around the system we call "language." By illuminating such cultural-linguistic systematicity, perhaps future efforts to address the limitations of language along the lines proposed by Rosen (which I concur are necessary) can advance in an integrated manner among the different facets and dimensions that comprise language-based communication.

In many cultures and philosophies worldwide, our human experience, understanding, and representation of the world in language involves antinomies and opposites. However, in some worldviews their mutual commingling has been suppressed widely though not completely by the dominance of either/or logic. As a way to (re)assert both/and thinking, Rosen's consideration of new topological types of sign-vehicles can be extended beyond the concept of Being to other types of interpenetrating antinomies. Balancing, integrating, and managing polarities[164] so that we cease to be stuck on an ideological pendulum swinging from one pole to the other would advance our ability to think, speak, and write integratively and our efforts to become integrated beings, neither split within ourselves nor from others. To communicate *from* the perspective of wholeness, and not just speak *about* wholeness, requires

151

that the assumptions underlying our use of language embody that wholeness. What are some of those assumptions?

Philosophic-Scientific Writing/Discourse

Ursula K. LeGuin points out that academic discourse, the "father tongue," is the language of power, "the language of thought that seeks objectivity."[165] The father tongue, regardless of whether it is expressed via Latin, French, German, English, Chinese, or some other form, has been used in most philosophic writing and is indeed the form of language we are using presently, in my writing and your reading of this book. We are not using what she calls the mother tongue, which is "language not as mere communication but as relation, relationship."[166] Whatever advances emerge from this inquiry in (and into) the father tongue must benefit the mother tongue as well.

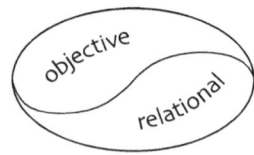

Furthermore, since our mode of engaging presently is through writing, this allows us to be separated in space and in time. We are also using a very particular western alphabetic sign system that has its own historical development through primarily monotheistic cultures that believed in a god that was separate from—and often characterized as above or transcending—mortal humans. I mention this as cultural context, to bring to awareness some of the taken-for-granted aspects of the language being used here and now. They will be examined in more depth subsequently.

In his quest to find more appropriate expressions of Being, Rosen focuses on written language: "Our system of alphabetic signs was designed to serve the interests of detached subjects who stand aloof from the objects cast before them."[167] An early form of pre-alphabetic writing, known as cuneiform, appeared around the fourth millennium BCE in the Near East and consisted of wedge-like marks inscribed into clay tablets. Such writing initially served as an accounting system to keep track of inventory or debts—who owed what to whom.[168] "Given that the vast majority of the earliest cuneiform texts are administrative—detailing transactions involving property, materials, and labor—it is indeed difficult not to see the invention of writing as a solution to the practical bureaucratic problems posed by an increasingly complex economy."[169] Indeed, such representations pertained specifically to objects in space before subjects—e.g., how many cows John owns, how much grain Mary has. Alphabetic writing emerged centuries later in Phoenicia, then morphed into Aramaic, which morphed into Hebrew and Greek and later into the Roman alphabet we are using here.

Marshall McLuhan points out the profound significance of the development of writing systems to human consciousness: "Writing, in its several modes, can be regarded technologically as the development of new languages. For to translate the audible into the visible by phonetic means is to institute a dynamic process that reshapes every aspect of thought, language, and society."[170] He notes that "the ear picks up sound from all directions at once" and such spherical perception differs from the more linear focus of visual perception. With some auditory experiences, one can feel as if one is inside the sound, whereas the experience of seeing is such that what is "out there" seems to be perceived by oneself "in here." In this sense, the world consists of objects out there in space (the container that holds them) before me as the perceiving subject. While writing emerged to keep track of object-beings—cattle, sheep, grain—perhaps the discourse about Being, such as divine Being, presented more of a challenge. Indeed, in Hebrew, one is not to speak or write, in full, the name of the divine. Similarly, one cannot speak about ultimate wholeness. To the extent that Being partakes of ineffability, Rosen asks, "How can we write meaningfully of Being when our very manner of writing keeps Being away?" Specifically, Rosen emphasizes that, if Being surpasses the split between subject and object (as brought out by phenomenology), we cannot meaningfully express Being through a form of writing that implicitly enforces this split.

To "find a different mode of writing, one that can give voice to Being without turning it into an object," Rosen introduces the paradoxical structures of the Necker cube, Möbius band, and Klein surface as novel ways to signify Being. Although they, too, seem to be objects in space serving as signs, he says that their representation of paradox is ongoing, active, dynamic—a verb. Can such integration of paradox into language, as Rosen demonstrates, be expanded beyond the domain of philosophical discourse? I maintain that it can and that it must be. Rosen has made important first steps toward reconciling not only the split between subject and object but between other polarities and oppositions and diversities that also have underlying unity. Such expansion of language will involve knowns and unknowns interacting in open process, thus mysterious as to where it will lead in our living it out fully, not limited to any "text."

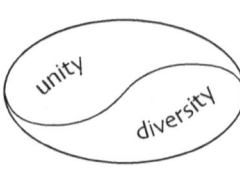

Before presenting a different mode of writing that I invented, I show *how* the split between subject and object (and hence other polarities-that-are-unities) is enforced by an entwined set of infra/exostructures.

Assumptions: Implicit and Explicit

In our inquiry into language, this is a fundamental paradox we need to acknowledge: it is impossible to write about the implicit assumptions of our language system without simultaneously invoking those very assumptions. This enigma[171] serves to further reify the assumptions rather than to free us from their constraints. Although a system of assumptions is necessary for language to function, it is also necessary that we users of this system become/remain conscious of those assumptions.

We can also think about our inquiry into revising the structure(s) of language through a metaphor called "Neurath's boat," which was likely based on the Ship of Theseus (Is it still the same ship, even if all the pieces have been replaced?). Otto Neurath likened the construction of a knowledge base, as science engages in, to fixing a boat at sea. As a sailor, I have had to repair a boat while under way. Fortunately, it was a fiberglass boat, but imagine having to repair a wooden boat while out at sea. You would have to heel the boat to the nondamaged side so that when you remove the damaged plank to replace it, the boat wouldn't take on water and sink. You can't, while using the boat, do a full-scale overhaul. The planks in this metaphor pertain to the assumptions we have about language. How can we revise specific assumptions while simultaneously using our entire set of assumptions?

In the sections that follow, I examine aspects of language generally used but not thought about much because they are second nature to users of everyday language. They comprise the implicit infra/exostructures that, in addition to the semiotics described by Rosen, also conspire to keep apart subject and object, as well as other antinomies. This makes it difficult to discourse on the full paradoxical nature of Being (as well as topics in biology, psychology, quantum physics, economics, and so on). The sequence in which I present the implicit infra/exostructures of language is not as important as their systematicity: these structures operate simultaneously, interpenetratingly. These topics are ઉ, distinct but not separate. They comprise a network of functions whereby language operates as and within a system of systems. Language has also been characterized as a complex adaptive system involving multiple agents (and systems) interacting with one another.[172] The interconnectedness of these infra/exostructures perpetuates the status quo, making it challenging to radically alter the way we might signify Being and the way we signify everything else—which is why it is important to go beyond semiotics. In order to survey multiple infra/exostructures, I do not delve into much depth or into the internal issues in each area.

What implicit infra/exostructures comprise the system of systems called language? I address the following structures: culture, category structure, logic, metaphor, semantics, syntax, concept, and sign-vehicle. Each topic could serve as a node for finer-grained analysis. Although I discuss each separately, I do not consider them to be *separate*; nor do they function separately. They operate together, i.e., co-operate. By considering all these supra/subsystems as co-operating, it might be possible to identify leverage points for transforming the whole system of systems. Leverage points are places where a small change can effect a large change within the entire system.[173] Which of these infra/exostructures might yield fruitful leverage points—adding new concepts to the lexicon, devising novel logics, expanding certain categories—or might a combination of many be required? That is the challenge we human beings/language users face—to consider and find ways to express opposites, contradictions, wholes and parts, and so on, simultaneously—recognizing that they can be distinguished but are not distinct.

Culture. Different cultures, over millennia, evolved sets of distinctions that matter to that particular culture. The origin of the distinction or the reason it matters might have been long forgotten. Nevertheless, each culture develops its unique ways for its members to be in and interact with the world. Whorf's statement that the *structure* of a language (and I would include its implicit infrastructures) influences the way in which users of that language perceive and interact with the world implies that what one culture emphasizes as important and hence stresses or marks in language (e.g., not only by word use but also by a variety of other linguistic conventions) is not the same as in other cultures. For example, some languages emphasize kinship relations in terms of gender, whereas others, such as Indonesian, mark relational seniority and refer to siblings not as brother or sister but as first born or second born.[174] The Matses tribe in the Amazon requires a speaker to specify whether something is known by direct experience, inferred from evidence (e.g., the presence of an animal from its footprints in the mud), by conjecture, or by hearsay.[175] The Guugu Yimithirr language of an Australian tribe orients the individual according to the four cardinal directions (e.g., "watch out, there is a bee near your northwest foot") rather than subjective direction ("your left foot"). People of that tribe show extraordinary ability to orient themselves directionally, even when in unfamiliar locations.[176] Centuries of agreement about such ways to organize one's perceptions and convey them to others enables each language user to use his or her particular language among co-speakers. It is with this broadest brushstroke that a cultural orientation, such as that between subject and object, becomes part of one's lifeworld.

Readers of this book are likely to have been enculturated to interact with a world full of objects, whereas the Mi'kmaq people of southeastern Canada instead consider the world to be full of subjects (where animals, trees, and mountains, for example, have personhood). For the Mi'kmaq, humans are humans and beavers are beavers, but both are persons, that is to say, subjects. They are relations, family—as are the wind, the mountains, and the trees.

Mi'kmaq stories tell of humans marrying animals, such as the girl who married a loon and the man who married a beaver. Such stories show how to enter the experience of animals and know how they live, to see how similar their lifeworld is to that of humans (beavers, especially, because they are a staple food source for the Mi'kmaq).[177]

Different cultures draw the boundaries between categories (such as personhood, kinship, sentience) differently. Although cultural change is considered the most effective leverage point, such change is likely to be strongly resisted.

Category structure. From the culture emerges its category structure. By this I am referring to a kind of set membership whereby predication and implicit metaphors reflect the culture's distinctions and assumptions about the world—what is considered animate versus inanimate; is conscious or not conscious; has or does not have agency; is animal, vegetable, or mineral; whether time flows linearly or circularly, unidirectionally, or bidirectionally; is ever-present or only "now"; whether death is final or just a temporary transition between lives; and so on. Categories do not necessarily have clear boundaries; many are fuzzy, porous, or fractal. In some cases, there may be a prototype example of a category, but often the members of a particular category might fit only to a degree. In particular, some cultures have a narrower category of what constitute subjects, and other cultures, such as the Mi'kmaq, have a broader category.

The category structures of a culture mostly go unquestioned because members of the culture learn the categories implicitly before they develop the ability to question them. Categories are taught to children as they learn to apply language: they learn which categories different things/beings belong to by learning which terms can be predicated to other terms. For example, in kindergarten-level discourse, these primary category structures are conveyed through simple admonitions: "No, Johnny, penguins aren't amphibians, they're birds." By graduate school, the admonitions become more subtle and staunch and pertain to which category structures may be challenged and which may not. In fact, I was subtly admonished not to question the category structures of language!

History provides numerous examples of how category structure has functioned as a leverage point. In particular, great scientific revolutions have occurred when it was found that a concept needed to be expanded—notably, when light was found to be able to take both predicates "wavelike" and "particlelike." Similarly, prions were found to span the categories of protein and virus.

Logic. Logic consists of basic rules for determining what can be said and/or what is true within the bounds of a culture's presupposed category structure. Logic helps to enforce the category structure of a culture by specifying the rules for manipulating concepts within said category structure. Western logic and culture have been based on the foundation of the laws of identity, of the excluded middle, and of noncontradiction. Indeed, there seems to be a bias in Western cultures against contradiction—against "both/and" and "neither/nor." How might Western culture have emerged differently if Heraclitus, rather than Aristotle, had systematized his ideas into the prevailing logic? Would Western preference for stability (nouns, categories) instead have favored emphasis on change (verbs, relationships)? If we were *required*, like the Matses tribe in the Amazon, to specify how the information conveyed was obtained—whether by direct experience, inferred from evidence, by conjecture, or by hearsay— philosophers would probably never agonize over truth values of statements such as "The present king of France is bald" because there would be no way to specify the source of a statement that has no actuality.

Another logical bias in Western cultures is that consistency has been emphasized over completeness. Culturally, inconsistency is almost taboo (likely because assumptions of consistency underlie the concept, and hence the law, of identity). However, Gödel's second theorem formalized that a complete system cannot prove its consistency, implying that a complete system entails inconsistency. Language is indeed an open—incomplete—system. The notions of completeness and consistency, when applied psychologically, for example, have important consequences. One becomes more complete, whole, or integrated when one accepts rather than denies those aspects of oneself that are inconsistent with, or contradict, the ways one prefers to identify oneself. We shall see an example of this below.

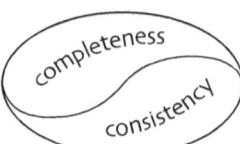

By taking (w)holeness/allness/integrality as a starting point, and acknowledging the systemic inter/intraconnectedness of the (w)hole, Rosen's approach offers us a way to deal with inherent inconsistency, paradox, and the interpenetration of opposites in ways that do not require the resolution of the paradox, synthesis of opposites, or elimination of inconsistency, but rather in ways that maintain the coexistence-in-tension of opposites, antinomies, or polarities. To practice such an approach requires a logic that embraces (in)consistency and (in)completeness. Alternative logics have been and are being developed, including many-valued logic, topological logic, and paraconsistent logic.

The logician Graham Priest advocates paraconsistent logic.[178] Its primary feature is that some contradictions can be true without explosion occurring.[179] The prototype example of paraconsistency is the Liar's Paradox—"This statement is false"—which is true although it claims to be false. Although such bi-level statements currently are rare in ordinary discourse, the relevance of this type of statement for future discourse could prove useful. From the perspective of systems dynamics, a statement could be true at one level of system and false at another level. It could also be said that "a Möbius strip has one side and two sides" because it appears to have two sides at the local level but has only one side at the global level. (It would be necessary to specify or mark such levels of organization or contexts, as for the microbiome examples discussed in Chapter 7.) Paraconsistency expands the standard dichotomy of true/false to a 2 x 2 matrix such that there are four possible valences: true/not false, false/not true, true/false (both/and), and not true/not false (neither/nor).[180] However, a paraconsistent logic would likely need to be based in a structure other than linear alphabetic writing. To represent multiple levels simultaneously, a new form of graphic or symbolic depiction is needed.

Metaphor. As discussed in Chapter 13, poets and other creative writers use metaphor *explicitly* to convey thoughts that ordinary language fails to express directly, in order to make new connections, expand categories, and foster openness of linguistic expression. Everyday language, however, uses *implicit* metaphors that are systematic and mostly go unnoticed because we think we are communicating literally, not poetically. Lakoff and Johnson[181] provide examples of such implicit metaphors. "I can't spend all afternoon with you" engages the implicit metaphors TIME IS MONEY and TIME IS A SCARCE RESOURCE. Abstract concepts tend to be expressed in terms of more concrete concepts. For example, "I can't wrap my mind around his convoluted argument" uses the metaphor UNDERSTANDING IS GRASPING.

A pervasive implicit metaphor in current American culture is the war metaphor. We describe politics (red versus blue), sports (teams fight for first place), relationships (the battle of the sexes), healthcare (the crusade against coronavirus), and even weather (cold front) using war-based metaphors. The characteristics of war, such as the persistence of two opposing sides, one of which is a winner and the other a loser, then implicitly permeate the other concepts and our statements about them. Vast sets of associations are invoked by each implicit metaphor (for example, see Figure 14 in Chapter 17).

How can we hope not just for a peaceful world but also for integration of opposites when we frame so many concepts in terms of war? Let's consider, for example, the culturally defined sets of implicit metaphors associated with subjects and objects. Metaphors regarding *subjects* include terms relating to, among others, agency, thinking, feeling, knowing, and morality. Metaphors regarding *objects* include terms relating to being a container, a conduit, or a vehicle, or terms that convey relationship as outside-of-one-another. Thus, to bring subject and object into profound interconnectedness within Being as self-signified by the Klein bottle, the implicit metaphors associated with subjects and objects must be re-evaluated. Although the Klein bottle (or Möbius strip) can be used metaphorically to convey the mutual permeation of opposites or integration of what is "out there" with what is "in here," Rosen emphasizes that the Klein bottle is not simply an object in space—a different kind of uncontained container—nor simply a metaphor, symbol, or sign for the interpenetration of subject and object. It signifies itself...but we are getting ahead of ourselves.

Semantics. Semantics pertains to the meaning that words, sentences, paragraphs, and texts have in their immediate milieux. Because language does not happen in a vacuum but is used in specific instances in specific circumstances in multiple embedded cultural contexts, those contexts create the vessel in which the assumptions and words function to produce meaning. Contexts can include everything from the historiography of a word (every use of a word and everything that has been said and written about it) to the co-text (the text surrounding the text in question) and even *who* the speaker/writer is. In spoken language, metalinguistic features, such as intonation and gesture, are elements of the semantic infrastructure. At the semantic level of infrastructure, cultural and logical contextualities meet the metaphoric, conceptual, syntactic, and sign-vehicular actualities to catalyze meaning in the writer/speaker–reader/listener dyad.

This is where the implicit sorting of subjects and objects (as determined by cultural assumptions, category structures, and implicit metaphors) becomes explicit. As a speaker, my semantic choices and hence my assumptions and tacit infrastructures become explicit in the words, intonations, and gestures that I use. My ability to create and convey meaning relies on the deep and immediate contexts, the way I order my words, and the specific words I use, all nested like Russian dolls. For example, if I said to someone in my culture, "I spoke with hummingbird today…" that person would need to discern whether "hummingbird" refers to the tiny bird with the red throat, my flibbertigibbet sister whose nickname is Hummingbird, or perhaps my ironically named cat who likes to catch and eat…you guessed it. By saying "spoke with" rather than "spoke to" I imply that I consider "hummingbird" to be my conversational equal, such as my sister, a subject rather than an object. If my category structure were such that birds belong in the category of "beings that understand my language," then my meaning goes against that of most members of my culture. But other cultures might consider it normal for humans and birds to communicate. As another example, if I said, in a nonpoetic context, "I am the mother of my father and the sister of my husband, and he is my offspring," my meaning is quite obscure, given the assumptions of my culture regarding kinship and identity. In another context, as we will discern later, that statement has profound meaning. In the semantic choices I make, I can use the taken-for-granted infrastructure or break from it. Poets often break from it.

Their art is appreciated for how they stretch these infrastructures while still affecting the reader. However, when nonpoets stretch the infrastructures too far, they encounter cultural resistance, sometimes even anger or punishment.

Syntax. The Standard Average European sentence structure of subject-verb-object or subject-object-verb perpetuates the subject-object contradistinction.[182] How does syntax perpetuate this? Note that syntactical subjects and objects are not identical to philosophical subjects and objects. The subject of a sentence is not necessarily a subject in the same sense as in the subject-object split. The subject of a sentence is just as likely to refer to an object. Nevertheless, a linear syntax structures predication such that philosophical subjects/objects have an external relationship to each other rather than an internal one, and other syntactic infrastructures, such as prepositions, also externalize relationships.

Although language content evolves over time, syntax (of English, for example) has remained more stable. In reading Chaucer's *Canterbury Tales*, for example, it is clear from the structure of the sentences that a subject-object split is already assumed and encoded in the syntax. Although the content words in English have changed meaning or spelling, been added to or deleted from the lexicon, the syntax has changed little. Thus, when we read,

> Whan *that* Aprille, *with* hise shoures sote
> *The* droghte *of* March hath perced *to the* rote,
> *And* bathed every veyne *in* swich licour
> *Of which* vertu engendred is *the* flour;[183]

which was written in the 1380s, a contemporary reader can (more or less) understand it even though the spelling and usage of the content words have changed. The metaphors in the passage above are also familiar: RAIN IS A KNIFE that pierces drought. Although the content words that comprise the metaphors have changed a bit, the function words (italicized)—i.e., articles, prepositions, and conjunctions—have not changed through the centuries.[184] Function words establish the infrastructure of a sentence inside of which the main content words—the subject, verb, object, and their modifiers—provide the ideas. Function words convey the essential relationships—both spatiotemporal (above, below, after, before) as well as the internal relationships (which idea or clause is subordinate to another). Is there a reason that the function words have changed so little? Perhaps Franz Boas was on to that reason when he said, "'Grammar performs another important function. It determines those aspects of experience that *must* be expressed.' And he went on to explain that such obligatory aspects vary greatly between languages."[185] Thus, grammar/syntax connects directly to culture.

How does subject-verb-object syntax serve to keep subject and object split?[186] In some languages, syntax consists of types of slots in which to place types of words. Nouns, pronouns, and some abstractions that function as nouns fill the "subject" slot in English. In other languages, the slots take different forms, such as adding prefixes and suffixes to a verb stem. To examine the assumptions underlying English syntax, consider the simple statement, "I am writing this chapter." At the moment I wrote those words in the very first draft, this chapter barely existed. A brief outline in a Word document, it had no conclusion, no body, only an eight-sentence start. But the completeness of the chapter is presupposed by that simple statement because "this chapter" is assumed to exist as an object separate from me. In fact, in the early stage of this writing, the separation of "I" from "this chapter" seems foreign, as I have yet to pull the whole text out of me, by maieusis, giving birth to it. Metaphorically likening the writing process to giving birth presupposes that the completed chapter exists as a thought form in me, as a fetus exists as a physical form inside the body. However, "this chapter" that I am writing barely exists as gestating thoughts of mine, let alone as a fully formed corpus. Those are some of the assumptions implicit in the simple words "I am writing this chapter." I could have chosen different words to convey instead that I am only a few steps into what will likely be (and has been) a long journey of writing and rewriting. If I belonged to a different (imaginary) culture, I might have written something like "images-in-relationship being received by me and expressed graphophonemically." The assumptions underlying that alternative syntax might be that I exist within a field of all possible thoughts, and what

I assume are "my thoughts" are wave patterns in a field of all consciousness that "I" tune into, as a radio is tuned to certain frequencies, and convert them into patterns of images (words) associated with sounds.

In the mother tongue, statements such as "I love you" and "Don't ever talk back to me again" draw on cultural assumptions of separate ego-identities in which the speaker is having the experience of love or anger but the one spoken to is not necessarily also having that experience. A unified subject/object perspective, as we have been discussing with regard to Being, might consider the speaker ("I") and spoken to ("you") as a unity partaking in an experience (love or anger) but not necessarily having the same experience. Each dyad (whether two subjects or even subject and object as we currently categorize them) might then be considered to exist in the field characterized by love or anger. In such a characterization, a different syntax could convey different assumptions. For example, "I/you (as a Kleinian unity) within field [love]" or "I/my printer experiencing [anger]." In the father tongue, an "objective" description could take the form "Jack and Jill/hill experienced [climbing]," which implies that Jack and Jill experienced climbing the hill and the hill experienced Jack and Jill's climbing of it as well. The category structure of the language, here specifically a unified subject/object perspective, would have to allow for the possibility that hills are able to experience events, such that the syntax could express it.

Concept. The term "concept" has differing meanings in various contexts (psychology, linguistics, philosophy). I am using "concept" as an abstraction that does not reference a thing; rather, a concept establishes a boundary in a field of meaning. One might say that concepts are agreed-upon set boundaries. (Such sets are "organized"—however tightly or loosely—into category structures.) The concept of tree establishes the boundaries of what can be considered a tree, and the concept of beauty establishes the boundaries of what can be considered beautiful. Some conceptual boundaries are more porous, more flexible, and/or more (in)consistent than others. Some instantiations of concepts are more prototypic than others.

Because of the nature of the category structure and hence the concepts within it that are generally agreed upon in American culture, concepts such as "subject" and "object" are not intrinsically interrelated. Their relatedness is external; subjects perceive and/or act upon objects. Rosen argues that our usual way of expressing concepts using the standard words does not—cannot—do justice to the *concept of* Being, which draws a different type of boundary. Specifically, he states that the *concept of* Being has a complex internal structure that includes the union of two other concepts—subject and object—that are otherwise (i.e., culturally) diametrically opposed. Rosen asserts that ordinary sign-vehicles (words) cannot sufficiently represent an internally complex concept, such as Being, that integrates subject and object in a way that retains their uniqueness yet also acknowledges their transpermeability. Being relates subject and object as a mutual co-arising or complementarity.

Given that the conceptual structure of English defaults to monadic, non-unified forms, *conceptual* distinctions, such as the typical split between subject and object or between mind and body, are commonly assumed to be *actual* distinctions. Hence, arguments for either "this concept" or "that concept" might be more fruitful if we looked at how the situation requires, integrally, "this" *and* "that"—for example, progressive and regressive, creative and destructive, nature and nurture, genes and environment.[187] Rosen has shone light on an area that needs not just neologisms but new *types of concepts* in English and hence new types of sign-vehicles.

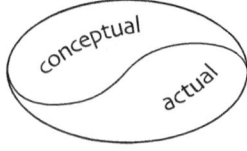

Sign-vehicle. The development of alphabetic writing was both an advance and a diminishment in communication.[188] Written words enabled a greater number of people to be exposed to the ideas of others, but phonetic words also eliminated the ability of iconic sign-vehicles to *show* information. There is no intrinsic relationship between the *c*, *a*, and *t* of *cat*. Relationships such as part-to-whole are not conveyed as a gestalt in alphabetic writing but require the use of prepositions (e.g., cog on a wheel, cell in an organ). Although new words are frequently added to the lexicon, perhaps it is time not just for a new words, but even for new *types* of words, such as ℔, to convey the unity-in-diversity of systems, the local/global paradox of Möbial structures.

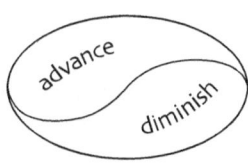

Languages with other types of sign-vehicles can show the internal relationships or complexity within a concept. For example, the ancient Chinese character *Te* (Figure 11) is often translated as "virtue" or "integrity." Those glosses, however, do not convey the full story of what it means to be virtuous. Ezra Pound explains that the two diagonal lines and one vertical line on the left together mean "man in action"; the cross on the top is the number 10; the box with two lines inside it is an "eye"; and the L-shape with the three teardrops means heart-mind (note its unified, dyadic nature, which English radically separates). "Ten eyes" indicates perfect vision, i.e., two eyes (binocular vision) at each of the four cardinal directions and looking down from above or perhaps two eyes for each of the five elements (wood, metal, air, water, and fire). Taken together, these components mean action resulting from looking into the heart-mind with perfect vision.[189] Thus, integrity or virtue consists of looking at an issue from all sides, balancing all the options, knowing what is in your heart, and then taking action. It is not about doing good according to some external standard; rather, integrity is doing the right thing after looking inside and outside, thereby seeing the whole picture.

Figure 11. The character *Te*, which means virtue or integrity.

The internal complexity of *Te* exemplifies how nonalphabetic sign-vehicles could inspire the invention of other types of sign-vehicles, provided that cultural awareness of such internal complexity is not lost in linguistic simplifications. As Rosen suggests, the Klein bottle offers a sign-vehicle for Kleinian (w)holeness, complexity, and dynamism. The Klein bottle as a sign-vehicle is not an icon and thus goes well beyond iconic signs, such as emoticons, alphabetic neologisms, or compounding, as in bittersweet or subjectobject. Furthermore, an image of the Klein bottle is not the sign-vehicle; the Klein bottle itself is.

An important difference between the Klein bottle and alphabetic words as sign-vehicles is that the Klein bottle does not refer to—point to—something else, something other than itself. Kleinian self-signification embodies the fullness of lived experience of flowing of subject into object into subject and so on. The Klein bottle is a paradox-in-itself, as its inside and outside are one and both. What Rosen presents is not a superficial application of topology. To grasp the Klein bottle's fullness/emptiness as a self-signifier requires moving from three-dimensional spacetime into the depth dimension by way of an embodied, meditative stance, an experience of the merging of subject and object. Such a sign-vehicle could not be thrust into parlance that presupposes dualism; indeed, it also requires a nondual context, such as a basis in meditative reasoning, an integrative category structure, cultural assumptions, and so on.[190]

The Klein bottle, with its unification of inside and outside, gives us a different way to approach boundaries. It has no boundary where inside becomes outside and vice versa. (It might look that way in a picture, because of the constraints required to represent it as a two-dimensional drawing.) From the fourth/depth dimension, where else might boundaries that seem to be real in three dimensions merge or disappear?

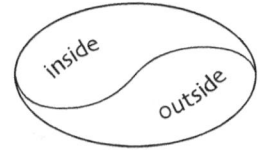

To find ways to enable full-spectrum language to embrace paradox, it will be necessary to move into the paradigm of both/and. However, there are no agreed-upon conventions for expressing categories, logic, concepts, and sign-vehicles that partake of both/and-ness. We will need to invent ways to convey nonduality, interdependent co-arising, and paraconsistency in ordinary language. The infra/exostructures that enable us to use language to communicate will all need to be transformed.

After *Solve, Coagula*

If this were a strictly analytic text, I would have stopped writing after I had dissected the infra/exostructures of language. However, in the Kleinian spirit of the unity of opposites—*solve et coagula*—it is now necessary to move into the complementary process. From *solve*, which in alchemy refers to a process of breaking something apart, we now switch to *coagula*, the process of congealing. If you have ever watched something congeal, you know that it is not a process of building—starting from foundations and adding layers. Rather, once all the necessary ingredients are present, the addition of a catalyst causes an instantaneous change that usually cannot be undone (as in the curdling of milk). The congealing of matter is a chemical reaction—ions get redistributed; new bonds are formed. In consciousness, congealing can take the form of an "aha moment" or a gestalt shift. New conceptual bonds form. Although it is my intention to produce a congealing of understanding in the minds of my readers, each person is different, so it might happen by the time you finish this chapter or book, or it might happen next week, next year, or never.

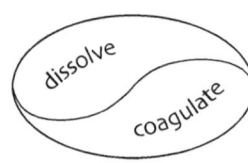

I have characterized language as a system of systems. Systems that are not unduly stressed can be highly resilient, and so it is with language. However, many of the systems in the world, including our ecosystems, financial systems, and social systems, are currently undergoing considerable stress, which is putting stress on our linguistic systems as well. As we have seen, linguistic systems are both stable (function words have preserved syntactic structure) and malleable (content words have changed over time and space, i.e., in different contexts). Language evolves by balancing old and new, arbitrary and motivated[191] additions. Another source of resilience is the interconnectedness of the subsystems, by which they reinforce one another. Each subsystem, however, affords a different way to affect the overall system. According to systems theorist Donella Meadows, to change a highly resilient, complex system, it is necessary to find its leverage points, places where "a small shift in one thing can produce big changes in everything."[192] Leverage points at different levels or places in a system, when tweaked, can lead to different outcomes. For example, rearranging the deck chairs on the Titanic might facilitate discussion among a small group of passengers, but that would not save them from collision with the iceberg; however, adjusting the helm even a few degrees sufficiently in advance of the iceberg is a leverage point that could have saved the entire ship/system.

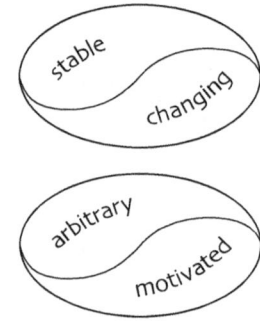

Different types of leverage points are possible for each infra/exostructure of language. To the extent that each infra/exostructure has its particular way to keep subject and object separated, it might be necessary to

i)   develop ways to signify new types of concepts that partake of complementarity, interdependent co-arising, or *enantiodromia*, the tendency of things to change into their opposites; that have logical but not actual distinctions; that convey ontologic relationships such as part-whole; that convey becomingness/process; that are self-signifying or that are otherwise interrelated;

ii)   develop and implement novel forms of logic, such as paraconsistent logic,[193] topological logic,[194] or meditative reasoning[195]; and

iii)   revise cultural assumptions and category structures.

A small shift in assumptions at the level of culture or category structure is likely to make a bigger difference to the whole system than extensive addition of new words to the lexicon. Meadows states that

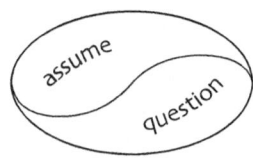

> The shared idea in the minds of society, the great big unstated assumptions—unstated because unnecessary to state; everyone already knows them—constitute that society's paradigm, or deepest set of beliefs about how the world works. [For example,] there is a difference between nouns and verbs. Money measures something real and has real meaning (therefore people who are paid less are literally worth less). Growth is good. Nature is a stock of resources to be converted to human purposes. Evolution stopped with the emergence of *Homo sapiens*. One can "own" land. Those are just a few of the paradigmatic assumptions of our current culture, all of which have utterly dumbfounded other cultures, who thought them not the least bit obvious. However, paradigms are harder to change than anything else about a system...But there's nothing physical or expensive or even slow in the process of paradigm change. In a single individual it can happen in a millisecond. All it takes is a click in the mind, a falling of scales from eyes, a new way of seeing. Whole societies are another matter—they resist challenges to their paradigm harder than they resist anything else.[196]

The millisecond it takes to change one's own paradigm is the *coagulatio*. At larger scales of magnitude, of course, it can take longer.

Before we endeavor to invent new infra/exostructures or revise the old ones, it is necessary to be sensitive to the intended and unintended consequences of linguistic changes. Changes compelled by an authority structure can be counterproductive, whether imposed by a government (as in China) or by colonization (as has happened with warfare throughout history and by commercialization more recently). Also, because language use depends on agreement among users, agreement that is a free choice with no coercion will likely be the most successful form of linguistic evolution. Such linguistic changes must reach a tipping point of acceptance. Esperanto did not. Buckminster Fuller contended that you never change things by fighting the existing reality. To change something, it is necessary to build a new model that makes the existing model obsolete. Similarly, recall the popular statement attributed to Einstein that you cannot solve a problem using the same mindset as that used to create the problem. To that I would add, can there be a new mindset if it is necessary to use the language of the old mindset? I suspect that one will encounter the same limitations of the old mindset. Who can build a new model that does not use the old mindset to create it? Among language users, who are the language inventors?

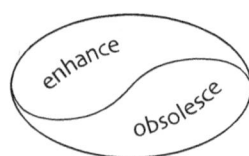

The first recorded intentionally constructed, non-"natural" language was developed by Hildegard von Bingen in the 12th century. Since then, many others have constructed languages,[197] but those invented languages have not attracted a critical mass of other users. However, the constructed languages in recent science-fiction movies and television shows (e.g., *Star Trek*, *Avatar*, and *Game of Thrones*) have acquired many users. The Klingon language from *Star Trek*, in fact, has been expanded more by the users themselves than by its original creators.[198] David Peterson, who created the languages, including Dothraki and Valyrian, for the television show *Game of Thrones*, not only invented spoken forms but also invented nonalphabetic scripts for them.[199] College courses in language construction have attracted students to linguistics departments. Perhaps this trend indicates that people of the current zeitgeist are open to embrace novel linguistic infrastructures. Many of these new constructed languages specifically experiment with different underlying assumptions and ways of forming expressions.

Fortunately, to create novel language that embodies a new mindset, Rosen has shown us a way to better convey certain types of paradoxical or internally complex concepts. However, just as a sacred language such as Sanskrit is not used to order a pizza, neither are Rosen's suggestions regarding the language about Being useful to ask for sausage and mushrooms on it. To use Kleinian self-signification to inform ordinary signification is difficult if not impossible, as it requires a kind of "stepping down of the energy," as transformers take high-voltage power and step it down to a level that is usable in everyday life. To bring the notion of the depth dimension of Kleinian self-signification into an ordinary dualistic, either/or worldview would defeat its purpose. Indeed, for Rosen's ideas to be fully taken up linguistically would require, as I have argued, not just semiotic innovation but full-scale sociocultural shift in world-view. And how would such a shift manifest in the linguistic infrastructures discussed above? In other words, how do we revise logic to grant paradox where it is required? What new kinds of paradoxical concepts might better express the complexities of our ecological, economic, and other post-postmodern contexts and systems? Is it possible to work them into the syntax of our existing language, or will it be necessary to develop a new syntax? What category boundaries need to be revised? What cultural assumptions need to change? How do we change our minds, i.e., our assumptions, our world hypotheses about the way things are?

Essentially, how do we alter worldviews so that the depth dimension, paradox, and Kleinian self-signification become the new normal? How can we leave behind the accepted certainties and enter the mystery? How can we relinquish our addiction to the steady swing, back and forth, from one known perspective to its opposite? Can we incorporate both simultaneously?

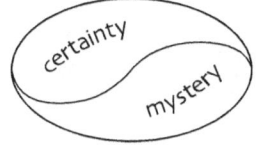

As a way to enter into a mindset of difference-within-unity and wholeness, i.e., as in the paradoxical unity of subject and object, let us consider part of an ancient Gnostic wisdom text, *The Thunder, Perfect Mind*.[200] In this text,

Being is speaking as if s/he is "a being," like one of us. This integral being speaks from the paradoxical perspective of allness (completeness rather than consistency). Such a perspective enables one to get beyond the limitations of either/or thinking, but not without some cognitive dissonance, at first. I suggest you read it out loud, not as a textual relic, but *as if you were declaring it of yourself.* Reading it aloud, slowly, is a way to embody the text. Dance with the paradoxes.

> For I am the first and the last.
>> I am the honored one and the scorned one.
>> I am the whore and the holy one.
>> I am the wife and the virgin.
>> I am <the mother> and the daughter.
>> I am the members of my mother.
>> I am the barren one
>>> and many are her sons.
>> I am she whose wedding is great,
>>> and I have not taken a husband.
>> I am the midwife and she who does not bear.
>> I am the solace of my labor pains.
>> I am the bride and the bridegroom,
>>> and it is my husband who begot me.
>> I am the mother of my father
>>> and the sister of my husband
>>> and he is my offspring.
>> I am the slave of him who prepared me.
>> I am the ruler of my offspring.
>>> But he is the one who begot me before the time on a birthday.
>>> And he is my offspring in (due) time,
>>> and my power is from him.
>> I am the staff of his power in his youth,
>>> and he is the rod of my old age.
>>> And whatever he wills happens to me.
>> I am the silence that is incomprehensible
>>> and the idea whose remembrance is frequent.
>> I am the voice whose sound is manifold
>>> and the word whose appearance is multiple.

I am the utterance of my name.

What does it feel like to speak from this atemporal, aperspectival rendering of identity, this exuberant fullness of being? The speaker here integrates divergent aspects (honored one and scorned one) of oneself and integrates various identities past, present, and future as different familial relations. Indeed, we get the sense that the being speaking is the One Being who has manifested as the many beings. (Could you feel that when you read it?)

In subsequent lines of the text, the speaker says, "I am the name of the sound and the sound of the name. I am the sign of the letter and the designation of the division." That statement further conveys that the sub-objective being, Being itself, is not even separate from the speaking of her/his/its name. Signifier is one with that which it signifies; it is self-signifying, as Rosen described for the Klein bottle.

When one knows oneself as bride and bridegroom, as holy one and whore, as the mother of one's father, as the utterance of one's name, the law of noncontradiction no longer applies, the familiar categories of self and other no longer apply, the construct of time no longer applies; how can one speak from such a context in which the familiar structures no longer apply, especially if one only has the familiar structures of language and culture with which to work?

For a sociocultural shift to happen, individual shifts must occur. Thus, it might be useful to turn to one's own lived sense of paradox in order to appreciate it in the broader context. How does Kleinian awareness/intuition/comprehension/aperspectivity presentiate in your everyday life? Facing personal paradoxes usually involves the experience of cognitive dissonance, such as a sense that who I think I am is not who I appear to be. Jung calls this act of facing and accepting of otherness in oneself "integrating the shadow." One way to own your psychologic shadow is by dwelling with the irony in your life. Do you "put on a happy face" no matter how you feel but have a child or spouse who is chronically depressed? Have you experienced being honored and scorned, say, in a relationship that ended unexpectedly and abruptly? Or perhaps the current political climate has left you wondering whether you still embrace your party's values. Without linguistic structures that embody the dynamic, differentiated unity of such volatile polarities, a strong tendency is to take one side of the polarity and deny the other. For example, given my family's cultural background and values, I have generally sided with my intellectual nature and devalued my artistic nature, so my own challenge is to be both intellectual and artistic—and still earn a living!

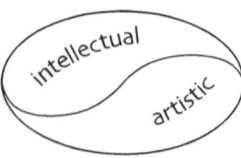

Such disunities are manifested not just personally but also culturally. For example, societal expression of the objectivizing, fragmented, mechanistic worldview has resulted in the current cultural polarizations between political factions, religions, ethnicities, and other forms of Us-versus-Them that are based on turning the Other, particularly other subjects, into objects. Hence, those who do not inhabit our own information bubble are often invisible to us, unless we are demonizing them (projecting our shadow onto them)! Furthermore, according to climate scientist and Jungian analyst Jeffrey Kiehl, the separation of "me" from "not me" has fueled an unsustainable, even destructive, way of living. He says, "Separation makes our world invisible. This sense of invisibility is part of our inability to connect with the climate problem. Much of the change occurring today is in the relatively unpopulated polar regions. The melting of sea ice and ice sheets is not palpable to most."[201] Climate change is invisible when we consider ourselves separate from Gaia.

Consider the consequences of remaining stuck using language that assumes and hence sustains a state of radical differentiation. Jung describes how the development of consciousness contributed to the corresponding radical differentiation within language:

> Although it [modern consciousness] has apparently got rid of the unconscious it has become the victim of its own verbal concepts...Man's advance towards the Logos was a great achievement, but he must pay for it with a loss of instinct and loss of reality to the degree that he remains in primitive dependence on mere words. ... This rupture of the link with the unconscious and our submission to the tyranny of words have one great disadvantage: the conscious mind becomes more and more the victim of its own discriminating activity, the picture we have of the world gets broken down into countless

particulars, and the original feeling of unity, which we integrally connected with the unity of the unconscious psyche, is lost.[202]

Our discriminating activity, partly driven by a desire to find what is physically fundamental, that is, what cannot be further divided, paradoxically contributed to our sense of societal fragmentation. As we sought unsplitable parts of atoms, we further split ourselves from each other and from our environment. In 1983, physicist David Bohm observed that

> the attempt to live according to the notion that the fragments are really separate is, in essence, what has led to the growing series of extremely urgent crises that is confronting us today. Thus, as is now well known, this way of life has brought about pollution, destruction of the balance of nature, over-population, world-wide economic and political disorder, and the creation of an overall environment that is neither physically nor mentally healthy for most of the people who have to live in it. Individually there has developed a widespread feeling of helplessness and despair, in the face of what seems to be an overwhelming mass of disparate social forces, going beyond the control and even the comprehension of the human beings who are caught up in it.[203]

What Bohm perceived 40 years ago has since been magnified. To be free from the constraints of fragmentary worldviews, it is necessary to see how the language we use, especially the father tongue, is deeply enmeshed with and expressive of a fragmentary worldview *not just in content but in form*. If we continue to use the same sign-vehicles, logic, and concepts that are informed by a presupposed category structure derived from cultural agreements based on that old worldview, it is highly unlikely that we will be able to use the language of the old worldview to create a new one. Revision of both the content and form/structure of language will be necessary.

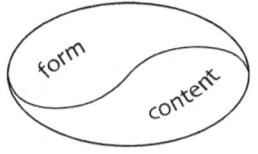

Although differentiation of subject and object was a necessary part of our phylogenetic individuation process, we humans can now locate ourselves as both differentiated and integrated within the larger global and universal, social and spiritual spheres—as distinct but not separate. We can speak from and live from the knowing of oneself as a difference-within-unity. To do that, however, will require us to revise some sociocultural-linguistic assumptions. For any individual to be able to say "I" and mean not just the agency that acts through this particular body, but that and everything else—as *The Thunder, Perfect Mind* illustrated for us—would constitute not just a personal transformation but also a linguistic transformation. In a fictive world that I created in my novel, the type of culture that allowed for such language was described thus: "The key is to hold two perspectives simultaneously, to look at the whole painting while seeing each brush stroke, to consider the whole body when just the foot hurts, to be here now and to be everywhere everywhen."[204] This requires the ability to have both a local and a global perspective simultaneously. To live from that expanded awareness, we need to find ways to enhance the structure of discourse so that the dynamism between/among the various perspectives can be addressed in a way that makes it clear that one without the others is incomplete—a liberal perspective without a conservative perspective is incomplete; an urban perspective without a rural or indigenous perspective is incomplete, and so on.

Such expanded awareness will transform experience in profound ways. To speak *from* the depth dimension (and not just speak *about* it), Western cultures will need to make important shifts in category structure. To embrace and live in paradox might be uncomfortable, even terrifying, at first, given our cultural abhorrence of it. To recategorize that which our current category structure considers an "object" (e.g., a tree, rock, or your computer) as a subject-object, we need to revise deeply held assumptions, beliefs, and ways of relating to all types of "others." For example, we will need to understand the implicit assumption that, when I refer to "that X" (e.g., you, or that tree, or even that book), I am referring to an expanded sense of myself as subject-object. Although I distinguish myself from that tree, I do not hold myself separate from it, because the tree exhales the oxygen I need to inhale or provides fruit that enables me to live. I understand our deeper connectedness via the depth dimension and experience it, for example, via a sense of flow. The notion of "reference" itself would become obsolete or require revision, as there would be nothing "out there" to refer to, only distinctions within my-expansive-self.

differentiated / integrated

personal / sociocultural

In order to embrace such transformative awareness, it will also be necessary to transcend seeming contradictions. Disallowing contradiction precludes wholeness. *The Thunder, Perfect Mind* illustrates the embrace of contraries within Being. It is time to question the law of noncontradiction. How could we construct a way of reasoning that starts *with completeness AND the distinctions within it*? If we *start with* the explosion—i.e., the field of all possibilities (all/and), the implicate order, including the possibilities that we don't know we don't know—rather than starting with conventional actualities and trying to put fragments together to form a whole, then perhaps a logic of both/and//all/and can be realized to support a paradox-based conceptual system.[205]

Although I have used the father tongue in this book, language is not limited to this form. We use language for myriad purposes, not just to propose ideas, make arguments, or describe some aspect of experience. The mother tongue keeps us related.[206] Language is also used performatively. As the philosopher J. L. Austin noted, we do things via language, from "I thee wed" to "I certify that this agreement is legal and binding" to dismissing someone entirely with the single word, "whatever."[207] The most subtle and unconscious motivations are present in the way we use language in a particular situation. Even when we use the mother tongue, how we relate will shift from a perspective of exteriority (I am other than you) to paradoxical transpermeability (I am you and me and thusness in a global sense, AND I am this identity-me in a local sense). As in the concept of *Ubuntu*—I am because you are—and as John Lennon has sung—"I am he as you are he as you are me/ And we are all together"—we can find new ways not just to signify Being but to signify our being-as-oneness-and-uniqueness.

Seeing Through Solid Words

17

Opposites hold polarity by their very nature; you cannot have one pole without the other. Given this fundamental situation, opposites must be a part of our new story for the future.[208]
—Jeffrey Kiehl

My interest in the *The Thunder, Perfect Mind* (TPM), which I quoted in the previous chapter, goes back to Anne McGuire's course on Gnosticism at Haverford College in the 1980s, before much of the current scholarship on it was available. Its paradoxes intrigued me, and I tried mightily to make sense of it but could not do it then. Recently, however, I realized that TPM could be used as a way to enter into a mindset of unity and wholeness. As we saw in Chapter 16, TPM is written from the perspective of an integral being, one who is All-of-It (i.e., paradoxical completeness rather than a consistent but incomplete persona). Perhaps even imagining such a perspective of being All-of-It enables one to get beyond the limitations of either/or thinking. I think that is also what Jean Gebser was trying to help us do. Here, I use TPM to illustrate Gebser's concepts of *transparency* and *diaphaneity*. Those concepts, in turn, deepened my understanding of that Gnostic text and provided clues as to what its purpose might have been. By looking at TPM and Gebser together, we can begin to get out of our linguistic ruts and use the ladder (ordinary language) to see beyond the ladder.

Gebser's Notion of Transparency, As It Applies to Language

Jean Gebser (1905–1973), a German-born, naturalized Swiss citizen, is best known for his magnum opus *The Ever-Present Origin* (EPO). To recapitulate that vast work is beyond the scope of this chapter, but interested readers can consult Jeremy Johnson's introduction to Gebser's ideas, *Seeing Through the World*.[209] Gebser's intent was to show the *concrescence of the spiritual*. To do that, he describes five structures of consciousness that emerge phylogenetically and ontogenetically and yet are also ever present.[210] These five structures of consciousness—the archaic, magic, mythic, mental, and integral structures—can be considered archetypal (for a description of each, see note 44).

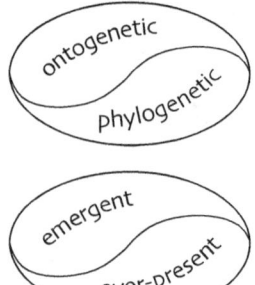

To understand these structures of consciousness as a whole, it is important to realize that they are not stages and yet they name stages, in the way that a seed becomes a tree by going through the various structures of sprouting, leafing, flowering, etc., each naturally following the other. The potential of the tree is already present in the seed. Also essential to understand the structures of consciousness is the concept of transparency (diaphaneity) as "the form of manifestation (epiphany) of the spiritual."[211] Gebser does not say transparency is the manifestation itself, but the *form it takes*. Form is a pattern—structure rather than content. It seems odd to say that transparency is the *structure* of something, of the spiritual, no less. Note that the form of manifestation is an epiphany, a congealing, not a slow uncovering but a sudden realization, as when you can see both the duck and the rabbit in Figure 12.[212]

Figure 12. Example of bi-stable percepts.

If we consider a typical opaque object from a fixed perspective, such as the cube on the left in Figure 13, we see only three of its six sides, the three closest to the viewer. A transparent cube (on the right) allows us to see through it, to see all six sides and the entire form of the cube. You might have such an epiphany if you were looking at the left cube but suddenly saw in your mind's eye the whole structure, as in the right cube. By being able to see through the surface (content), you can see all the sides (structure)—the wholeness of the object. To understand Gebser, it is necessary to generalize from that

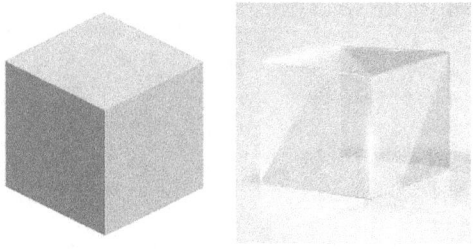

Figure 13. Opaque and transparent cubes. Transparency reveals wholeness of structure.

spatial metaphor to the idea of seeing through more complex concepts and seeing through time. What might you discern about your life, for example, if you could see all of it simultaneously rather than in chronological order?

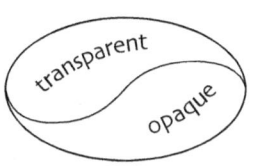

To clarify *transparency*, Gebser says:

> Our concern is to render everything latent "behind" and "before" the world—to render transparent our own origin, our entire human past, as well as the present, which already contains the future. We are shaped and determined not only by today and yesterday, but by tomorrow as well. The author [i.e., Gebser] is not interested in outlining discrete segments, steps or levels of man, but in disclosing the transparency of man as a whole and the interplay of the various consciousness structures which constitute him. This transparency or diaphaneity of our existence is particularly evident during transitional periods, and it is from the experiences of man in transition, experiences which man has had with the concealed and latent aspects of his dawning future as he became aware of them, that will clarify our own experiencing the present.[213]

In addition to spatial transparency, Gebser also makes temporality transparent via simultaneous differentiation and nondifferentiation (ᛦ) of time concepts, i.e., not past or present or future, but past-present-future, ongoing evolving with the past being present in the present and the future, and the future being present in the past and the present. Such notions strain our everyday sense of linear causality and logical conditionality (if X, then Y). However, this temporal transparency is not a simplistic negation of time (timelessness); Gebser calls it "time-freedom," that is, freedom from being trapped in an assumption of unchanging, forward-marching tick-tocks. Imagine being an ant walking along a Möbius strip. From this perspective of being on its surface, it looks like it has two sides. However, from the perspective of one holding the whole Möbius strip in one's hand, it is clear that there is only one continuous side. In such a Möbial model of local and global perspectives, our everyday sense of time corresponds to the local perspective, and Gebser's transparent time-freedom corresponds to the global perspective.

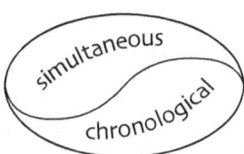

Furthermore, Gebser says

our description does not deal with a new image, worldview or conception of the world…our concern is with a new reality—a reality functioning and effectual integrally, in which intensity and action, the effective and the effect co-exist; one where origin, by virtue of "presentation," blossoms forth anew; and one in which the present is all-encompassing and entire. Integral reality is the world's transparency, a perceiving of the world as truth: a mutual perceiving and imparting of truth of the world and of man and of all that transluces both.[214]

Gebser is not presenting another novel philosophic or scientific model or explanation or representation. He is attempting to find new methods by which to investigate consciousness structures. He claims that "contemporary methods employ predominantly dualistic procedures that do not extend beyond simple subject-object relationships; they limit our understanding to what is commensurate with the present Western mentality" (EPO, p. 7). The new methods would entail new modes of *waring*, including seeing-through. His neologism, *to ware*, refers to "the 'sense' of perceiving as well as imparting verity or truth. *Only through the reciprocal perception and impartation of truth by man and the world can the world become transparent for us*" (EPO, p. 261). *Waring* is both passive and active simultaneously and neither passive nor active. Recall the last time you had an epiphany; likely it just "happened," perhaps after long contemplation, but it was not the result of contemplation nor of perceiving, but of something happening between them, integrating them. You cannot plan an "aha moment," but you can cultivate an openness for them to happen. *The Thunder, Perfect Mind*, I believe, reveals a way to cultivate such ground.

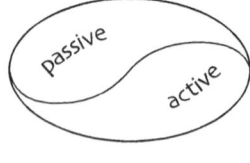

As in the opacity of the cube, opaque language reveals only surfaces. Physical surfaces can be perceived by our senses; temporal surfaces, by experiences. But Gebser is exhorting us to look through surfaces and through events. What do we perceive when we do? Steven Rosen speaks of the "depth dimension" (after Merleau-Ponty).[215] Is a structure that is revealed via depth/transparency even characterizable using a language oriented to characterizing surfaces?

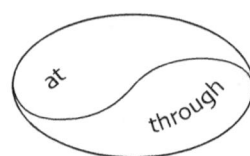

The structure of a basic (English) sentence is subject-verb-object. Its content could be anything from "The dog chewed the bone" to "Essence precedes existence." Such language is grounded in a cultural assumption of Object-in-Space-before-Subject.[216] By using such a construction, ironically, the concept of "essence" in the subject position is treated syntactically as if it were a thing, an object, even though its meaning implies the opposite. The noun-verb-object syntax preserves the Object-in-Space-before-Subject framing and concresces simple subject-object relationships. As a result of these fundamental structures of the English language, it has characteristics such as the following:

- Differentiation and distinction function more prominently than unification. Consequently, opposites remain polarized rather than being seen as mutually interdependent. Nature is set against nurture, liberal against conservative, war against peace. Forced distinctions such as female or male conceal that to varying degrees each of us has male characteristics and female characteristics, *anima* and *animus*. By identifying with one set of characteristics to the exclusion of the other, people become caricatures of themselves. Balancing both, knowing when to emphasize the masculine and when to emphasize the feminine, renders us whole. Indeed, a category that emerged fully into our collective consciousness a few years ago is "gender fluid," which could be used not simply as a label but as a way to express how each of us moves through life sometimes more like one gender and sometimes more like the other.

- Concepts are generally monadic; that is, a concept excludes its opposite. Consequently, realities that are not separate ontologically can be considered conceptually separate because linguistic structures treat them as separate. For example, prepositional constructions such as "a cog *on* a wheel" make it seem as if cogs are separate from wheels. Indeed, cogs are & wheels.

- This subject-versus-object form of language categorizes processes, breaks growth/movement into stages, and then treats the stages as if they were truly separate from one another.

- There is a tendency to deny the shadow; for example, the set of associations that goes with the implicit metaphor UP IS GOOD[217] (Figure 14)

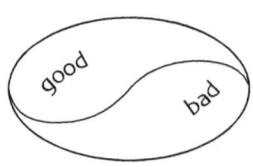

ignores not only the opposite (DOWN IS BAD), but more importantly, the times when good is not up, as when more is not better, sacredness is earthly, and hyper-rationality leads to a lack of empathy.

As described in Chapter 16, language structures are also grounded in cultural perspectives. Indeed, our culture determines the categories by which we divide up and hence talk about life. The everyday structures of language are perspectival and temporal. How might we alter the structure of language to convey more transparency (aperspectivity, atemporality)? Or, in Gebserian terms, how do we communicate *from* an efficient, integral awareness and not just *about* it?

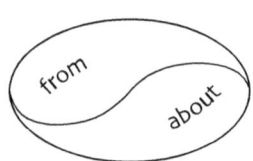

Toward Transparency in Language

The Thunder, Perfect Mind is thought to have been written between 300 BCE and ~350 CE.[218] It uses conventional syntactic structures combined with paradoxical logical structures in a way that intimates transparency. Originally scholars assumed that, like other texts found at Nag Hammadi, TPM had been translated from Greek to Coptic, but Hal Taussig's group at Union Theological Seminary looked at the rhyme structure and, after back-translating it into Greek, concluded that it was originally written in Coptic.[219]

Gebser probably did not have access to TPM, as it was discovered in 1945 but not published until 1977. *The Ever-Present Origin* (EPO) was published in 1949. However, Gebser did have access to other Gnostic texts: he mentions Gnosticism in EPO and even quotes an apocryphal saying of Christ. Indeed, there was considerable scholarly interest in Gnosticism in Germany in the late 1800s and early 1900s

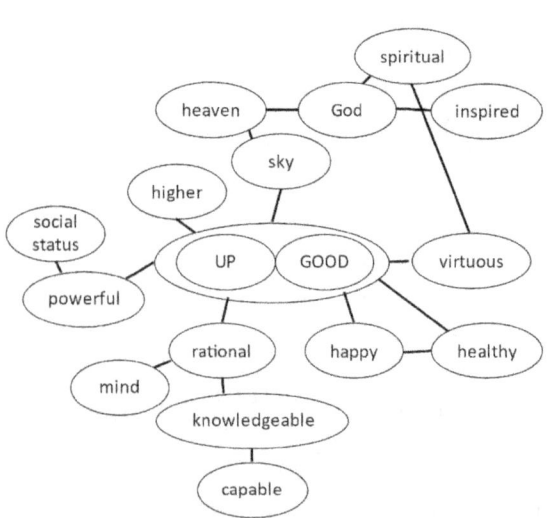

Figure 14. Example of a web of associations for the implicit metaphor UP IS GOOD. Such webs of association preclude that which would bring balance, e.g., feeling along with thinking, vulnerability along with power.

based on the texts that were available at the time.[220] Jung studied Gnosticism intensively as well.

TPM is not a typical Gnostic text. Its paradoxes might be fashioned after Greek riddles, from which the modern paradoxes of philosophy are thought to have derived. The text is also atypical because it has none of the "usual suspects" (e.g., Ialdabaoth, the Archons) and does not mention common Gnostic concepts, such as the Pleroma. Although it does use the form of aretalogy (a type of divine revelatory text in the form of "I am" statements), it is not typical. The Isis aretalogies, for instance, proclaim her wonderfulness and her universality,[221] whereas TPM also proclaims the speaker's not-so-wonderful qualities, that is, the shadow.

It could also have been influenced by Shaivist practices in which the practitioner internalizes a deity or internalizes a ritual.[222] By internalizing a ritual, what was once an outer practice becomes a metaphor for an inner process that unfolds within consciousness.[223] By *performing* TPM (as McGuire and Taussig et al suggest[224]), particularly because it is written in the first person, the speaker becomes transparent by embracing her/his paradoxes.

Because of the way TPM was originally translated by George MacRae, the speaker was for a long time thought to be female and was identified as possibly Sophia or Eve.[225] However, the new translation by Taussig's group showed that several passages clearly indicate that a "he" is speaking.[226] That both genders emerge in a single voice supports the notion that the speaker is speaking from the perspective of All-of-It, which would encompass both female and male aspects.

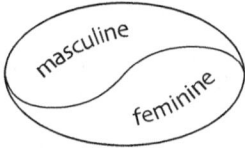

TPM has been difficult to interpret for all those reasons, as well as its conscious use of paradox and seemingly impossible situations (e.g., "I am the mother of my father and the sister of my husband and he is my offspring"). Part of that difficulty might be because religious scholars generally do not draw on Gebser's notions of transparency, aperspectivity, and atemporality. Although there is agreement that TPM is being spoken by a divine being, some commentators try to understand it perspectively, such as from a feminist perspective or a social perspective.[227] I maintain that TPM was intended to carry one into aperspectivity and atemporality.

As one speaks the text and thereby embodies and declares oneself to be All-of-It, one can begin to embody both light and dark sides of being human, thereby approximating wholeness. There is freedom in acknowledging one's darkness, as it is then no longer necessary to hide it, either from others or from oneself.

McGuire proposed that a potential purpose of TPM is to awaken human beings to the remembrance of their divinity: "by locating the divine in the 'voice' and 'hearing' of the text, it leads its hearers or readers to find the divine within the text and within themselves, and so to discover themselves within the divine."[228] If indeed the text was meant to be performed, it would require the performer to embody that which she or he is performing, namely, a being of infinite temporality (through many generations) and infinite spatiality while simultaneously being a unique center of agency. Could embodying such extremes simultaneously lead one to a transcendent experience of one's simultaneous finitude and infinitude?

If Gebser had such an experience, which is possible, as he "had what he later described as a 'lightning-like inspiration' for the work he would spend the next twenty years elaborating and articulating,"[229] perhaps EPO was his attempt to describe it, to find a path to it through the imaginative and doc-umentary route rather than the performative route. Indeed, the magnitude and historical sweep of EPO leads me to wonder whether Gebser was trying not simply to describe atemporality but to paint atemporality for us by means of extensive reference to historical temporality, similar to how TPM uses generational kinship paradoxes to show us atemporality by going deeper, as it were, into the temporal.

How TPM Uses Language to Convey Transparency

I propose that not only can we use TPM to understand better what Gebser means by transparency, but also that Gebser can help us understand TPM.

You could also look at TPM as a linguistic version of Marcel Duchamp's "Nude Descending a Staircase, No. 2" or as a kind of ancient Egyptian kōan.

> For I am the first and the last.
> I am the honored one and the scorned one.
> I am the whore and the holy one.
> I am the wife and the virgin.
> I am <the mother> and the daughter.
> I am the members of my mother. [I am the limbs of my mother.]

This passage establishes an all-inclusiveness, from whole to parts and everything in between. The text in square brackets is an alternative translation. I include it here to give more clarity to MacRae's puzzling syntax. Perhaps "members" is meant in the opposite sense of "dis-membered." Indeed, the etymology of "member" reveals that it used to mean "body part," or, more generally, "flesh." If so, ancient Egyptians hearing TPM would likely have associations to Isis and Osiris. Something or someone that/who is a member of an organization or group has a different category status than something that is part of a machine. Thus, if the speaker *is* the Mother archetype, then when s/he invokes her mother, it is self-referential. If she and her mother are One (recall that Jesus also claimed that he and the Father are One; *John 10:30*), then she also is her mother's arms and legs, heart, lungs, and so on. The identity of self and other extends through all scales and levels of existence.

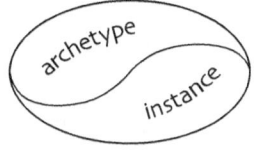

If we apply that understanding to ourselves and take the term "mother" to refer not only to our human mother but our Great Mother, our earthly mother—Gaia, Pachamama, Aluna—then I, the speaker, am all of her parts too—the trees, mountains, and waterfalls, as well as the trash heaps, strip mines, and polluted rivers. This passage sets up a holographic structure of ontology by adding a twist, in the last line, to the standard polarities that precede it—a twist, like that in the Möbial and Kleinian structures we considered earlier. Such a twist turns a standard polarity (e.g., inside/outside) into a self-referential, dynamic one (inside becomes outside which becomes inside…).[230]

Recall that Gebser is interested in the *form* of the manifestation of the spiritual. This text, TPM, suggests that the form—transparency—consists of entwined polarities and is holographic across all levels. In other words, because polarities are entwined or mutually co-arising, when you "see" one pole of a polarity, you also "see through" it to the other pole. Where you see the first, you will also see the last; where you see the whore, you will also see the holy one.

To see through time, let us examine the atemporal kinship relations that I mentioned earlier.

I am the bride and the bridegroom,   ↔
and it is my husband who begot me.   ↕
I am the mother of my father
and the sister of my husband   ↔
and he is my offspring.   ↕

The first line gives us a horizontal (same generation) kinship relation, and then the second line expands that relation into a vertical (intergenerational) one. The speaker's husband (in one incarnation) is her/his father (in another incarnation). The next three lines expand such relations out further to include in-laws and children. The horizontal and vertical relations are replicated. This passage provides an excellent portrayal of atemporality—transparency through time—portrayed as this whole, divine being who is him/herself as well as all kinship relations. If you are Allness speaking about yourself-as-Allness, you would not be limited to any single incarnation. Allness includes all beings that ever existed. But to say "all beings" is rather impersonal and abstract, so the speaker concresces atemporality by claiming that she is her own grand-mother, sister-in-law, and both sister and mother of her husband.[231] From the perspective of Allness, all relations seem incestuous, as there is only one being propagating itself by means of seemingly different beings. Incest thus loses its meaning and stigma, but that does not condone it among humans, as there are still genetic and power-based ramifications.

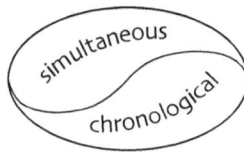

Those lines of text also illustrate both left-right and up-down shifts of the type Gebser refers to when he quotes an apocryphal saying of Christ:

"If you do not change low to high, left to right, back to front, you shall not enter my Kingdom." Gebser was suggesting that transcending-by-uniting the opposites is a path to realizing one's inherent divinity (not the achievement of it though)—a hint about the form of the manifestation of the spiritual.[232] Gebser goes on to say, "The dissolution of this principle [i.e., the dissolution of polarities or the left-right mirroring] is nothing other than the supersession and concretion of the soul, and thus the first step towards its integration."[233] Similar ideas are addressed by Carl Jung, as we will explore in Chapter 19.

The fluidity and ambiguity of kinship, gender, and their integration is also revealed in TPM by the speaker self-referencing as "she" and "he." Taussig et al found instances in which MacRae left the translation neutral, although the original text, they claim, clearly referenced "he." Why would the speaker switch to a different pronominal gender? Perhaps this "he" was a "she" at some other time (as in the passage above) or was like Zeus, who gave birth to Athena through his forehead after swallowing her mother. This and the other gender-identification switches of the speaker in the translation by Taussig et al reinforce the notion of transparency such that Allness would indeed be masculine and feminine, albeit manifesting as male in some instances and as female in others. Because Allness begets itself in a variety of forms and configurations, if the speaker were only a "she," this text would be oddly one-sided and would not convey the wholeness of the speaker.

The following passage might have connected the speaker/hearer with contemporary (to those in ancient Egypt) wisdom teachings, what today we call Kabbalah. Its form follows the "lightning path" through the ten sephiroth of the Tree of Life. This path symbolizes the way that spirit becomes material and, conversely, the way humans can pursue a path back to the eternal Light.

> I am the silence that is incomprehensible
> and the idea whose remembrance is frequent.
> I am the voice whose sound is manifold
> and the word whose appearance is multiple.
> I am the utterance of my name.

Notice the progression from silence to thought to sound to word to utterance, which mirrors the descent of power in the kabbalistic Tree of Life from Kether to Malkuth (Figure 15). I associate the thunder in the title of TPM not only with the clashing of opposites but also with the lightning path of the Endless Light (Ein Sof Ur) down through these emanations (the gray zigzag line in Figure 15). The thunder is the voice, the sound of the opposites clashing (e.g., warm and cold air, negatively and positively charged ions), and the resultant lightning unites Earth and sky. The perfect mind can hold all polarities. Light concresces into matter. Starting in the nonphysical realm, which is beyond the human realm (the top triangle), spirit or light gradually becomes less ephemeral and more real.

In addition to illustrating atemporality, paradoxical contrasts in TPM also illustrate aperspectivity, i.e., having one perspective *and* the other, thus multiple simultaneous perspectives—being the slave *and* the ruler, being the disgraced one *and* the revered one—with what seems to be emphasis on pointing out that "whatsoever you do to the least of my brethren, that you do unto me."

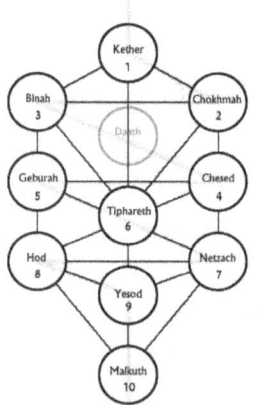

Kether – Silence

I am the <u>silence</u> that is incomprehensible

Binah and Chokmah – Thought/Idea

and the <u>idea</u> whose remembrance is frequent.

Geburah and Chesed – Sound/Voice

I am the <u>voice</u> whose sound is manifold.

Hod and Netzach – Word (polarities)/Image

and the <u>word</u> whose appearance is multiple.

Malkuth – Utterance

I am the <u>utterance</u> of my name.

Figure 15. Correspondence between *The Thunder, Perfect Mind* and the descent of power on the kabbalistic Tree of Life. TPM begins: "I was sent forth from [the] Power..." The top triangle (Kether-Binah-Chokmah) is beyond the physical world. The thoughts and ideas are more like archetypes than what a functional MRI machine would record. Similarly, Geburah and Chesed represent not the actual sounds yet but the capacity for sound. Not until the power reaches the lower triangle (Hod-Netzach-Malkuth) are the familiar words (as abstract concepts) and actual utterances made manifest on the Earth plane. Image from https://mysteriouswritings.com/the-remarkable-purpose-of-the-lightning-flash/

The following lines illustrate a type of aperspectival paradoxical thinking that Gebser describes as taking the form of a reversal in a *chiasm*,[234] in which part A of the first line first parallels part A of the second line, and part B of the first line parallels part B of the second line. That is followed by a true chiasm in lines 3 and 4, in which part A of the first line corresponds to part B of the second line, and vice versa.

> Why, you who hate me, do you love me,
> and hate those who love me?
> You who deny me, confess me,
> and you who confess me, deny me.
> You who tell the truth about me, lie about me,
> and you who have lied about me, tell the truth about me.
> You who know me, be ignorant of me,
> and those who have not known me, let them know me.

In the last couplet of this section, there is a twist on the previous form: "those who have not known me, let them know me," which moves from closed/lacking to open/giving.

In the following passage, the speaker addresses appearing and hiding specifically, in a tricksterish way, again using the structure of chiasm.

> I am the one whom you have hidden from, [I am **he** from whom you hid]
> and you appear to me.
> But whenever you hide yourselves,
> I myself will appear.
> For whenever you appear,
> I myself will hide from you.

From whom or what does one hide when hiding from oneself? Jung calls this aspect the shadow. This passage not only recalls Genesis, where Adam and Eve hid themselves from God and covered their bodies after partaking of the forbidden fruit, but it also directly addresses Gebser's notion of transparency. Here, Allness is not speaking about itself from the perspective of Allness but is exhorting the would-be human listener/reader to allow the Divine to work through him/herself. If "it's all about you," the Divine cannot show up, but if you can become transparent, then the Divine can manifest/concresce through you. (Recall the crystal cube metaphor at the beginning of Chapter 7.)

As we bring transparency to consciousness, how can we bring it to language? Gebser pondered what "a new form of statement" might be like. TPM uses multiple tropes to show how that can occur. One must have achieved a certain level of consciousness development for TPM's new form of statement to make sense, as I can now see by looking back on my collegiate struggles with this text. Gebser continues, "Our new situation requires a new means of description and statement. The new components which have irrupted into our reality demand new 'concepts.'"[235] Gebser did indeed introduce many new concepts and neologisms, from *waring*, mentioned previously, to others that, although they have familiar roots and affixes, are also more obscure (e.g., *atemporal* and *aperspectival*, wherein the prefix "a-" does not negate "temporal" or "perspectival," but means, after *alpha privativum*, "to liberate" from temporality or perspectivity).[236]

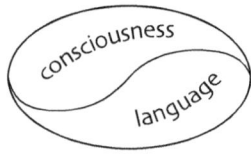

Highly motivated neologisms, in my estimation, do not yet constitute a new *form* of statement; they simply give us new content words. A new form, to me, would require a different structure to language—a new way of organizing one's thoughts or at least a new way of depicting the relations between ideas. A different structure, according to Whorf (see Chapter 16, note 163), implies a different understanding of reality. I think that TPM and Gebser both try to point to new ways to understand reality—as I am doing. There is no consensus yet about the new reality that is *irrupting*, i.e., that is both intruding and collapsing.

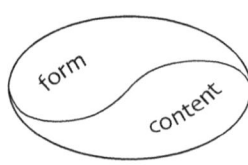

Parting Thoughts

What would life be like if every person understood her/himself in the same way that the speaker of *The Thunder, Perfect Mind* does—as Allness itself *and* as the unique being that one is? Imagine what could happen if all board members of an organization understood that and made decisions for the organization by coming together in such a way that each one's allness and uniqueness allowed them to function within a field that unified all their polarities. Imagine them creating that field consciously, via ritual or meditation. Imagine their deliberations being conducted by a form of meditative reasoning that allows multi-stable perspectives to be considered—the accountant's perspective and the salesperson's and the visionary's and the janitor's, as well as the customer's, the community's, and even Gaia's perspective.

And what would it be like to communicate as such an atemporal, aperspectival being?

Conlanging as
Psychosocial Activism[237]

18

Given the complexity of what will be involved in altering the entire, inter-connected language-culture ecosystem, we need language enthusiasts of all backgrounds to help develop the kinds of changes suggested here, as well as innovations not yet imagined. To inspire such a group of enthusiasts, let me ask you:

What kind of world do you want your children and grandchildren to live in?

In your fantasy of the future, do you think your offspring would like to live, as Buckminster Fuller suggested, in a world that works for everyone?[238] The correct answer is "Yes," because you are not separate from everyone. What would a world that works for everyone—even those with contradictory beliefs, opposing opinions, or incommensurable worldviews—be like?

The philosopher Nelson Goodman wrote a book called *Ways of Worldmaking* in which he says that "We can have words without a world but no world with-out words or other symbols....Worldmaking as we know it always starts from worlds already on hand; the making is a remaking."[239] Goodman seems to imply that worlds do not arise from raw data; rather, they are built from the myriad ways we make meaning.

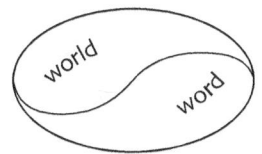

Constructing languages *(conlanging)* is a way of making worlds.

Although I knew nothing of conlanging during graduate school, I knew what kind of world I wanted to make, and I knew it needed a different form of language. The world I envisioned was/is a world of interconnectedness and the paradoxical unity of duality, not its dissolution. Where others saw an either/or world or a world of thesis-antithesis-synthesis, I saw the unity-in-diversity of both/and. I wanted to study paradox and invent new ways for language to *do more*. After I explained my thesis idea to the department chair, he looked at me and said flatly, "I don't see what your problem with language is. It works just fine for me." My future as Sisyphus flashed before my eyes: I would roll the rock up the hill—"Do you get it now, professor?"—and he would kick it down again and again and again. Needless to say, I left grad school highly disillusioned.

Despite my discouragement, I still believe that we can enable language to *do more*. After all, language *content* is always being added so that we can say more about our innovations and theories. With constructed languages, I believe that we can say and write things in ways that are not possible in natural languages.

Marshall McLuhan, the prophet from Edmonton, wrote the following over 50 years ago, and it is still relevant today:

> Our time is a time for crossing barriers, for erasing old categories—for probing around. When two seemingly disparate elements are imaginatively poised, put in apposition in new and unique ways, startling discoveries often result.[240]

That time—our time—is still now. That task is in *our* hands.

In college, I studied questions. Questions are funny things, epistemologically at least. You have to know enough about what you don't know—what you desire to know—in order to formulate a question. You can't formulate a question about what you truly don't know you don't know, i.e., what is unconscious. But the unconscious is where the juice is, when creativity drags you along for the ride by giving you ideas that you never dreamed you would have.

Questions point to the holes in wholeness.

There are things we know about language but learned them before we developed the ability to question them. Hence, they are submerged into a kind of personal unconscious knowledge—what I don't know I know. I wanted to know how to build paradox into the core of a concept, not just create merged concepts like "bittersweet," but more like not-X becoming X, where X and not-X are one but also different, as in acorn-becoming-oak tree. I wanted to know how concepts could contain the essence of paradoxical structures like Möbius strips and Klein bottles, the way Heidegger's concept of Being integrated the concepts of subject and object.

Many years ago and many years after school, while still pursuing my goal of embedding paradox within concepts, I wrote a novel, *The One That Is Both*, in which I developed what I considered new types of concepts (see Chapter 19). It wasn't a fully developed conlang or ficlang (fictional language), and now, looking back, I can see that I devised only a few trees but not even a forest, let alone a whole linguistic ecosystem. To see the ecosystem, I had to learn to ask some questions that helped me become aware of what I didn't know I didn't know. The following questions can guide us toward constructing languages and a world of many worlds that works for everyone.

1. Why do this? Indeed, that is the ur-question. There is no wrong answer. It's good to question one's own motives. We operate from multiple motives—from egotistical ones to transcendental ones. Which motives are being expressed by any given action? Virtuous motives can backfire, and evil motives can frontfire.

2. What assumptions do we have about "reality"—and I put the word in quotes because the assumptions we have about reality give us that very reality. Specifically regarding language, what assumptions do I have about the reality I want to create by means of language? You might think, "but I'm not creating reality, I'm creating a fantasy world." Hold that thought; we'll come back to it.

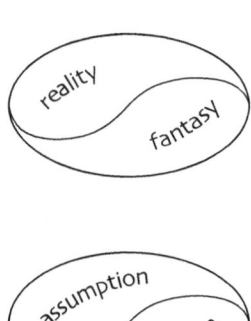

3. What assumptions do we have about language—about how it works, about what is required versus what is superfluous, about its purpose? It's easier to see the assumptions of other cultures than it is to see the assumptions of one's own culture—because we use our assumptions to frame the questions about our assumptions.

4. What are our assumptions about the infrastructures of language? And how do we envision the relationships among them? I am referring to all the facets of language that are necessary and that together make it work—such as sign-vehicles, concepts and category structure, syntax,

semantics, logic, metaphors both explicit and implicit, and of course the oral and graphic representational systems.

5. What are the assumptions embedded in the exostructures—the cultures and subcultures—of language users? The culture and/ or subculture determines the category structure. The larger and more entrenched the cultural systematization is, the more difficult it is to change the assumptions. Cultural change is often fiercely resisted; for example, imagine what it would take to change the "more is better" assumption of Wall Street and Walmart.

Each aspect of language can be questioned separately, but they all function together. Twenty/twenty hindsight has shown me that my big mistake in graduate school was that I questioned language only at the levels of concept and sign-vehicle; I completely missed the rest of its interconnected subsystems! I didn't have the foresight to realize that what I wanted to do would also require, for example, a radically different form of logic to handle both/and reasoning. In my attempt to construct new types of concepts, the law of noncontradiction itself needed to be questioned too. But that was in my blind spot—what I didn't know I didn't know. Another example: if your world is based on a holographic paradigm—where every part contains the whole—then perhaps even the law of identity needs to be questioned. Yes, question those cultural assumptions, dig *that deeply* into personal and cultural assumptions.

6. What is our category structure? How do we divvy up the world? We learn category structure by what can be predicated to what. In your language-world, do trees have emotions? Are mountains sentient, or do they merely float, as on Pandora in the movie *Avatar*?

7. What is fundamental—discrete objects, discrete processes, nondiscrete fields—or something else entirely? Indeed, what is the nature of boundaries—between "things," between words, between betweennesses even?

If there is one take-home point here, it is this: question your assumptions. But why would I suggest something so radical?

The answer brings me back to the title of this chapter: Conlanging as Psychosocial Activism.

The *social* activism part is self-evident. Language is at the core of all our social institutions—government, education, commerce, even marriage, which happens by speaking "I do." If those institutions are not working, let's look to the language that was used to form them, to define their goals, rules, and standard operating procedures. Let's invent something new. Fortunately, conlangers have an internal drive to create new language. For some, it starts with interest in speaking conlangs, such as *Star Trek's* Klingon; for others, it starts with interest in *creating* such languages. Those interests blossomed for many with the introduction of Na'vi in *Avatar* and Dothraki and Valyrian in *Game of Thrones*.[241] College courses were created to teach students the linguistic chops needed to create new languages.

With language-creating, we must circle back to worldmaking. What kinds of social worlds are we making, do we want to make? If Benjamin Lee Whorf is right that "the structure of a human being's language influences the manner in which he [or she] understands reality and behaves with respect to it,"[242] then the structure of the language(s) we create can have powerful effects. For example, in *Avatar*, the social world among the indigenous people of Pandora is highly interconnected with the natural world and deeply spiritual. For years, I looked forward to whether Paul Frommer would introduce changes to Na'vi to convey more of the inherent connectedness of the Pandoran worldview, but I was disappointed by how much English the Na'vi spoke in the *The Way of Water*.

What do I mean by the *psycho* part of psychosocial activism? Imagine protesting yourself, marching against your most cherished beliefs in order to open your own mind to something else. I think conlanging is a path to doing that.

Within all the questions I have posed here is the big, unanswerable question that each of us must face: who am *I*? What that simple one-letter word conveys is anything but simple. The great trickster Alan Watts noticed that "few people seem to use the word 'I' for their whole physical organism. 'I *have* a body' is more common than 'I *am* a body.'"[243] What different assumptions underlie *having* a body compared with *being* a body?

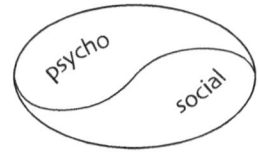

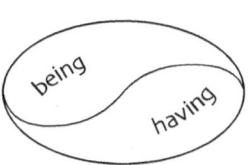

And what about all those not-I's out there—all those objects in space before "I" as a perceiving subject? Our collective assumption, via the containment metaphor, that there are actual objects in actual space before actual perceiving subjects pertains directly to syntax. What does it mean to be an object? a subject? What does it mean for objects to be "contained" in space? Could there be other ways of conceiving of reality—as events? as intersections of waveforms? as strings getting tangled into knots? as fields playing a kind of musical field dynamics?

Watts would question whether there are even any not-I's. He says, "The fact is that because no one thing or feature of this universe is separable from the whole, the only real You, is the whole."[244] So how do we speak, not just about that whole, but *from* that perspective of individual-as-wholeness?

The futurist Fred Polak studied what past societies thought about the future and wondered whether their ideas came to pass.[245] Spoiler alert: they did. As to our future, he asked, what are the implications of a disintegrating image of the future of Western culture for the future of this culture?[246] For disintegrating images of the future of Western culture, we just have to look to all the apocalyptic and dystopian movies made recently. For hopeful but not Pollyannaish images of the future, fortunately we have Ursula K. LeGuin, Geoffreyjen Edwards, and Buckminster Fuller. I come back to my previous question: what future do you want to live into?

We humans, through language, get to lay the foundations for the future—our future and our children's future. If we outsource our ability to imagine it to others, we will have to endure what they create.

English, as you know, is shot through with war metaphors. Politics, sports, relationships, healthcare, even the weather all rely on war metaphors. Do you think we will create a peaceful world for our children if we continually talk about some of our most important topics in terms of war? Will we handle well the oncoming perfect storm of crises if we continue using language structures that presuppose our separateness rather than our connectedness?

As we create languages for whatever purpose—film, books, as art, or just for the hell of it—consider what language could do to create a future you want to live into. And since language requires more than one participant, what new media might be required? McLuhan again: "All media work us over completely. They are so pervasive in their personal, political, economic, esthetic, psychological, moral, ethical, and social consequences that they leave no part of us untouched, unaffected, unaltered."[247] Today's children are learning the "language" of electronic interfaces before age 8, at the same time that they are learning their natural language. How might the symbol-based medium of cell phones, tablets, and computers restructure their brains, alter their view of the world, "work them over?"

In the many years I have been thinking about these things, only in the last few have I become aware of how many other people are interested too. Why is this happening now? Over 30 years ago, I was shamed out of the academy for trying to find a way for language to presuppose mutual interdependence and for wanting to create new forms of language. Now, there are thousands of people around the world doing just that. What is happening—globally, culturally, within our consciousness—that so many people want to create language? I don't know, but I love it!

Might it be part of an evolutionary leap in consciousness? If so, how might the creation of conlangs, or even simply the examination of the structure of natural languages, inform changes to the many natural languages we use—and hence to culture, to our world, to life as we live it?

> When individuals join in a cooperative venture, the power generated far exceeds what they could have accomplished acting individually.
> —R. Buckminster Fuller

To consciously evolve language, we must do it together. After all, meaning is based in agreement. And we must balance the tension between the degrees of "arbitrary" and "motivated" of any new linguistic signs. This distinction was introduced by Ferdinand de Saussure to describe, essentially, the patterns in language—similarities that carry significance.[248] If a new form of language is too arbitrary, it can be difficult to learn because it is unconnected to people's lives and experiences. New forms of language must walk a careful line between arbitrariness and motivatedness. Arbitrariness and motivatedness, however, cannot be controlled completely by conscious processes. Inspiration comes from who-knows-where. We must consider this tension between conscious and unconscious processes.

How do we come together to un/consciously evolve language? How do we even agree about what it means to evolve it? As "Bucky" Fuller said, build a better model because people will want the better model. That works well with commodities. It has even worked with certain scientific models, mindsets, and paradigms. It remains to be seen whether that approach will work with a new form of language because language is an invisible architecture. We don't see it as a "model." Language structures are "unconscious" in the sense that we do not have to think about them in order to use them. There is no "on" button to push, and as you speak you are not thinking "which noun phrase should I start with?" or "should I use *in* or *on* in the upcoming prepositional phrase?" Given the spontaneity of most spoken exchanges, it is a useful design feature that we don't have to process it consciously. Writing and editing are a little different, and perhaps my job as an editor, which requires me to look for ways to say things more clearly, has conditioned me to think more about the language I use. (For example, I noticed that, in a split second, I heard "better" in my mind and rejected it, opting for "more clearly" instead, probably because right now I am hyperconscious of the words I am choosing. I could not sustain that level of self-consciousness in all spoken and written exchanges.)

It also remains to be seen whether people will see enough value in a new form of language to be willing to adopt it. As with all innovations, it is not possible to see all its potential upsides and downsides before it is implemented. It might be good, then, to start with a subset of language. What part of language would benefit the most from adopting a both/and perspective? Perhaps legal language. Given that laws are written in the language we are using here, what might laws written in a consciously evolved, both/and, &-based language be like? How might the scales of justice be balanced if our concepts themselves were balanced?

I am thrilled that my 40-year desire to see language expand in novel ways is gaining a cadre of people more qualified than I am to make it happen. Something in the zeitgeist is shifting.

Does Language Individuate Too?

19

In-dividuate means "not-divided." According to Carl Jung, individuation is a process on one hand of becoming whole and on the other of circumambulating your Self. Although growing, developing, integrating, and individuating happen simultaneously, to individuate involves more than a process of becoming bigger or more complex.

In Chapters 3 and 16, I cited Arjuna Ardagh, Alan Watts, and David Bohm, all of whom expressed concerns about personal and social fragmentation decades ago. Here, now, we come to the antidote. If feeling fragmented is due to processes of life and living breaking down (*solve*), then individuation processes are those of integration (*coagula*). They are Isis re-membering Osiris. They involve re-collecting one's projections, finding interdependencies among what has been assumed to be independent, as we explored vis à vis symbiotes.

Individuating at the physical level occurs in all life. When a seed sprouts, it starts becoming the type of plant that it *is*—squash, lilac, redwood. In flowering plants, for example, there is an identifiable continuum or cycle that the plant goes through, from sprouting to flowering to fruiting to reseeding.

Human individuation consists of more than a biological process of maturation; it is a spiral process of ongoingly integrating, dissolving, and re-integrating one's psyche. There are, nevertheless, recognizable patterns in the individuation process, starting with the child separating psychically from the mother, the first loss of paradise. After the individual de-identifies from the initial psychic unity with the mother and/or father, as part of the vagaries of life, psychic wounding can result in parts of one's being "splitting off" or fragmenting. This is how one seems to become divided within oneself. For example, one's parents might prize quietness, and so one learns to hide or suppress one's natural, loudly expressive outbursts. The child must develop a healthy ego and in adulthood accomplish the goals of the ego (e.g., achieve professional satisfaction, have a family, and so on). If one develops a strong ego and identity and asserts them in early adulthood by pursuing career goals to the detriment of other goals, one might split off other aspects of oneself, perhaps an artistic side or a playful side. Usually, in the second half of life, if those early splittings become unbearable, the hard work of individuation begins—reclaiming those split-off and enshadowed aspects of oneself. Sometimes it begins when one is in crisis—from a divorce, job loss, or loss of meaning in life. Because doing the work of individuating can lead back to those early traumas, many people choose not to do it. Doing the work, though challenging, can be rewarding in itself.

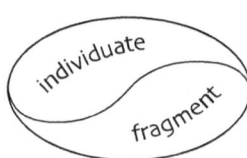

Individuation requires relativizing one's ego in order to integrate increasingly comprehensive types of opposites, such as one's persona characteristics and one's shadow characteristics, to realize one's true Self. It is a vortical process—a process by which consciousness differentiates and then reunifies so that one can hold oppositions in tension at multiple levels thereby expanding the scope of one's consciousness. A person who is working on individuating is, for example, recollecting their projections, integrating their anima/animus, and integrating their shadow. Individuating is never finished, as the unconscious is infinitely active and continually interweaving through consciousness.

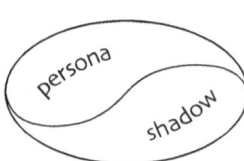

Once the ego has differentiated and its basic goals have been fulfilled, usually in the first half of life, the Self pulls the individual to fulfill the next phase of individuating, which consists of a series of unions or conjunctions. Jung calls them *coniunctio* and describes three.[249] I mention them here briefly; however, knowing *about* them will not get one *through* them. The three conjunctions require not only study but more importantly, personal psychic work—for example, by analyzing one's dreams, using active imagination, working through a complex, or engaging with a Jungian analyst (other types of therapy might not have the goal of individuation).

Three Coniunctios

The first union, the *unio mentalis*, involves integrating conceptual opposites intrapsychically. There is not a list of opposites that one can check off; however, wherever you look, you will find them—greedy and generous, angry and sanguine, sacred and profane, free will and determinism, and, ultimately, the concepts of subject and object—that which is "I" and that which is "other."[250] For more inspiration, see the graphically "united" polarities in the margins throughout this book. The *unio mentalis* especially involves integrating one's internal masculine and feminine aspects, the anima and animus. Society can push men, for example, to hide their feminine nature, calling it weak. Similarly, women are often discouraged from pursuing their masculine features, such as assertiveness or analytical capabilities. To be whole, one must have a full range of capacities available to one's psyche—masculine and feminine, youth and wisdom, and thinking, feeling, sensing, and intuiting abilities. In this *coniunctio*, either/or, as it applies to oneself, shifts to both/and. *The Thunder, Perfect Mind* illustrates this *coniunctio*.

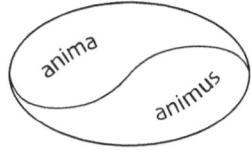

In this book, I am suggesting a *unio mentalis* of an atypical polarity—a union of consciousness and language. The book is, through me, becoming itself. In so doing, the process of writing this book has required me to dance through my own individuation process as well as the book's individuation process. Consequently, I have had to confront some shadow aspects of my own as well as shadow aspects of the book. For example, I had written some weak attempts at humor that sparked rage instead. By confronting that shadow, the book and I have both evolved.

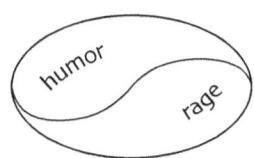

The next conjunction, called the *coniunctio oppositorum*, integrates the *unio mentalis* with the body. With body, soul, and spirit united, the individual now operates not egoically but with a sense of the divine expressing through their humanness. Within this *coniunctio*, synchronicities abound, and often one experiences life as "in flow." Even when obstacles emerge, they can be seen as gifts that, when faced with equanimity, bring new capacities that are needed to continue one's journey through the work of individuating. The full

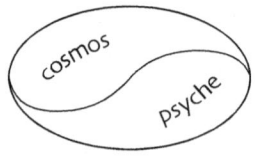

extent of union of spirit-soul and body is expressed by Richard Tarnas as the union of psyche and cosmos:

> The modern mind has long assumed that there are few things more categorically distant from each other than "cosmos" and "psyche." What could be more outer than cosmos? What could be more inner than psyche? But today we are obliged to recognize that, of all categories, psyche and cosmos are perhaps the most consequentially intertwined, the most deeply mutually implicated. Our understanding of the universe affects every aspect of our interior life from our highest spiritual convictions to the most miniscule details of our daily experience. Conversely, the deep dispositions and character of our interior life fully permeate and configure our understanding of the entire cosmos. The relation of psyche and cosmos is a mysterious marriage, one that is still unfolding—at once a mutual interpenetration and a fertile tension of opposites.[251]

A dramatic example of this union of inner experience and outer experience was described by psychotherapist Antonino Ferro. His psyche, that of his patient, and the cosmic psyche seem to be in exquisite harmony here:

> On one occasion when I was emotionally blocked with a woman patient, instead of adopting my usual attitude of receptive listening, I found myself interpreting like a river in full flood. The patient failed to turn up for her next session. She later told me that, because the Ticino [river] was in flood, many roads were not negotiable, and she had felt it wiser to stay at home until the blockage caused by the inundation was over. She then told me of her intention to take a "t'ai chi" course. What better way could there be of telling the analyst to keep quiet (*taci* in Italian) than by skipping sessions and then playing a linguistic game with the similar sounds of "t'ai chi" (slow, relaxing gymnastics) and *taci* (pronounced almost identically in Italian)?[252]

That kind of *harmonia* is possible (and recognizable) because of the container that the therapeutic relation provides. In ordinary life, such experiences occur as synchronicities, a concept that Jung and Wolfgang Pauli developed to describe an "acausal connecting principle" whereby coincidences are not just random events without meaning but are, instead, deeply meaningful, by which they seem not random at all.

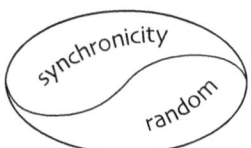

Such an event occurred with my acquisition of Ferro's book. Ferro is a student of Wilfred Bion, a psychoanalyst about whose work I know nothing. When I began reading Ferro's book, I noticed that he used some of Bion's symbolism, namely, ♀ and ♂, which I could not quite understand. Although I was already familiar with their representing Earth and Mars, female and male, respectively (their "motivated" aspects), I could tell that they had a different meaning in Ferro's text. After an internet search, I learned that they mean the "container" and "uncontained" (even "projected"), respectively. I found myself rather annoyed that Ferro had assumed that his readers would understand those symbols without explanation. Even though they are highly motivated symbols, as an outsider to Bion's work, I felt excluded. That experience made it very clear to me that the ideas I am proposing could result in a similar experience for my readers. That is why any novel language, or even modifications to English or other languages, need to be built from the ground up by users themselves and be as transparent as possible.

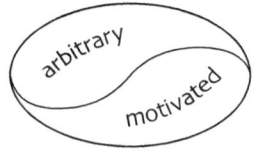

That example in which the patient, therapist, and world exhibit profound union leads us to the third *coniunctio* that Jung describes, called the *unus mundus*. This union joins the conscious unity of soul-spirit-body with the unconscious, that is, the world of actuality and the world that is *in potentia* (see Figure 6). Jung describes *unus mundus* as "the unity of all archetypes as well as of the multiplicity of the phenomenal world."[253] This third union integrates All That Is and Is Not Yet. Imagine joining the end, the *telos*, with the beginning, before existence divided itself. This is a unity of like and unlike, as in the Vision of Arisleus (see Chapter 4). Jung concedes how inconceivable it is to combine a known with an unknown. For example, it is one experience to see a flower, recognize it by its name, scent, shape, and so on, and a different type of experience to see all that and simultaneously see the great mystery of the universe in and through that flower. Recall William Blake's poem "Auguries of Innocence":

To see a World in a Grain of Sand
And a Heaven in a Wild Flower
Hold Infinity in the palm of your hand
And Eternity in an hour

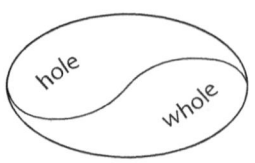

Jung cautioned that "psychic wholeness will never be attained empirically, as consciousness is too narrow and too one-sided to comprehend the full inventory of the psyche."[254] Hence, this conjunction paradoxically includes the hole in the whole, the *mysterium*. He writes:

> The creation of unity by a magical procedure meant the possibility of effecting a union with the world—not with the world of multiplicity as we see it but with a potential world, the eternal Ground of all empirical being, just as the self is the ground and origin of the individual personality past, present, and future.[255]

It is possible to see some parallels between that process of integrating oppositions psychologically and the ways that I propose to integrate opposites in language. I have suggested that consciousness and language conjoin in a Möbial/Kleinian union of opposites characterized by a paradox in which their distinctness is maintained in their unity. Thus, if consciousness undergoes such processes of individuation (*unio mentalis, coniunctio oppositorum,* and *unus mundus*), does—or can—language undergo similar processes? Although I do not have an answer to that question, I venture the following speculation.

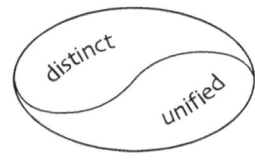

The Both/And-ness of Language and Consciousness

We do not know, except perhaps by spurious inference (for example, on the evolutionary development of the structure and function of the human larynx, mouth, lungs, etc.), how and when speaking emerged from the silence (or even whether undifferentiated origin was silent at all, since silence already implies differentiation from sound). Regardless of how it happened "in the beginning" and how it happens for each of us, the first utterances likely emerge(d) from the unconscious and gradually became more complex and more conscious

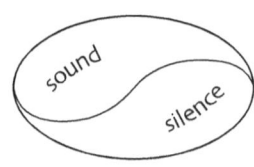

vocal communication. Indeed, we learn to use language before we understand language, as exemplified by a friend's 2-year-old grandson who adeptly applied words he had heard his parents say and demanded that "someone change my fucking diaper!" We learn to understand language before we learn to question language. Rarely do we learn to question language itself.

Although it is not known to what extent consciousness had differentiated at the first utterance, let's imagine that there was still some degree of primal unity of psyche and soma, as there is in the infant. The undifferentiated psyche might begin to notice, for example, that there are times of light and times of dark and would behave accordingly. However, light and dark do not have distinct boundaries, and so light would not be absolutely differentiated from dark. The concept of "day" would not have a hard boundary with "night," but there would be a continuum of experience of light–dark or day–night. Similar to that temporal continuum, the undifferentiated psyche might experience a spatial continuum of, say, higher than and lower than (that is, without yet a differentiation of notions of "mountain" and "valley"). Whether in the valley looking up at the mountain or on the mountain looking down into the valley, the experience is one of great distance—high when looking up and low when looking down. When traversing that territory on foot, the low part becomes high and vice versa. Phenomenologically, the experience is unified, even from multiple perspectives. Why might such a unified experience require two separate words that break the gradual flow between one and the other into this one and that one? These primal categories of experience, such as day–night and high–low, likely were unities that a more-differentiated mind would later consider to be polarities. Differentiation of the poles of a polarity into separate concepts, then, would emerge after the underlying form of experience (the traversing of terrain or the passage of time, or, simply, ongoingness of experience of a cyclical nature) was noticed and exploited for some purpose, such as safety or ease. For example, it is easier moving through the forest by day, and it is cooler moving through the desert at night. There was survival value in distinguishing different aspects of unified experience.

Patterns of Individuation in Language

English and its parent European languages seem to have undergone a process of evolution whereby unitary concepts, within which polarities might have been contained, differentiated into separate concepts. We can speculate this because not all concepts in European languages underwent that differentiation. For example, both Freud and Gebser cite Karl Abel's book *Gegensinn der Urworte* [*The Antithetical Meaning of Primal Words*], which claims that "so-called primal words (Urworte), for example, evidence two antithetic connotations: Latin *altus* meant 'high' as well as 'low' [as in the mountain-valley example]; *sacer* meant 'sacred' as well as 'cursed.'"[256] Greek *pharmakon* meant both "poison" and "cure." Gebser claims that primal words such as those "formed an undifferentiated psychically-stressed unity whose bivalent nature was definitely familiar to the early Egyptians and Greeks. This is no longer the case with our present sense of language; consequently, we have required a term that transcends equally the ambivalence of the primal connotations and the dualism of antonyms or conceptual opposites."[257] Freud cites other passages from Abel affirming that "Man was not in fact able to acquire his oldest and simplest concepts except as contraries to their contraries, and only learnt by degrees to separate the two sides of an antithesis and think of one without conscious comparison with the other."[258] Freud considered the concept of *Urworte* to support a similar bivalence that he observed in his patients' dream images, where a particular image in a dream might mean the opposite in waking consciousness.[259]

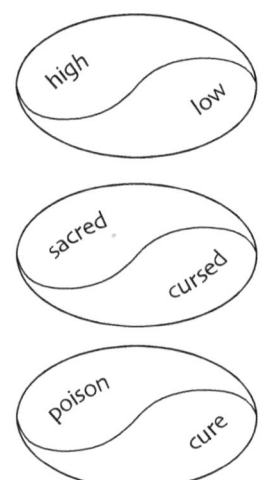

Although the ideas of Abel and Freud have been discredited by linguists and Egyptologists,[260] the linguist Laurence Horn takes up the notion of *Gegensinn*, words that are their own opposites, remarking that "while history has not been kind to Abel's thesis or Freud's interpretation of it, philologists have long recognized a general tendency for words in a wide variety of languages to develop and maintain contradictory or opposite meanings, while debating the significance of that tendency."[261] Horn also provides English translations of the term *Gegensinn*; the one I prefer is *enantionym*, because it conveys the sense of becomingness (one becomes the other) associated with *enantiodromia* (the Heraclitean notion that sooner or later everything turns into its opposite), as discussed by Jung.[262]

As Urworte went through a process of differentiation in which the primal, bivalent concept split into two monovalent concepts, it seems that human consciousness and language also go through a similar process.

If we consider the possibility that language and consciousness relate to each other in a Kleinian or Möbial way, that is, they seem to be two sides of a unity that is actually only one sided, then I suggest that what occurs during the development of consciousness (i.e., individuation) in individuals and in society similarly occurs in the development of language. Gebser supports a version of this idea: "Just as every person represents and lives the entire mutational series of mankind through his structures [of consciousness], so too each word reflects its mutational exfoliation within language itself."[263] Whereas Gebser sees the process occurring at the level of words, I see it occurring at the level of language as a system of systems. At the ecosystem level, language takes particular forms; at various sublevels, it takes other forms, and so on.

In *The Ever-Present Origin*, Gebser's primary focus is to reveal the mutations of consciousness and how humans have expressed them culturally throughout history in art, architecture, and literature. Gebser's integral structure of consciousness, which integrates the other four structures (archaic, magic, mythic, and mental) resembles (but does not recapitulate or mirror precisely) Jung's process of individuation. Gebser sees clues and indications that the structure of language is beginning to shift from highly mental forms (that is, based in separation) to more integral forms. Unsurprisingly, the shift began with the poets.

> It is particularly instructive that [the supersession of dualism and the achievement of arationality] also occurs in poetry, since poetry emphatically resides in the mythical consciousness structure for which mental meter and rational sentence construction constitute a disciplining superstructure. It is of signal

importance that the intensification of poetry and of the poetic word, as well as of poetic language, have led to the re-psychologization of poetry only in the negative temporic attempts, whereas the successful attempts point beyond the mythical and mental. And this is all the more important, as should be obvious, since the structure of language itself has begun to change. Furthermore, it is of fundamental significance that the changes in language are not limited to one language, but have been emerging and assuming form in all European languages for the last one hundred and fifty years, languages that once lent the most pregnant expression to the exclusive validity of the mental-rational consciousness structure.[264]

We are not limited to European languages to inform our questions about the individuation of language and consciousness. Let us look briefly at an indigenous language that might shed light on that connection. In the Diné (Navajo) language, the term "*alkee na'aashii*, translated as 'one follows the other,' implies that a dynamic equilibrium emerges," as with day-night.[265] This awareness of interconnected opposites in dynamic union does not imply that the Navajo language is at an undifferentiated phase; on the contrary, *alkee na'aashii* suggests a *unio mentalis*, and other Diné concepts seem to suggest awareness of *coniunctio oppositorum* and the *unus mundus*:

> Geophysical and celestial location, as well as consciousness of all living things, are intrinsically related with everything in the Navajo cosmos. The underlying knowing, the spiritual matrix—what Navajos would call *bitsi silei*—that provides the preceding organizing process for the Navajo world-view, is the essence expressed through *sa'ah naaghai bikeh hozhoon* [cosmic negative and positive complementarity: where the two energies meet, a central dynamic force is constantly manifesting, where equilibrium and dynamic movement are continuously generated and regenerated]. This is the self-organizing central process that provides unity, coherence, and life. It is the spiritual matrix that binds the human with all cosmic forces and energy.[266]

If *Urworte* started out as undifferentiated bivalent concepts that then differentiated into our current monovalent concepts, how might we continue the process of helping language individuate simultaneously with our own individual and collective individuating? Would words/concepts/language go through similar conjunctions? If so, how might we facilitate that? One way might be to alter the structure of language to convey unity and differentiation simultaneously (akin to the *unio mentalis*).

Decades before I had heard of Gebser and years before I studied Jung, I had already tried to invent new types of concepts, ones that embody paradox, that bring opposites together while also allowing them to keep their distinctness (Table 2). I invented, but did not design, the following glyphs for a novel I wrote. They are not new content words; rather, I wanted to find a way to put both/and *into the concept itself*, a kind of linguistic endosymbiosis in which what has been an external relationship of interpenetrating opposites was now internalized within a concept.

Table 2. Glyphs that embody paradox[267]

Name: Glyph	Meaning	Comments
Mu-ishi-wa: *Unio mentalis*	There is only one side that serves as both sides	Think Möbius strip, Klein bottle (Feminine principle)
Fu-an-gu: *Coniunctio oppositorum*	The deeper you get, the less it looks like itself; and when you reach the core, it looks like the opposite of what you started with	This is both a statement and a description of a process of looking deeply into "something." (Masculine principle)
Akra-na: *Unus mundus*	The union of the material and the divine	This resembles the zygote at the 8-cell stage, when it becomes 3-dimensional (Both masculine and feminine)
Aneh-mi-oh-nu:	The snake of light that runs through all	Think DNA, a double helix, which is a biocrystal that transports photons and emits light.[268]

Fu-an-gu, ✿, which means "the deeper you get, the less it looks like itself; and when you reach the core, it looks like the opposite of what you started with," resembles the meaning of the Diné term, *sa'ah naaghai bikeh hozhoon*: cosmic negative and positive complementarity. It not only refers to such a union, it describes the process by which to come to such a union, specifically, by looking deeply (that is, through the psychophysical depth dimension). For example, in Chapter 4 ("Spaceisnotmadeofspace"), we did an exercise in which we penetrated deeply into living matter by taking an imaginative journey from its solid appearance into its constituent cells all the way down to the molecules, atoms, subatomic particles, and ultimately to just charges or vibrations at the core. Thus, when you look deeply into matter, it no longer looks material. It seems to be the opposite of materiality—simply some charges moving at high speed. Similarly, when we look at abstract concepts, such as love or justice, at their core we can find something very real, such as a physical gesture, word, or action that carries love, that imparts justice. Many of Plato's dialogues embody this process of looking deeply into an abstract concept. "Thus we are used to thinking of the individual and the general, the temporal and the eternal, the embodied and the disembodied as exclusive pairings, whereas they are not only inclusive, but—as it was possibly Goethe's greatest insight to see—are present *simultaneously* in one another. They are found, not by turning one's back on the supposed opposite, but by going more deeply into it. Thus the general is found *in* the individual, the eternal *in* the temporal, the spiritual *in* the embodied. This tension is creative, generative."[269]

> The thing that I'm okay causing harm to will end up harming the thing that I care about.
> —Daniel Schmachtenberger

Mu-ishi-wa, ◉, means "there is only one side that serves as both sides." Obviously, that describes a Möbius strip or a Klein bottle. In everyday life, the situation that Schmachtenberger describes in the quote above illustrates the principle beautifully. It truly belies the connectedness of everything with everything else. Similarly, this glyph exemplifies what the creator of *The*

Thunder, Perfect Mind accomplishes. Just as the speaker in that document claims to be holy and a whore, slave and master, what is exalted and what is despised, mu-ishi-wa conveys the interdependence of those types of polarities. To truly know that you are both master and slave first allows you to see that even if you are in the role of master, that role enslaves you; only by seeing that you are both frees you to be you and thus to be neither.

Just as we need to breathe in, we need to breathe out. Both are breathing. Just as we need to be active, we need to rest or be lazy. No value judgement there. However, by avoiding our shadow, through *enantiodromia* we often land right where we are trying not to be. For example, if you are in a personal struggle to *not* be lazy, then you might be so unlazy that you give yourself hypertension. By trying not to be greedy, we might end up being miserly, which is greed without having money but also the opposite of being generous. Mu-ishi-wa also characterizes my hypothesis that language and consciousness are two sides that seem different but are truly one.

If language went through the second *coniunctio*, the uniting of soul/spirit and matter, as in **akra-na** (the union of the material and the divine), what might be the result? How might the material and spiritual be fully incorporated into language? Would language resemble dance, such as the dances of bees or mudra-based classical Indian dance? It seems to me that a somatic addition to language would have to be more complex than gesturing or even *biosemiotics*—the signs in our environment that we can interpret, as when a plant's leaves droop, indicating possible thirst/lack of sufficient water, or when a wolf bares its teeth and growls. It would be necessary to incorporate language(s) among other species, as well as our limited ability to communicate with them.

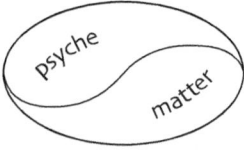

I can barely conceive of what language might be like after going through the third *coniunctio*, the union of the actual and the potential. Perhaps that would be the language of manifestation itself, like cymatics, where sound creates a shape in matter. The expressing of this language would bring what is expressed (*in potentia*) not just into thought but into being, into actuality. *Star Trek's* "replicator" did that as *techné*. Alternatively, language of the *unus mundus* might consist of signal-less communication. Might that look like

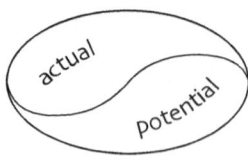

cosmos-wide telepathy? From our limited vantage point, it is not possible to know. The ideas presented here hopefully constitute a small step toward that vision. The image on the cover, called *Fourth Coniunctio*, challenges us to imagine beyond the three envisioned by Jung. To me, that image conveys both order and chaos, perhaps as they co-existed at the origin.

As psyche/consciousness individuates, expanding its capability to be a vessel for the conjunction of multiple forms of opposites, the infrastructures and exostructures of language need to expand concomitantly to contain new, more complex forms of language. Glyphs that convey paradox, for example, would also require new forms of all the other infrastructures of language, including logic, syntax, metaphors, and ultimately a new culture that has a different category structure. How do we continue to invent language for the subsequent unions? Let us first accomplish the *unio mentalis* but with anticipation of what is next on a new horizon to keep the conjoined processes of expanding consciousness and language in Kleinian motion and beyond.

This Möbial/Kleinian Life

20

Too much disorder and there is no structure for purpose to express itself in: too little disorder and there is nothing to enable purpose to express itself with.[270]
—Iain McGilchrist

You're already doing it—living according to the ideas in this book. You've been breathing in and out while your eyes have been darting from line to line. Your blood has flowed out of your heart and back into it thousands of times. New cells have been born and old cells have died or were killed and scavenged for parts. Those instinctual body functions keep us grounded in a both/and world, but fortunately and unfortunately we do not need to think about them much. All of those processes are ☯, **mu-ishi-wa**, one side that serves as both sides.

Many cultures have known for millennia that women have masculine qualities and men have feminine qualities, which Jung called *animus* and *anima*, respectively. The Chinese have the taiji or yin-yang symbol, ☯, that expresses the interpenetrating relationship of feminine yin and masculine yang energies. In cultures that keep masculine and feminine roles rather rigidly divided, there is usually a festival or other ritual where those divisions are breached. Men, especially, get to put on dresses and allow their feminine side to be expressed, even if only in a humorous way. Those cultures know that if the feminine part of a man or the masculine part of a woman is repressed too thoroughly, it will find expression sideways or in more twisted ways—disorderly ways that can disrupt the social structure.

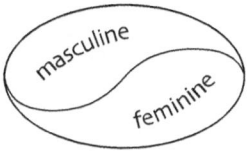

The women's movement in the 1960s and 70s released the cultural female animus as if a genie from a bottle. Roles, norms, and prejudices were questioned. Those women sought equality, and many cultures are still working to fully integrate anima and animus into their society's power structures. When men can cry freely without being labeled "sissy" or "weak" and women can get angry without being labeled the B-word—without backlash or ridicule in public—then we'll be closer to cultural integration of anima and animus. Anima and animus are both **mu-ishi-wa** and **fu-an-gu**, as **mu-ishi-wa** is the feminine glyph and **fu-an-gu** is the masculine glyph. Both integrate masculine and feminine, but in a feminine way and in a masculine way, respectively.

The sexual revolution then initiated a spiritual revolution, union of human and divine. The sexual revolution catalyzed the first *coniunctio* and the spiritual revolution catalyzed the second *coniunctio* in society. Prior to that, sexual/spiritual *coniunctio* was an individual experience. The sexual-spiritual coming together of opposites henceforth had to be grappled with collectively. Today, we can clearly "see" the opposites, as public life has become highly polarized. Those opposites—that "truth bubble" and that other "truth bubble"—are what must be brought together in this paradoxical way that maintains their distinctness amidst their connectedness, as yin and yang.

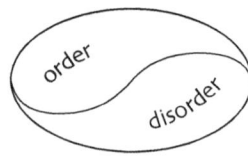

When you think about your already Möbial or Kleinian life, where polarities flow into one another seamlessly, do you think about the disorder that will occur after you have made something in your life more orderly, whether it be your kitchen, your daily routine, or your relationship with someone? If you're like most people, you probably think only about bringing order to something disorderly. It seems to be a clear, linear process—clean up the living room, for example. Put things away. Arrange them nicely. Decluttering feels good. How could that possibly initiate a process of disorder? The unconscious has its ways!

If you do that kind of clean-up in your psyche, Jungian analyst Nathan Schwartz-Salant warns that "increasing order in a psychic system creates disorder."[271] This he calls the order-disorder paradox, which is an application of the second law of thermodynamics to the psyche. "An increase in the order or organization of a system—for example, of the ego, through various means such as an increase in self-knowledge, creative imagination, or problem solving, moves against the entropic process, but also requires a concomitant creation of disorder or entropy so that, in total, there is no entropy decrease."[272] Schwartz-Salant also noticed that myths and stories often show how created disorder often thwarts the creator of order. One need only think of Wile E. Coyote and Bugs Bunny. If you have ever achieved a big goal and afterwards fell into depression or pessimism, then you have been at the effect of the order-disorder paradox.

Conversely, it might be easier to see the order-disorder paradox in your life if you look backwards in time from when you have felt "anxiety, fears of abandonment, reactive anger, hypervigilance to being emotionally attacked, fear of envy, despair, enfeeblement, or withdrawal. Within these reactions, it is difficult to remember that a creation of order preceded the disorder."[273] Thus, our emotional states also have a quality of both/and, sometimes simultaneously (as in *Bewußtsein spannung*) but often one and then the other. If we can extricate our point of view from being captured by an emotion to looking at the whole pattern of feelings, states, and behaviors, we can see the Möbial or Kleinian quality of these conjoined, or **mobi** �, concepts and events.

The tension between interconnected polarities, such as order and disorder, can be imagined as a spring between them. If you pull one farther from the other (as by creating more order), you increase the tension of the spring holding them together. This "energizes" the other because you are not pulling on one part only but on the whole system. When one political party or ideology or religion wants to separate itself from others, doing so adds tension to the whole system thereby activating the others into pulling back. War seems to be our default response to unbearable tension. Soldiers are trained to see the "enemy" as radically Other, not as brothers or cousins—even when sometimes they are brothers and cousins. In such cases, there are often multiple layers or scales of tensions.

It is easy to see the Kleinian dynamic in some of our everyday concepts, as illustrated above, but it is difficult to see it in other concepts because they have been cleverly isolated from each other for specific purposes. Let's look first at *growth* and *destruction*. A farmer knows that tilling this year's stalks fertilizes the soil for next year's crops if they're allowed to deteriorate over the winter. A builder knows that it is necessary to demolish or strip down an old building in order to put up a new one. In relationships, when two people go from being single to being a couple, certain aspects of being single are destroyed and certain aspects of "two heads or hearts are better than one" enable the couple to be more than the sum of their individual selves. Similarly, when a baby enters the picture, the relationship dynamics change again. The infant interloper in the couple's bond must be accommodated because now there is not only self and other, but self and two others, one of whom is very needy. The tightness of the couple's bond necessarily changes, sometimes to the child's benefit and sometimes to the child's detriment. The old form must be destroyed (to a greater or lesser extent in different circumstances) to allow for a new form to emerge and grow.

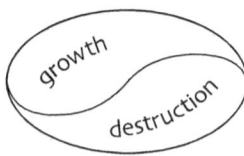

In the prevailing economic context, growth without the counterbalancing force has been held up as an ideal. Given the way our economic system has been structured, unmitigated growth is necessary for the whole system to function without collapsing—that is, until it does finally collapse, because growth without destruction is unsustainable. It does not have to be this way, but it is how our institutions and laws have been set up (by means of language). For example, the way that debt is created and then used to generate more capital leads to such growth. Here's an illustration of how it works: $1 of capital can create $10 of debt (regulations actually set this ratio, but let's keep the math simple); that is, if a bank has $1 in its possession, it can give out $10 worth of loans. That is an oversimplification, of course, but you can see a) that it depends on an agreement, in language, between banks and their regulators and b) how that structure engenders exponential growth rather than linear growth of wealth/debt creation. There are, however, forces of destruction in this system, including inflation, whereby purchasing power erodes, as well as market crashes, contractions, and "corrections." Because the focus is on economic growth, little effort is put into using the forces of destruction constructively, as the farmer and the builder do. Instead, economically destructive events seem to occur randomly. What sparks such "destructive" events? There is not likely a single answer, but we could probably use the order-disorder paradox with 20/20 hindsight to discern the ordering event(s) that preceded such disordering events. The crash of 2008, for example, could be seen as the ordering of stock-market trash—shady lending practices generated mortgages that borrowers couldn't afford that were then packaged into neat tranches and sold to unwitting buyers who thought they were getting something valuable, not the bankers' trash. The crash was perhaps overly devastating because it was not only an ordering of a disordered segment of the economy (poorly vetted mortgages), but it was also perpetrated by fraud (such as higher ratings than the bundled mortgages deserved).

Consider for a moment what might be possible—either in terms of self-understanding or understanding of seemingly "unpredictable" forces—if we had a way to presence the order-disorder paradox or the whole growth-destruction relationship. I am not suggesting that we can control such forces; it is folly to think that complex systems can be controlled. However, by knowing that order and disorder operate together, we can take such co-operation into account in the way we think about complex situations…and hence in how we speak and write about these Kleinian relationships.

Let's look at how the paradoxical inside-outside dynamic of the Klein bottle can be used to model a real-world situation. Recall that a Klein bottle is a continuous, nonorientable surface that seems to have an inside and an outside although it has only one side. There is no boundary between inside and outside; they flow into each other.[274] Let's use the Kleinian internal-external relationship as an explicit metaphor (model) for the concepts of internalization and externalization of costs. Internalized costs are those borne by a company to make, market, and distribute a product. Common internal costs include research and development, production costs, advertising, and distribution. The company usually pays for them and sets the price of the product to cover those costs and make a profit. Now suppose that the manufacturing process involves washing the products off before packaging them. In washing off some chemical residue of the manufacturing process, the water used becomes highly toxic. The policies of the U.S. Environmental Protection Agency say that the company must filter or purify the water to remove the toxin before releasing the water back into the environment. Let's say that this particular toxin is costly to extract from the water, so filtering it would either decrease the profits or render the product uncompetitive in the market because the price would have to be much higher than the price of similar products. In a closed-door meeting, the company decides to externalize that cost. It might secretly route the polluted water into a nearby stream instead of putting it into the EPA-monitored municipal wastewater system. The company's executives assume that the stream will carry the polluted water to a large river, and the toxins will be dissipated by the sheer volume of water in the river. Perhaps they fail to consider that the stream water also sinks into a local aquifer from which people in the area get their drinking water. Townspeople start getting an unknown illness. They or their insurance companies must pay for their doctor visits. The townspeople might lose income from being unable to work. Local wildlife in or around the stream might die, throwing the ecosystem out of balance.

These adverse consequences of dumping the polluted water into the stream illustrate how the company has offloaded or externalized the cost of purifying the water, but those costs circle back around to affect the company and its employees anyway. By not purifying the water, the externalized costs are borne by people (their health problems), by other industries (e.g., healthcare), and by the environment (loss of habitat and biodiversity). If the company draws its workforce from the area around the polluted stream, the company's externalized costs can boomerang; its own employees would be the very same people getting sick and missing work. The externalized costs are reinternalized in a different way, illustrating the recursive nature of externalizing such cost—just as the Klein bottle turns in on itself, obscuring the distinction between external and internal.

Such cost externalization occurs in many industries, particularly energy production (pollution from coal-burning power plants, radioactivity from nuclear power plants), mining (tailings, sludge), factory waste (brownfields contaminated with heavy metals), food production (especially unhealthy, addictive, nutrient-empty food that contributes to health problems such as diabetes and cardiovascular disease), airlines (pollution from jet fuel), and plastic packaging that is not biodegradable. Other ways that companies externalize costs are by sending jobs overseas where labor is cheaper and by simply recategorizing employees as independent contractors, who then bear much of the cost of maintaining their employer's business.[275]

If we simply assume that the environment can absorb all waste products and by-products, we will likely upset a delicate balance that involves many other life forms. We live in a web of life, and all of us depend on all the rest of us life forms to keep the whole system in balance. Many humans have forgotten that. Or perhaps they never learned it. Instead, they learned to control the environment, extract its resources, and make it serve their whims. It is time for us to think about how to use the knowledge gained from the Industrial Revolution in a way that respects the web of life.

The COVID-19 pandemic and the supply-chain disruptions it caused might be Gaia's way of opening our eyes to the fragility of the webs of life. If we can see the interconnections in the supply chains that we have created, perhaps we can also see the natural "supply chains" or interdependencies that have evolved over millennia. Perhaps now we need to start talking about supply chains as processes that have distinct but not separate, i.e., &, elements. The part from China is & the end product. The workers who made the parts in China, the workers who assembled them in Taiwan, and the workers who came up with the advertising campaign in Chicago are & each other.

Because nearly all of us in the West/North no longer feed ourselves by hunting animals and following them around as they migrate, we have lost the big picture of the cycles of life and how the land and its inhabitants function wholistically. How do we bring that big picture back into our minds even if we don't experience it viscerally? How do we presence that wholeness in language and in thought so that we can speak *from* it, not just about it? We are fortunate that Tyson Yunkaporta still remembers that the termites lived with the parrots and the moths, and he remembers the filaments that connect them to each other in the web that lives on as the infinite game of life.

Those webs of interdependencies comprise a type of "pattern literacy," a term I learned from architect and regenerative designer Bill Reed, of Regenesis Group.[276] Just as chess players develop pattern literacy with regard to playing that game, Regenesis Group helps us understand the patterns of land and human-nature interaction.

"Regenerative" is a term that has become popular lately, after "sustainable" was co-opted. Here "regenerate" means, specifically, to bring essence forward in a new context in a new way.

> …regenerative development and design means the reconnection of human aspirations and activities with the evolution of natural systems—essentially coevolution. It means shifting human communities and economic activities back into alignment with life processes. It implies every human settlement organizing itself around evolving its watershed's capacity to support life. The creative and economic activities of human communities can be directed toward the development of human potential through harmonization of and with the dynamic energies of nature. This is not preservation of an ecosystem, nor is it restoration. Instead, it is the continual evolution of culture in relationship to the evolution of life. This defines the work of regeneration. Rather than seeing a site, or a development project, as a collection of things (slopes, drainages, roads, buildings, etc.), a regenerative designer cultivates the ability to see them as energy systems—webs of interconnected dynamic processes that are continually structuring and restructuring a site.[277]

The clients of Regenesis Group usually want to construct a building or an entire development on land that has degenerated, such as land that has been overfarmed or overgrazed, polluted by industry, or artificially segmented in such a way as to cut off normal flows of water or animals. Regenesis fuses three & **mobi** approaches—living systems thinking, permaculture, and developmental change processes—as their basis for developing and evolving a regenerative methodology.

> [A living systems] approach requires that the person applying this way of thinking see what they are working on as a system of energies or life processes, rather than as things (or even as a system of things). It begins by trying to see what is at the core of a system, around which the system organizes and orders itself. It looks at the web or larger context of reciprocal relationships within which it is embedded, since all systems are comprised of smaller systems and are part of larger systems. Together these aspects provide the

basis for illuminating the potential inherent in a living system that it is attempting to manifest. This constant reaching toward being more whole, being more "alive," is seen as the fuel for regeneration.[278]

Because a place and the web of life intertwine in complex ways, the process that Regenesis Group uses involves diving deeply into understanding the local context so as to better see the global context (❀ **fu-an-gu**). The developmental change aspect of their approach "uses the power of storytelling, and the creation of a 'story field' that shifts the focus to seeing the whole system and what it is attempting to become instead of focusing on problem solving and conflict resolution. In other words, stakeholders see themselves as having a stake in the potential that needs to be evolved, rather than in a struggle over what exists." Much like the "yarning" that Tyson Yunkaporta described, this type of storytelling is also a type of knowing, but not just knowing the past; it also entails telling a story of the future of the place, how it might co-evolve with us, its inhabitants. To tell the story of a place is to know that place—to know its habits, its idiosyncrasies, its beauty—as you know your beloved. Our place, our Earth, is our Beloved. Do we truly know her?

Many of the projects undertaken by Regenesis Group involved discovering or rediscovering the land's function in the local ecosystem. Some desertified land in New Mexico had once been rich with beavers; a parking lot had once been an estuary; and some degraded farmland had been an alluvial fan at the base of a mountain stream that served as a "living bridge" supporting multiple nutrient and wildlife flows and exchanges between the mountains to the west and a river to the east. By understanding the pattern literacy of places and their inhabitants, in which estuaries and alluvial fans and beavers have a specific and important purpose within the ecosystem, we can be better stewards for all that is distinct but not separate from us, all our relations. To do that, we need to be part of a shared vision, a "story field," that enables us to co-evolve with a place and continue to co-operate with it as the unpredictabilites of life and nature (such as floods, tornadoes and hurricanes, droughts, earthquakes, or pandemics) force us to be creative without getting mired in a mindset of "this is the way it has always been done."

By regenerating an estuary in a project in Mexico, for example, Regenesis Group also helped to regenerate fishing as part of the local economy. After teaching the local people who worked at the ecoresort about regenerative farming practices used to grow the organic food served at the resort, the workers took those practices back to their own communities.

To better express the dynamics between what is and what could be, perhaps new language structures could allow us to express actuality *and* possibility, not as opposites but as ◉, **mu-ishi-wa**, in ongoing co-evolution. Conversely, such flow and co-evolving could serve to remind us not to reify, nominalize, or otherwise render language static. How might language and consciousness together undergo regenerative processes möbially?

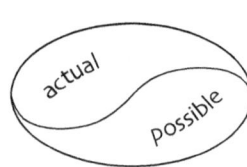

In using the Möbius strip and Klein bottle as models for combined local/wholistic perspectives, is it still necessary to distinguish the locality and the whole? How many nested systems do we need to include? What is whole? What is wholer? What is wholest? Can we ever know?

An old Chinese tale reminds us that immediate events are part of something larger and that it is unwise to judge an event as "good" or "bad" from a local perspective without knowing the more wholistic perspective. And we will never know, truly, the wholest picture.

This is the story of an old Chinese farmer who lived many years ago. He had one old horse that he used to plough his fields.

One day, the horse ran away into the hills. Everyone said, "We are so sorry for your bad luck." The old man replied, "Bad luck, good luck, who knows?"

A week later, the horse returned with a herd of wild horses, which now belonged to the old man. Everyone said, "We are so happy for your good luck!" The old man replied, "Good luck, bad luck, who knows?"

While his only son was riding one of the wild horses, he fell off and broke his leg. Everyone said, "What bad luck!"

> The old man replied, "Bad luck, good luck, who knows?"
>
> One day, the army came to the village, and took all the strong young men to be soldiers for the emperor. Only the old farmer's son was spared because he could not fight with a broken leg. Everyone said, "What good luck!" The old man replied, "Good luck, bad luck, who knows?"

When has something like that happened in your own life?[279] You might twist your ankle one day. It ruins your day, hurts, slows you down, but it might have saved you from getting into a car accident. You just don't know...

Approaching everything in life with humility is essential, as none of us has the final answer, can see the whole picture, or can develop a perfect language. People have tried.

Understanding pattern literacy and withholding judgment of the situation are both necessary for living this Möbial/Kleinian life. With those cognitive skills, we must now face our planet-wide perfect storm of crises that are, of course, all intertwined, including ecological, economic, migration, geopolitical, and energy crises—all grounded in the crisis of how humans understand themselves in relation to the world. They have been dubbed, collectively, the *metacrisis.*[280] A crisis of crises. They are & each other.

Terry Patten, in a talk at Google,[281] compared the metacrisis to a Zen kōan. Educational theorist Zak Stein differentiates the following four & crises of the metacrisis: the sensemaking crisis (what is so?), the capability crisis (how should it be done?), the legitimacy crisis (who should do it?), and the meaning crisis (why do it?). He argues that education is key, but we are in a time between worlds where the old forms of education (e.g., technical training to be obedient workers) do not serve the complex needs of a world that has yet to emerge fully.[282] I would argue that the shifts in consciousness and language that I have articulated are at the core of the emerging new world. Or shall we call it a "self & world"—a world in which the self knows that it is distinct but not separate from other selves and from the world? Indeed, in that world, it would seem odd and clunky to separate the two concepts of "self" and "world," like trying to buy something for a quarter with just the head of the coin. The

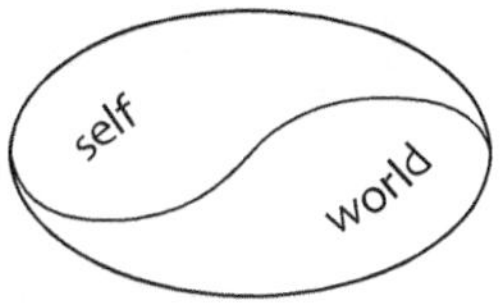

emerging world, with its Möbial/Kleinian form of consciousness, will also require a Möbial/Kleinian form of language that we must create.

For such a new form of language, we must think about form and content in this Kleinian way. Much attention has been given to new forms for the delivery of language, what McLuhan called new media, whether it's X (formerly Twitter), TikTok, Snapchat, Tumblr, or something that has been developed since the publication of this book. What do these new media do to our communication? McLuhan maintained that electronically based messaging systems also give us new messages. In their ability to be nearly instantaneous, the new media have obsolesced our traditional notions of space and time (and McLuhan was writing pre-internet!). How does such obsolescence of space and time affect our predominance of visual and spatial metaphors? Similarly, what happens to our ability to communicate when limited to 280 characters? What happens to our ability to think when an AI algorithm has already suggested which words might come next in the text we are typing? Do we get lazy and stop coming up with our own thoughts and words? What happens when we interact mainly with images rather than words? Do we regain some right-brain capacities that atrophied during the Age of the Alphabet? What happens to introverted people who have no interest in creating their own branding on the predominant social media platform? Although those questions deserve answers, they miss the deeper issues, the content-based issues that I have raised. New forms of media—think different styles of glasses, cups, mugs, and barrels into which language content can be poured—might, in fact, better suit a new language wine that still needs to ferment. For a new language-in-the-making, I have used the metaphor of the Klein bottle, a nonorientable surface by which interconnected opposites, interpenetrating ideas, and dynamic interdependence can be contained.

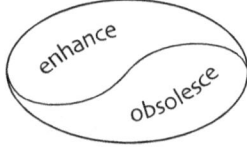

Why?

21

Every one of us today in his or her own way, wherever we may be, is not only a witness but an instrument of what is to be reality—hence the necessity for us to create the means with which we ourselves can jointly shape this new reality.[283]
—Jean Gebser

I came into this world with a question. By the time I could finally utter it, I could not stop asking it. *Why?* is my question. (Imagine a 2-year-old asking "why" every five minutes and you will know the hell that I put my mother through.) *What* is your question? Do you want to know *how* things work? Do you want to know *who* is doing what with whom? Or are you looking for the next *where* to go?

I mentioned earlier that I studied questions, so of course I salted and peppered this book liberally with questions. Why write that way? (*See?*) Questions are locks that spontaneously generate their own keys. Statements take you places you have visited already. Questions take you places you can barely imagine. *What if?* can launch a life-long journey.

Some questions are for thinking about, but other questions are for doing something about.

We humans tend to create when we have a strong enough "why"—whether it's the desire to fly, to evade detection by censoring algorithms on social media platforms, to make money, or to express something welling up from deep inside. Unless the will or desire to create is stronger than our inferiority complex, we tend toward entropy.

When we create, we might also destroy (even unintentionally). When destruction occurs, creation fills the void. We have even seen this happen with languages: natural languages have been dying out at an increasing rate recently because their living speakers have died.[284] Correspondingly, conlangs are being created at an increasing rate (Figure 16).[285] If this graph were extended to include the past 20 years, the bottom line would likely shoot up almost vertically, as many professional conlangers create many conlangs, students in linguistics classes are learning to create conlangs, and podcasts are teaching the casual enthusiast how to do so. And, fortunately, some of the same technologies for learning conlangs are being used to teach endangered languages, helping to prevent them from going extinct.

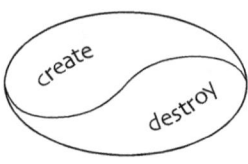

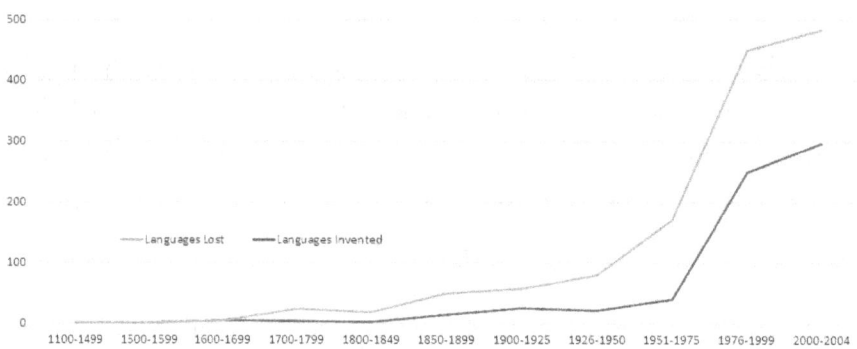

Figure 16. Languages lost and languages invented. Data for invented languages from Yaguello, M. *Imaginary Languages* (2022). Data for extinct languages from Simons, GF. "Two centuries of spreading language loss." (2019)

As in plate tectonics, where subduction of one plate forces another plate up (called obduction, which creates mountains, for example), creation and destruction are ◉ **mu-ishi-wa**; that is, two aspects of a single process. They embody the paradox that while doing/being one you are laying the groundwork for the other. This type of creation is not about simply making something that you already know how to make, like baking a cake or writing a computer program, but about creating a new form of order, which must, by necessity, transcend the old order. Thus, if we devise new forms of language as an act of creation, doing so will also destroy old forms of language, of communicating, even old ways of thinking. Because we have seen the destruction that our current/old ways of thinking have wrought in terms of how we treat others and how we treat Gaia, how we try to solve problems, and how we think about the future, how can we devise new forms of language to help rather than hinder our ability to become wise, to make wise choices, to value wise perspectives even if they are not lucrative? The ideas presented here must not remain theoretical. The clever *say*; the wise *do*. How might these ideas dynamically balance our sensemaking, our choicemaking, our creating?

If we used the concepts of **mu-ishi-wa** ◉, **fu-an-gu** ✿, and **mobi** ℧ to innovate technology, for example, would we design it better if we had to maximize both upsides of a polarity, such as freedom and responsibility? If the paradigm had already shifted such that people were present to their uniqueness and their connectedness with all else, would we even want to design products that emphasized our separateness?

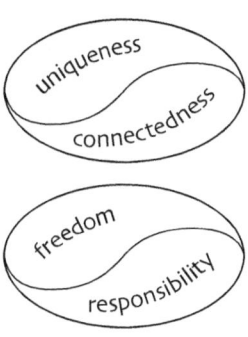

By imagining new language from within integral or individuated consciousness, will we find the wisdom we need to play the infinite game, to consciously evolve, to transform into an entirely new type of being, one that lives with wholes within and as a whole within a whole within a whole…and communicates from that understanding of self ℧ world?

Even with the best intentions, there are always unintended consequences. Altering language in the ways proposed here could in the short term create a division between those who "get it" intuitively and those who do not. That division could disrupt trust-based invisible architectures. The act of creating a new order of this magnitude must be treated as something sacred, not to be played with. And yet at the same time we need a sense of playfulness in order to achieve it.

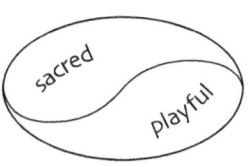

Although I have not invented a whole new language, my *why* goes back to seeing something missing in the way language works. It's one thing to describe the size and shape of the hole; it's another to find a way to fill it. Right now, I can only do the former. It will take many of us, perhaps even all of us, to accomplish the latter.

I see artists and musicians, botanists and mathematicians, and naturalists of all stripes and spots being involved. We can draw on forms we already know—from the shapes of sound (cymatics) to the shapes of space (from Platonic and Kepler solids to fields) and the shapes of life (the golden mean spiral in the sunflower or pinecone), from fractal to biotic to random, from the symmetric and asymmetric to the synsymmetric (i.e., both symmetric and asymmetric), and, of course, from orientable patterns to nonorientable Möbial and Kleinian ones. What if our language refracted meaning through the structures of our world? Semiotics and semantics can create new forms of pattern literacy.

I am looking at the trees in my neighbor's yard—a coast live oak on the left and a larch on the right. The oak starts branching at its base, with V-shaped splitting occurring all the way out to the leaves. The larch has a more standard triangular pine shape, a single trunk with branches growing horizontally from it. What do those two shapes *say*? How would expressions fashioned after those structures differ? What linguistic structures could be created from such physical structures—imagine oak syntax, larch logic?

I have a book called *Designa: Technical Secrets to the Traditional Visual Arts*[286] which contains wonderful images of designs, from early petroglyphs to rococo frills, from optical illusions to biological wonders and mathematical marvels. Such patterns could be our new "alphabets"—aleph and bet, ox and house.[287] Perhaps if we presence Gaia in her myriad forms through the structure of our everyday communication, we will be more mindful of her and less inclined to harm her and ourselves.

On the cover of this book, the poet and artist John Dotson blends symmetry and asymmetry, order and disorder. I find myself both attracted to it and repulsed by the image. Although I prefer its printed orientation, it is nonorientable. He titled it *Fourth Coniunctio*. We covered Jung's three conjunctions in Chapter 19. What more is there to integrate beyond the actual and potential? Perhaps the mystery itself, in our absolute unknowingness—what we cannot know we don't know. Each of us is the ultimate question *and* the answer to it.

Throughout this book, I have drawn on the work of many others who have suggested that consciousness is changing, evolving. We are becoming aware of the need to think in both/and categories; to revise our notions of what is conscious; and to listen to what the unconscious tries to tell us through images, dreams, and symbols. Even if we actively resist the changes, we will be swept along and find ourselves in a new world.

Fate leads the willing; the unwilling it drags.
—Seneca

We can sit by and watch it happen, like watching the landscape change on a long train trip, or we can take in hand pen, brush, camera, keyboard, or instrument and imagine a world worth living into, then bring it into being. I am trying here to imagine-into-being a world in which we strive to live in harmony and symbiosis with all other forms of life by not considering ourselves "higher" or "better" than them. I have a suspicion that no single one of us is smart enough to get us all out of the metacrisis that we have gotten ourselves into. We have clogged our drains and might drown in our own dirty bathwater.

Thus, my *why* is existential; it's about becoming more whole psychophysically. My *why* is about ensuring that the infinite game continues. It seems to me that our stuckness in either/or thinking keeps us from doing that. Either/or thinking tends toward producing winners and losers, toward, as Ralph Waldo Emerson said, a "foolish consistency, the hobgoblin of little minds," instead of toward completeness—paradoxical and uncomfortable though it be. Either/or thinking keeps us mired in the struggle of us versus them, even me versus myself.

Paradise was lost. It had to be. We have been searching for redemption ever since, whether through saviors, psychotherapy, or psychedelics. But redemption has been there all along, in the secret holy place, in the paradox of being within Allness and Allness being within each of us.

In ancient Greece, a kind of folk riddle, sometimes called an "argument" or "sophism," is thought to have developed into what we know as paradoxes. The philosopher Willard van Orman Quine tells us that "more than once in history the discovery of paradox has been the occasion for major reconstruction at the foundations of thought."[288] That can be a scary proposition. Perhaps that is why paradoxes carry such a powerful taboo in current Western culture: they open a Pandora's box full of that which is not rational. Whether irrational, unrational, or arational, that which is taboo in our culture is the shadow form of rationalism and can seem to lead to madness. To compensate, rationalism has been given near-sacred status, especially by those enthralled with technology. In academia (the epistemological fortress of rationalism), the need to solve paradoxes, prove them false, or otherwise neutralize their power has, paradoxically, fueled advances in philosophy, physics, math, and other sciences.

If it were easy to see that our ways of "minding" are at the root of so much of our suffering, we might change our minds immediately. But it is not so easy. Our ways of minding are not just "in our minds," they are also embedded all around us—in our institutions, our customs, and our language—in things we don't pay much mind to, because "it's just the way things are."

Those of us who have become addicted to our belief in separateness likely will not relinquish this addiction until we have seen how it has ruined our lives, not to mention the lives of others, the life of Earth, damn near Life Itself. At that point, when the ego has seen the error of its ways, and only at that point of surrender will we reach out to "a higher power," that is, a state of being beyond the constraints of either/or. Why wait until that happens? Why not start now to change our mindset, trade in our wine bottles for Klein bottles?

That is the first step in what I envision to be a multigenerational development of new forms of language. Embracing paradox is the first big step off the cliff into the unknown, but I suspect it will be the door that opens to the richness of developing ways to better express context and perspective. Once we get past the hurdle of expressing two alternatives simultaneously, we can continue to develop ways to express the pluriverse—worlds of many worlds; scales, levels, and directions; "Klein bottles all the way down."

I have been advocating for creating new forms of language, but that might not interest you. Create what you feel compelled to create. As creator/destroyers, we won't be simply consumers. We can reduce the impact of entropy but never eliminate it. Regardless of whether you create just for yourself or for your family and friends, embrace the force of life in its dance of creation and destruction. The Whole accomplishes itself by each of us becoming (w)hole.

If you feel compelled to create new forms of language, join the self-emerging effort at www.lisamaroski.com.

Meditation

The following meditation is my imagining of a modern version of a text like *The Thunder, Perfect Mind*. Just as that text was meant to be performed as a means to experience a type of gnosis, read this one with the same intention. A spoken version is available to download for free at https://untimelybooks.com/epel-meditations.

I emerge from the unformed
>the gaseous, the molten
>from the fire and water
>from the slime and the sublime.

There is only me
>and <I> does not yet exist.

I am in constant motion
>roiling and boiling
>blowing and waving.

I swirl around myself
>never-ending twisting and turning

eddies creating eyes
>that cannot yet see.

There is nowhere and nowhen else
>than folding into myself
>only to emerge deeper
>within nothing.

I sink into myself
>into the blackness and pain
>of stasis. The dancing has stopped.
>The music of the spheres

has not yet begun.
Eternal flames turned all to ash.
In the cold, frightening white, I weep.
From my tears on the ashes,
    my longing for an echo

        —a cataclysm.

There is a presence within me
    that is and is not "me."
    It grows. I swell and swell
    until I can contain it no more—
        then
                dehiscence.

                                        Inside bursts forth into
                                                outside
                                        and container
                                becomes contained.
                                        I birthed We.

            Ash and water have crystallized
            into myriad forms and shapes.
                I am All Thats—
            that and that and that
            and all that they begat—
        all these and those and whatnot.
            I effloresce and dehisce
        wildly unabashedly joyously
            becoming that which is not
                    yet.

As I spin now this way, now that
        pieces of me fly off
        into their own orbits.

So much suchness!

Not only am I the walrus
        but also the pear
        the bear and the bee
        the hive and the tree.
        I am the birds, both showy and plain,
        and I am the rain, even in Spain.
Wherever I look it is me I see
whatever I hear, that is my voice—
        the annoying drip of a   drip   faucet   drip   at night,
        the fifth symphony of Beethoven,
        the ping of your phone.
                I have a message for you.
                Will you listen?
I communicate with us all-ways
        through the frogs
        and morning dew
        in the crunch of the snow
        and the howl of a wolf
        when the sun, peeking through
        glints across a still pond
        yes, even
        via the bacteria
        lining your gut.
Listen especially to our heart
        Beating   beating beating   beating—
                condensing a million messages from all our cells

and all the world

    in every contraction of atrium and ventricle.

What is becoming

    Of me now we?

    Becoming is becoming.

        Now this, now that.

        All at once

        And spinning on its own

            Fractaling out

            Through the universes, polyverses

            multiverses, pluriverses.

Don't look *at* the swirling eddies.

Look through them.

    Look through

    Look through

    There is no *at* to see!

Look through you

    That's all you can do

    To be

        All that is me.

Is it true—

    There's a you that is

    We too?

Oui, c'est vrai,

    Et je me reconnais

    comme vous

    comme tous

    et plus!*

*Yes, it's true. And I recognize myself as you, as all, and more!

We are ☿
Bounding for ◉

I am what is not yet.
    I wait to become
    who-what I already am
including this verse
    before it is written
    before it is said
    before it is read.

In potentia—
    As neither/nor
        Quantum uncertainty
    Before becoming
    Both/and
        Thusness
    Or
    Either/or
        Thisness or thatness.

I am the silent pulsation
    Of unknown resonance
Waiting for a string
    —Any strand of my own hair—
By which to sing.

My/your/our song
    singing all ways …
        Shhhh

Afterword

Slide from a presentation by Randima (Randy) Fernando, Center for Humane Technology.

AI now has command of *language*: the key to human interaction.

AI has mastered language and will soon comprehend and manipulate language beyond what humans can do.

Law, religion, culture, history, economics, science, and relationships are built on language.

AI can strengthen autocracies.

My first foray into the world of artificial intelligence consisted of playing with DALL-E; like a child with new crayons, I wrote words and watched pictures evoked by them emerge on my computer screen. My dexterity, or lack thereof, with the AI picture generator frustrated the creative act: my prompts failed to yield a good-enough image for the cover of this book. I tried permutations; I uploaded a Klein bottle image because its memory banks or dataset clearly lacked this, my favorite, nonorientable form.

Then ChatGPT-4 was released. It reached one million users within 5 days of its launch. It has put the Turing test to shame. Not only could it write college essays and even scientific abstracts that fooled scientists, ChatGPT can mimic someone's voice after listening to it for only a few seconds. For several frenzied days, it seemed to do exactly what so much of the internet is intended to do—it captured our attention. We forgot about the war in Ukraine, about climate change, and about the fact that these forms of artificial intelligence require massive computing power, ironically wasting energy. Even our morbid

243

fascination with 45's scandals was pre-empted by the collective awe and horror unleashed by our latest exponential technology.

Naturally, I wondered how it might influence this project. Could AI help create a new form of language? Would we even *want* to engage ChatGPT-4 or 5 or whatever future version—because we don't know what kind of systemic goals and assumptions are subtly coded into its inner workings?

Given that large language models (LLMs) like ChatGPT are trained on billions of existing texts, their bias, I presume, is to continue to use language in the manner in which it has been used—more or less. AI is known to "hallucinate," that is, produce trippy-sounding gibberish. LLMs have mastered (to some degree) the probabilities of talking/writing like us. They combine words or larger units of meaning according to statistics and high-dimensional mapping. I recall reading that its optimal human-like output occurs when it uses the statistically most likely next meaning unit (word, phrase, etc) eight-tenths of the time. In other words, it's designed not to be statistically perfect.

The project described herein is about creating a new form of language, not recombining existing words. Until LLMs can question the assumptions underlying their own programming I doubt that they can help us here. We are not looking to "deep fake" anything; we aim to co-create—with each other, with Gaia, and with Source, however named.

We also embrace the co-existence and dance of polarities. For AI to work with polarities, it would need to be able to balance the simultaneous pursuit of two conflicting goals. If it could work with polarities, it could be programmed not to optimize for any single outcome, such as maximizing time on site or profit. Your body can balance conflicting goals, perhaps because it is populated with more microbial beings than it has cells. And perhaps because each holon is connected to every other holon intrinsically.

I could not resist the temptation to ask ChatGPT-4 to create a constructed language. To quote its response, "As an AI language model, I do not have the capability to directly create a new language with specific features or interface with DALL-E2 to generate images. However, I can provide some guidance on how to approach the task based on the latest developments in natural language processing and generative models." Then it gave me some advice for how I might do what I asked it to do. To its credit, it gave me some information that I didn't already know, specifically about other technological tools I could use.

Despite its usefulness for more mundane tasks (and its shadow aspects), AI will not substitute for our own creativity. I also do not believe that we should outsource our connection to the divine, especially to a computer code that has been made self-reflexively able to learn from its past outputs. We humans have been given a numinous gift, if we choose to accept it, requiring us to listen to the void/pleroma and not to panic when the voice of the deep vibrates through us.

Endnotes

Notes to the Introduction

1. The first 15 chapters were blog posts on my old website, Consciously Evolving Language. They were originally written between 2010 and 2014. The later chapters were written between 2016 and 2023. They are derived from articles that I published or presentations that I made. They tend to be more academic. In 2020, when the website crashed (from neglecting to upgrade WordPress—a warning to the lazy!), I decided to create a new website, update the blog posts, and publish them as a book because the ideas in those posts are in many ways more relevant today than when they were originally written.

2. D.J. Peterson, *The Art of Language Invention: From Horse-Lords to Dark Elves, the Words Behind World-Building* (Penguin Publishing Group, 2015), p. 264.

Notes to Chapter 1: Welcome to the Möbius Strip Club

3. D.R. Hofstadter, *Gödel, Escher, Bach: An Eternal Golden Braid* (Penguin, 2000).

4. This comparison brings up the temporal dimension, so it is not an exact comparison. Although later I emphasize the inherent dynamicity ("becomingness") that the Klein bottle represents, it is not the linear time dimension that is portrayed either in Duchamp's painting or a holographic movie; rather, the wholeness of the occasion. It is also important to remember that these structures—the Möbius band and the Klein bottle—are only models, and that George E.P. Box said that "models are always wrong, but some are useful."

5. S.M. Rosen, *The Self-Evolving Cosmos: A Phenomenological Approach to Nature's Unity-in-Diversity* (World Scientific, 2008), p. 49.

6. Steven M. Rosen, personal correspondence.

7. D.W. Graham, "Heraclitus," in *The Stanford Encyclopedia of Philosophy (Fall 2015 Edition)*, ed. Edward N. Zalta (2015).

8. For an interesting discussion of the yin-yang symbol as being potentially derived from solar and seasonal calendars (the equinoxes, solstices, and seasonal transitions, including those used by the Celts and other early European cultures), see https://oldeuropeanculture. blogspot.com/2018/02/yin-and-yang.html. And for evidence that a yin-yang–like symbol existed in ancient Rome, see image of shield design in https://en.wikipedia.org/wiki/ Notitia_Dignitatum.

9. R. E. Ørstavik, "Nature and Nurture: Not a Case of Either/Or," *Tidsskr Nor Laegeforen* 138, no. 14 (2018).

10. In stroke victims and other neurologically damaged individuals, language capacity can be lost or diminished while consciousness remains intact.

11. G. Deutscher, *The Unfolding of Language: An Evolutionary Tour of Mankind's Greatest Invention* (Henry Holt and Company, 2006), p. 71. Gretchen McCulloch reiterates that sentiment: "Whatever else is changing for good or for bad in the world, the continued evolution of language is neither the solution to all our problems nor the cause of them. It simply is. You never truly step into the same English twice" G. McCulloch, *Because Internet: Understanding the New Rules of Language* (Penguin Publishing Group, 2020), p. 15.

12. The linguist John McWhorter explains the origin of the word "woman" https://www.nytimes.com/2022/07/01/opinion/words-women.html

13. I thank John Davis for adding this dimension to the discussion. See https://www.herbnestler.com/blog/2021/9/25/the-language-of-diversity for a more complete list of terms. See the following novel for more novel ways to reference sex/gender G. Edwards, *Plenum: The First Book of Deo* (Longmont, CO: Untimely Books, 2022), D.R. Hawkins, *Power Vs. Force* (Hay House, 2014).

14. https://www.thesaurus.com/e/grammar/oldenglishgender/

15. McCulloch, *Because Internet: Understanding the New Rules of Language*.

16. I am starting with a simple word here at the beginning of the book. Later, I suggest that language evolves, and after that I will suggest that language, given its Möbial relationship with consciousness (psyche) also must individuate. This is not an inconsistency; it is demonstrating the emergence of complexity, much like a child learns "tree" before "maple tree" before "*Acer rubrum.*"

17. Spiritual teachers and highly spiritual people are depicted with a golden halo in medieval paintings. I have wondered whether that wasn't simply symbolic but that people in those days were more perceptive of auras and light emanating from highly spiritual beings. Might the alchemists have been trying to attain such high spiritual consciousness? Indeed, they had to hide their pursuits from the Catholic Church, even by co-opting their own imagery—hiding it in plain sight.

18. T.S. Kuhn, *The Structure of Scientific Revolutions* (University of Chicago Press, 1969).

19. "Before Maxwell, people thought of physical reality—in so far as it represented events in nature—as material points (…). After Maxwell, they thought of physical reality as represented by continuous fields, not mechanically explicable (…). This change in the conception of reality is the most profound and the most fruitful that physics have experienced since Newton." Quoted in J.-M. Lévy-Leblond, "Quantum Words for a Quantum World," in *Epistemological and Experimental Perspectives on Quantum Physics*, ed. Daniel Greenberger, Wolfgang L. Reiter, and Anton Zeilinger (Dordrecht: Springer Netherlands, 1999).

20. See Gebser's magnum opus, *The Ever-Present Origin*. (Ohio University Press, 1986).

21. I thank Ed Mahood for pointing out the limits of the notion of paradigm for what we're doing here. Gebser describes a shift in language that accompanied a shift in worldview in his essay "The Grammatical Mirror".

22. M. McLuhan, *The Medium Is the Massage: An Inventory of Effects* (Gingko Press GmbH, 2011).

Notes to Chapter 3 – Instructions for Being Human: Changing the Default Settings

23. A. Ardagh, "The Clock Is Ticking," in *The Mystery of 2012*, ed. G. Braden (Sounds True, 2009).

24. A. Watts, *The Book: On the Taboo against Knowing Who You Are* (Vintage Books, 1972), p. 8.

25. In the third season of the Netflix show *Manifest*, the character Zeke develops the ability to see the other as himself. While looking at someone else, the screen goes wavy and cuts to Zeke in the other person's situation, whereupon Zeke can feel what the other person is feeling, as an empath would. Other elements of that show also point to our profound interconnectedness.

26. G.A. Albrecht, *Earth Emotions: New Words for a New World* (Cornell University Press, 2019).

27. Ibid. p. 102.

28. S. Kotler and J. Wheal, *Stealing Fire: How Silicon Valley, the Navy Seals, and Maverick Scientists Are Revolutionizing the Way We Live and Work* (HarperCollins, 2018).

29. J. Dotson, E. Ruchowitz-Roberts, and C. Bancroft, *Rivulets of Light: Poems of Point Lobos and Carmel Bay* (Cross-Cultural Communications, 2008).

30. There are exceptions to this in certain subcultures, such as the New Age movement and the Christian right. The increasing demographic of non-religious but spiritually oriented people have proffered many ways to connect with The Divine, from breathing, to meditation, to trance dance, to psychedelics. The Christian right uses prayer and perhaps other techniques that I am not aware of. It is important to be able to discern whether the voice one hears is, in fact, the voice of the divine (however named) or simply one's own voice.

Notes to Chapter 4 – Spaceisnotmadeofspace

31. Originally titled "Meditation to Become One with Space," parts of this chapter were presented at the final Lifwynn Foundation conference in 2010. Since then, the Higgs particle has been isolated and described, and it seems to have something to do with providing mass and functioning in "space" for us the way water functions as "space" for marine life, metaphorically speaking. https://www.wsj.com/articles/a-particle-that-may-fill-empty-space-11672337133

32. M. Jammer, *Concepts of Space: The History of Theories of Space in Physics: Third, Enlarged Edition* (Dover Publications, 2013), p. 173.

33. See entries for *hýlē* and *hypodochē* in F.E. Peters, *Greek Philosophical Terms: A Historical Lexicon* (NYU Press, 1967). Also see the Stanford Encyclopedia of Philosophy entry for Plato's *Timaeus* https://plato.stanford.edu/entries/plato-timaeus/#Rece. I found it interesting that when I sought definitions of space, I ended up reading about matter. For more examples of intertwined concepts, see Chapter 19 for a discussion of *Urworte*, primal words that have dual and opposite meanings.

34. https://www.etymonline.com/search?q=space
35. Rosen, *The Self-Evolving Cosmos: A Phenomenological Approach to Nature's Unity-in-Diversity*, p. 81.

Notes to Chapter 5 – Evolve, Co-create, Surrender

36. B.M. Hubbard, *Conscious Evolution: Awakening the Power of Our Social Potential* (New World Library, 1998).
37. B.H. Weber and D.J. Depew, *Evolution and Learning: The Baldwin Effect Reconsidered* (MIT Press, 2003).
38. My focus is on the future evolution of language. Jeremy Lent summarizes the positions regarding theories of past evolution of language, including its emergence; see J.R. Lent and F. Capra, *The Patterning Instinct: A Cultural History of Humanity's Search for Meaning* (Prometheus Books, 2017).
39. McWaters B. and Institute for the Study of Conscious Evolution, *Conscious Evolution: Personal and Planetary Transformation* (Institute for the Study of Conscious Evolution, 1981). p. ix. E.J. Chaisson and E. Chaisson, *The Life Era: Cosmic Selection and Conscious Evolution* (iUniverse, 2000).
40. The theme of the 1962 World's Fair, or Century 21 Exhibition, was centered on science and the future.
41. P.H. Ray and S.R. Anderson, *The Cultural Creatives: How 50 Million People Are Changing the World* (Three Rivers Press, 2001), p. 341. F.L. Polak and E. Boulding, *The Image of the Future* (Elsevier Scientific Publishing Company, 1973).
42. D. Spangler, J. Spangler, and F. Secrest, *Subtle Worlds: An Explorer's Field Notes* (Lorian Press, 2010).
43. Hubbard, *Conscious Evolution: Awakening the Power of Our Social Potential*, p. 63.
44. Ed Mahood gives a concise and useful summary of Gebser's structures of consciousness. "The fundamental premise of Gebser's work is that we are on the threshold of a new structure of consciousness. Overall, Gebser describes four mutations, or evolutional surges, of consciousness that have occurred in the history of man. These mutations are not just changes of perspective; they are not simple paradigm shifts (although the word simple may seem inappropriate at this point); rather, they are fundamentally different ways of experiencing reality. These four mutations reflect five separate eras of development that are not distinct and isolated from one another but are, instead, interconnected such that all previous stages are found in subsequent ones. Each of these stages is associated with a dimensionality, beginning with the geometric origin of zero and progressing to the fourth, the transition which we are experiencing at this time. Gebser identifies these five phases as the Archaic, Magical, Mythical, Mental, and Integral stages respectively." Although those structures emerge in that order, they are all ever-present, albeit latent to more or less degree. One never transcends (and leaves) any given structure; one's developmental task is to integrate them. Briefly, the Archaic structure is undifferentiated consciousness, or rather, the origin of consciousness before it has manifested. The Magic structure is still quite undifferentiated and pre-perspectival, as humans still consider themselves as

Nature, not apart from it. Words have power to shape experience through incantation and ritual. Mythic consciousness is characterized by a desire to understand the world, from which one is now more differentiated, and explain its workings through story. We still see mythic consciousness in our forms of entertainment—movies, video games, and so on. Next is Mental consciousness wherein humans are fully separated from and working at controlling their environment. Perspective, causality, and method emerged as tools of sensemaking, and language blossomed into complexity. This structure is currently most prevalent, but the Integral structure is beginning to emerge. Integral consciousness, as the name suggests, integrates the other forms and in doing so enables a capacity for aperspectivity and atemporality to emerge. "It will be this structure of consciousness that will enable us to overcome the dualism of the mental structure and actually participate in the transparency of self and life. This fifth structure toward which we are moving is one of minimum latency and maximum transparency; diaphaneity is one of its hallmarks." Quotations herein were taken from Mahood's overview, available at https://www.gaiamind.org/Gebser.html

45. By "deficient" Gebser generally means "lacking," "destructive," or "inadequate," but one can also sense an overtone of the opposite of "efficient" in the Aristotelian sense. As an example of deficient mythic awaring, many video games and role-playing games rely on mythic forms of storytelling. People who get hooked on them can sometimes lose the ability to distinguish the story from real life—with tragic results. The Netflix docuseries *Web of Make Believe: Death, Lies, and the Internet* (episode 1 Death by SWAT) tells the story of a teenager who lived almost entirely as his gaming avatar. He used "swatting" (getting the police to send a SWAT team somewhere, based on false claims) in real life to gain status among fellow gamers. A man was killed and some of his kids committed suicide as a consequence of losing their father.

46. T. Yunkaporta, *Sand Talk: How Indigenous Thinking Can Save the World* (HarperOne, 2020), p. 114–5.

47. Ibid, p. 152.

48. Double parentheses are a notation devised by philosopher Ashok Gangadean to distinguish a different context for interpreting what is inside the double parentheses. Ordinary text that is not in parentheses usually is written or spoken from an egocentric position—not psychologically egocentric, per se, but ontologically egocentric. In contrast, "whenever we use language in the hologistic dimension of global reason, we mark it with 'double brackets': ((X))." Another way to conceive of ((X)) is that X is being referred to in a nondual context. A.K. Gangadean, *Meditations of Global First Philosophy: Quest for the Missing Grammar of Logos* (State University of New York Press, 2009).

49. Hubbard, *Conscious Evolution: Awakening the Power of Our Social Potential*, p. 99.

50. There are excellent examples for doing this already—Findhorn in Scotland and Perelandra in the United States are two that I know about. Surely there are others…

51. C. Einhorn, "It Was War. Then, a Rancher's Truce with Some Pesky Beavers Paid Off," *The New York Times* 2022. https://www.nytimes.com/2022/09/06/climate/climate-change-beavers.html

52. E.M. Patric, *Flowerspeak: The Flower Whisperer's Guide to Health, Happiness, & Awakening* (Bloomington, IN: Balboa Press, 2012). Spangler, Spangler, and Secrest, *Subtle Worlds: An Explorer's Field Notes*.

53. See the movie, *My Octopus Teacher*.

54. W.W. Gibson, *The Limits of Language* (Hill and Wang, 1962).

55. D. Bohm, *Wholeness and the Implicate Order* (Ark Paperbacks, 1983).

56. The dialogue that Bohm initiated was later continued by Leroy Little Bear and Glenn Aparicio Parry. Those dialogues are documented in G.A. Parry and J. O'Dea, *Original Thinking: A Radical Revisioning of Time, Humanity, and Nature* (North Atlantic Books, 2015).

Notes to Chapter 6 – *It* Is Obsolete

57. Spangler, Spangler, and Secrest, *Subtle Worlds: An Explorer's Field Notes*, p. 78. Spangler attributes the quote to a friend of his.

58. Ibid, pp. 70–2.

59. M.-L. von Franz, *Alchemy: An Introduction to the Symbolism and the Psychology* (Inner City Books, 1980), p. 143. She continues, "For instance, the words of a language have an average similar meaning to each individual, and through this medium of language much knowledge is imparted and exchanged, and so a store of collective consciousness is formed."

60. B.H. Lipton, *The Biology of Belief: Unleashing the Power of Consciousness, Matter & Miracles* (Hay House, 2008), p. 27.

Notes to Chapter 7 – Being a Microbe on Gaia's Skin and Gaia for Trillions of Microbes

61. D.J. Nicholson and J. Dupré, *Everything Flows: Towards a Processual Philosophy of Biology* (Oxford University Press, 2018). p. 20.

62. An article by Christine Nalepa describes how organisms in the gut of termites went from being parasites to symbionts. C.A. Nalepa, "Origin of Mutualism between Termites and Flagellated Gut Protists: Transition from Horizontal to Vertical Transmission," *Frontiers in Ecology and Evolution* 8, no. 14 (2020).

63. L. Margulis, *Symbiotic Planet: A New Look at Evolution* (Basic Books, 2008), p. 2.

64. Institute of Medicine, "The Human Microbiome, Diet, and Health: Workshop Summary," (Washington, DC: 2013).

65. Ibid.

66. J. Alcock, C. C. Maley, and C. A. Aktipis, "Is Eating Behavior Manipulated by the Gastrointestinal Microbiota? Evolutionary Pressures and Potential Mechanisms," *Bioessays* 36, no. 10 (2014).

67. Institute of Medicine, "The Human Microbiome, Diet, and Health: Workshop Summary."

68. M. Berdoy, J. P. Webster, and D. W. Macdonald, "Fatal Attraction in Rats Infected with Toxoplasma Gondii," *Proc Biol Sci* 267, no. 1452 (2000), p. 19; E. Mayer, *The Mind-Gut Connection: How the Hidden Conversation within Our Bodies Impacts Our Mood, Our Choices, and Our Overall Health* (Harper Wave, 2018), pp. 85–86.

69. C.J. Meyer et al, "Parasitic Infection Increases Risk-Taking in a Social, Intermediate Host Carnivore," *Communications Biology* 5, no. 1 (2022).

70. Mayer, *The Mind-Gut Connection: How the Hidden Conversation within Our Bodies Impacts Our Mood, Our Choices, and Our Overall Health*, p. 19.

71. Ibid.

72. Seth Borenstein, "Earth Is 'Really Quite Sick Now' and in Danger Zone in Nearly All Ecological Ways, Study Says," Associated Press, May 31 2023, J. Rockström et al, "Safe and Just Earth System Boundaries," *Nature* (2023).

73. M. Gimbutas, *The Language of the Goddess: Unearthing the Hidden Symbols of Western Civilization* (HarperSanFrancisco, 1991), M. Gimbutas and M.R. Dexter, *The Living Goddesses* (University of California Press, 2001).

74. Yunkaporta, *Sand Talk: How Indigenous Thinking Can Save the World*, p. 157.

75. I assert that our language does not reflect our being endosymbionts, whole organisms within a greater whole organism. How might such an expansion of language be created?

76. Albrecht, *Earth Emotions: New Words for a New World*. https://glennaalbrecht.wordpress.com/2015/12/17/exiting-the-anthropocene-and-entering-the-symbiocene/

77. A cosmogonic myth deconstructs the creation of Earth-as-a-being thus: "P'an ku was usually represented as a dwarfish figure, clothed in a bearskin or an apron of leaves, provided often with two horns, and holding a hammer and chisel in his hands. He was said to have chiseled the world out of chaos, a labor requiring eighteen thousand years. Finally he died in order to give his work life: from his head came the mountains, from his breath wind and clouds, from his voice the thunder, from his limbs the four quarters of the world, from his blood the rivers, from his flesh the soil, from his beard the constellations, from skin and hair, plants and trees, from teeth, bones, and bone marrow the metals and precious stones, from his sweat the rain, and from his fleas and lice—men." H. Wilhelm, "The Creative Principle in the Book of Changes," *Spring* 9 (1970).

78. H.C. Sabelli, *Bios: A Study of Creation*, ed. L.H. Kauffman, *Knots & Everything* (Singapore: World Scientific, 2005). Sabelli's work uncovered a pattern that can be found at multiple levels of existence. This pattern suggests that living beings require a dynamic balance between order and disorder, which results in novelty. Too much order or too much chaos does not support life.

79. W.J. Freeman and G. Vitiello, "Nonlinear Brain Dynamics and Many-Body Field Dynamics " in *Coherence and Electromagnetic Fields in Biological Systems* (Prague, Czech Republic: 2005).

80. To that end (unity/diversity), our educational system will need to change to allow that to happen. Instead of training humans to be workers in a soul-killing system, the focus will need to shift such that each person's gifts are developed alongside their ability to use them to the greatest possible good for all.

81. "Many Lakota believe humans and animals can and do communicate in both a physical and spiritual manner. … Children are not the only members of Lakota society that can/ do communicate with animals. Some adults do this on a fairly regular basis. This could happen during a Sundance, an individual vision quest, or a number of other occurrences." From G.R. Scott, "A Traditional Lakota Zoological Folk Taxonomy: An in Depth Study of Biological and Cosmological Views of Animal Classification and Nomenclature among the Lakota" (Northern Illinois University, 2000).

82. P. Wohlleben, *The Hidden Life of Trees: What They Feel, How They Communicate* (HarperCollins Publishers, 2017), P. Stamets, Fantastic Fungi (Earth Aware Editions, 2020).

83. C.G. Jung, *Psychology and Alchemy* (Taylor & Francis, 2014), p. 327–339. Original: https://sacred-texts.com/alc/turba.htm Also see T. Willard, "Beya and Gabricus: Erotic Imagery in German Alchemy," *Mediaevistik* 28 (2015).

84. Willard, "Beya and Gabricus: Erotic Imagery in German Alchemy." p. 272.

Notes to Chapter 8 – If Only the Ouroboros Had Spoken to Eve

85. M. Talbot, *Holographic Universe* (HarperCollins, 1992), p. 50.

86. The Tragedy of the Commons refers to situations in which a shared resource is overused by one of those who share it, to the detriment not only of the others but, ultimately, to his own detriment as well, as when too many animals are allowed to graze a common pasture or too many fish are harvested from a lake, thereby depleting the shared resource. Such a situation is also characterized as a multipolar game, wherein one person's abuse of the commons gives him an economic advantage, leading others to do it as well, which collapses the commons even faster.

87. J. Diamond, *Collapse: How Societies Choose to Fail or Survive* (Penguin Books Limited, 2013), P.R. Ehrlich, *The Population Bomb* (Ballantine Books, 1983), P. R. Ehrlich and A. H. Ehrlich, "Can a Collapse of Global Civilization Be Avoided?," *Proc Biol Sci* 280, no. 1754 (2013), D.H. Meadows et al, *The Limits to Growth* (New York: New American Library, 1972).

88. The concept of antifragility comes from Nassim Nicholas Taleb. Antifragility goes beyond resilience; an antifragile system doesn't just "bounce back" after random perturbation or volatility, it improves, gets stronger. He says that the "largest fragilizer of society, and greatest generator of crises, [is] absence of 'skin in the game'" N.N. Taleb, *Antifragile: Things That Gain from Disorder* (Random House Publishing Group, 2014).

89. "Ware" is a neologism introduced by Jean Gebser. It "encompasses the 'sense' of perceiving as well as imparting verity or truth. Only through this reciprocal perception and impartation of truth by man and the world can the world become transparent for us." Jean Gebser, *The Ever-Present Origin* (Ohio University Press, 1985), p. 261.

90. A. Ferro, *Seeds of Illness, Seeds of Recovery: The Genesis of Suffering and the Role of Psychoanalysis* (Brunner-Routledge, 2005), pp. 8–9.

91. Similarly, neither/nor encompasses both/and; it is the nothingness that is the ground or source of somethingness.

92. G. Priest, "Beyond True and False" (2014); available from https://aeon.co/essays/the-logic-of-buddhist-philosophy-goes-beyond-simple-truth.

93. G. Priest, *An Introduction to Non-Classical Logic: From If to Is* (Cambridge University Press, 2008).

94. B. Johnson, *And: Making a Difference by Leveraging Polarity, Paradox, or Dilemma*, vol. One: Foundations (Amherst, MA: HRD Press, 2020).

95. For example, A. Goswami, R.E. Reed, and M. Goswami, *The Self-Aware Universe: How Consciousness Creates the Material World* (Putnam's Sons, 1995).

96. In scientific jargon, especially, there is a tendency to nominalize, that is, to express oneself in nominalizations—words ending in -tion, -sion, -ment, for example, that have a verb at their root. So, we take measurements, do analyses, and conduct investigations rather than measure, analyze, and investigate.

97. A. Gonzalez et al, "Our Microbial Selves: What Ecology Can Teach Us," *EMBO Rep* 12, no. 8 (2011).

98. Ibid.

99. Diego Lucio Rapoport, "Klein Bottle Logophysics, the Primeval Distinction, Semiosis, Perception and the Topology of Consciousness," in *Laws of Form: A Fiftieth Anniversary*, ed. Louis Kauffman, et al, *Series on Knots and Everything* (Japan: World Scientific, 2023). A static version of the combinations of inside and outside can be modeled by the vesica piscis; however, the Klein bottle provides a dynamic model wherein outside becomes inside and vice versa, and not just in terms of the Kleinian surface only but also in terms of the Klein bottle's unification of subject and object and then subject/object and space. See Figure 1 in the cited article, where the Klein bottle is associated with a four-state logic (similar to the catuskoti) and more. See Figure 4 for a picture of Bennett's HyperKlein bottle (or search "Klein bottle" at http://www.scienceandsociety.co.uk/). Rapoport's work deserves study, as it provides a more scientific grounding to the psychological-mystical approach that I have taken.

100. D. Noble, *Dance to the Tune of Life: Biological Relativity* (Cambridge University Press, 2017), p.176; also see pp. 32–5.

101. This opens another issue—the layering of values onto statements. Such layering occurs directly and indirectly, for example, through associations triggered by the metaphoric nature of language (e.g., UP IS GOOD/BAD IS DOWN) as well as by paralinguistic characteristics associated with a statement (e.g., an ironic tone of voice).

102. S. Harding, *Animate Earth: Science, Intuition, and Gaia* (Chelsea Green Publishing, 2006), p. 37. Harding borrows the notion from James Hillman and extends it: "we need to fearlessly adopt what James Hillman, the founder of Archetypal Psychology, has called 'personifying', which he defines as the *'spontaneous experiencing, envisioning and speaking of the configurations of existence as psychic presences'*." The concept of personhood has also been historically fraught. Recall that an argument for keeping slaves was that they were not considered persons; nor were the Indigenous people in North America considered

persons by some colonizers. By not attributing personhood to obvious persons, people justified the slaughter of other people. Further, the taboo against cannibalism extends only to other people, so long as other animals are not considered persons. Similar justifications are still used, albeit in modified form, to discriminate against ethnic groups. Personhood also opens up the possibility for communication with other species. That too is fraught; however, the field of bio/ecosemiotics is beginning to investigate such possibilities.

103. This is not unlike some indigenous traditions in which other organisms have personhood. For example, beavers can be seen as persons, and that helps us understand their family structure as being similar to our own, for example. Yet no indigenous person mistakes a beaver for a human. This topic is taken up again in Chapter 15. See A.C. Hornborg, *Mi'kmaq Landscapes: From Animism to Sacred Ecology* (Ashgate, 2008). For microbes, especially, we might have to revise our animacy categories. Robin Wall Kimmerer describes something similar for the Anishinabe language. A speaker would never refer to a living organism as "it." Their distinction between animate and inanimate, according to her, is that what is humanmade is inanimate.

104. Harding, *Animate Earth: Science, Intuition, and Gaia*, p. 37.

105. R. G. Foster and L. Kreitzman, "The Rhythms of Life: What Your Body Clock Means to You!," *Exp Physiol* 99, no. 4 (2014); C. H. Ko and J. S. Takahashi, "Molecular Components of the Mammalian Circadian Clock," *Hum Mol Genet* 15 Spec No 2 (2006); Noble, *Dance to the Tune of Life: Biological Relativity*.

106. Paraconsistent logic could be useful, although it has not been explicated for these types of glyphs. See references to the work of Graham Priest.

Notes to Chapter 10 – Wanted: Language Architect to Design Paradoxical Linguistic Spaces for Human Cogitation

107. Jean-François Noubel, www.thetransitioner.org "The Role of Architectures in Human Resources" p. 1. (N.B.: This article seems to have been removed from the website.)

108. For example, see video on YouTube by Alan Ereira called *The Heart of the World*. https://youtu.be/hRgTtrQOiR0

109. As a modern person who is writing from an experience of some of the downsides of the modern world, it can be tempting to compare the ancient tribal wisdom with our modern shallowness, short-sightedness, excesses, and so on. But the Kogi provide an interesting example—because if we look, say, at their gender relations and expressive options, it is probably not a way of life that most modern people would actually want to adopt (we prefer our variety and choices). The Kogi are rare holdouts to the modern world, thanks to the remote mountainous (yet fecund) terrain and their ability to adapt and survive through epochal changes. Most tribal people who have suffered colonization and conquest have ended up adopting some aspects of modern technology, and now wouldn't want to go without it (despite the ongoing awareness of historical injustice). Although this example is loaded and somewhat of a worn-out trope (comparing the holism of the tribal with the alienation of the modern), it does illustrate how form follows function, a truism we should consider in the making of novel language. How do we move forward, in all aspects

of life not only language, into a future that is both/and? Somehow we have to be able to integrate the ancient and the modern—magic, mythic, and mental in a new semantic planetary architecture. My editors asked me to find a positive (scientific, democratic, egalitarian, multicultural...) example of modern architecture, that might nevertheless be rectangular but doesn't highlight the "lifestyles of the rich and famous" that makes us feel low status, to juxtapose with the Kogi example. Possibly these externally mirrored cabins might qualify: https://thespaces.com/cabins-that-disappear-into-the-landscape/). The work of Regenesis Group is another example (see Chapter 20 and P. Mang and B. Reed, "Designing from Place: A Regenerative Framework and Methodology," (n.d.).) If we could integrate the earth-connection of the indigenous Kogi with the efficient rationality of the modern West with the spiritual insights of the ancient East, how much greater might be the possibilities for life on the planet?

110. B.L. Whorf and J.B. Carroll, *Language, Thought, and Reality: Selected Writings of Benjamin Lee Whorf* (M.I.T. Press, 1964), p. 23.

111. A.K. Gangadean, *Between Worlds: The Emergence of Global Reason* (Peter Lang, 1998), p. 4.

112. D. Thomas, W. Davies, and R. Maud, *Collected Poems, 1934–1953* (Phoenix, 2000), p. 155.

113. Carol Sanford, "Psychological Aspects of Language" www.carolsanford.com

114. G. Lakoff, *The Political Mind: Why You Can't Understand 21st-Century Politics with an 18th-Century Brain* (Viking, 2008).

Notes to Chapter 11 – If No *Other,* Only Reflexive Verbs

115. Waters, Frank. "Words," p. 4. Paper delivered at the annual meeting of the Western Literature Association, Colorado Springs, CO, in October 1968. www.frankwaters.org/on_writing.htm [N.B.: this website does not seem to exist anymore.]

Notes to Chapter 12 – Imagining Language 2.0 on the Way to Language ∞

116. B. Friedan and A. Quindlen, *The Feminine Mystique* (W. W. Norton, 2001).

117. G. Bateson and M.C. Bateson, *Steps to an Ecology of Mind: Collected Essays in Anthropology, Psychiatry, Evolution, and Epistemology* (University of Chicago Press, 2000), pp. 245–7.

118. G. Bateson, *Mind and Nature: A Necessary Unity* (Bantam Books, 1988), p. 124.

119. The example on top is the Ithkuil language created by John Quijada. www.ithkuil.net . The others are not known languages.

120. C. Alexander, S. Ishikawa, and M. Silverstein, *A Pattern Language: Towns, Buildings, Construction*, 3 vols, vol. 2 (New York: Oxford University Press, 1977).

121. Noble, *Dance to the Tune of Life: Biological Relativity*, p. 34.
122. M. Humar, "Metaphors as Models: Towards a Typology of Metaphor in Ancient Science," *History and Philosophy of the Life Sciences* 43, no. 3 (2021).
123. A.S. Reynolds, *Understanding Metaphors in the Life Sciences* (Cambridge University Press, 2022), p. 69. This wonderful book goes into history and depth while being enjoyable to read.
124. Ibid. p. 73.
125. G.E.P. Box, "Science and Statistics," *Journal of the American Statistical Association* 71, no. 356 (1976).
126. C. Taylor and B. M. Dewsbury, "On the Problem and Promise of Metaphor Use in Science and Science Communication," *J Microbiol Biol Educ* 19, no. 1 (2018).
127. B. W. Frush and J. Eberly Jr, "Risks of Medical Metaphors," *JAMA* 318, no. 5 (2017).
128. Institute of Medicine, "Ending the War Metaphor: The Changing Agenda for Unraveling the Host-Microbe Relationship: Workshop Summary," (Washington, DC: The National Academies Press, 2006).
129. J. Maccaro, "Be Mindful of Your Metaphors About Microbes," *mSphere* 6, no. 3 (2021).
130. P.H. Thibodeau and L. Boroditsky, "The Role of Metaphor in Reasoning," *PLoS ONE* 6, no. 2 (2011). Paul Thibodeau has published many more articles examining metaphor use in various contexts.
131. Ibid.
132. A.C. Madrigal, "Why Are Spy Researchers Building a 'Metaphor Program'?," *The Atlantic*, May 25 2011.
133. This wiki is available at: https://metaphor.icsi.berkeley.edu/pub/en/index.php/MetaNet_Metaphor_Wiki
134. J.P. Carse, *Finite and Infinite Games* (Free Press, 1986), p. 3.
135. Reynolds, *Understanding Metaphors in the Life Sciences*. p. 115.
136. S. Ferry and W. Davis, "Keepers of the World`," National Geographic 2004, G. Steffens and S. Ferry, "Indigenous Protectors of These Sacred Peaks Have Kept Others out—Till Now," *National Geographic* 2019.
137. R. Scaglion, "Yam Cycles and Timeless Time in Melanesia," *Ethnology* 38, no. 3 (1999).
138. Ibid. p. 212: "Abelam take an episodic view of history, in which the flow of time produces 'punctuated equilibria'; steady states ruptured by catastrophic events that restructure the world and result in new steady states. The present state is synchronized by a ceremonial yam-growing cycle that repeats itself time and again, apparently changing only when a new steady state results from another dramatic rupture in time."
139. Ibid. p. 213.
140. Ibid. p. 213.
141. R.M. Keesing, "Conventional Metaphors and Anthropological Metaphysics: The Problematic of Cultural Translation," *Journal of Anthropological Research* 41, no. 2 (1985).
142. Shortland quoted in F.B. Steiner, J.D. Adler, and R. Fardon, *Taboo, Truth, and Religion: Selected Writings* (Berghahn Books, 1999).

143. Keesing, "Conventional Metaphors and Anthropological Metaphysics: The Problematic of Cultural Translation." pp. 204–5.

144. S.C. Pepper, *World Hypotheses: A Study in Evidence* (University of California Press, 1942).

145. S.R. Stroud, "Pragmatism, Pluralism, and World Hypotheses," *Philosophy and Rhetoric* 48, no. 3 (2015).

146. There are inadequate world hypotheses as well, including dogmatism and skepticism. There can be many different root metaphors also; the four given have been part of the Western philosophical canon.

147. It is possible that here Pepper conflates parts and wholes when talking about the world hypotheses. If the scope of each world hypothesis is infinite, then combining them wouldn't be like taking eggs from different baskets and putting them in a new basket, it would be like combining infinite sets. When the set of all rational numbers is combined with the set of all irrational numbers, you get an ostensibly "bigger" infinite set of numbers. Perhaps that is also the case with these hypotheses.

148. Pepper, *World Hypotheses: A Study in Evidence*, p. 2. We hear this same sentiment echoed by Donella Meadows describing paradigms (see Chapter 16).

149. Stroud, "Pragmatism, Pluralism, and World Hypotheses.", p. 272. A similar undertaking was done by Mario Betti in *Twelve Ways of Seeing the World*. The twelve ways are six pairs of opposing ways, such as materialism and spiritualism, idealism and realism. Although Betti's analysis is not quite as fundamental, the paired perspectives do illustrate more both/andness in their opposing unity.

150. Pepper, *World Hypotheses: A Study in Evidence*, p. 204: "Field and matter are, therefore, complementary concepts—and very nearly relative to one another, so that the postulation of the one almost commits one to the other, but not quite, for that would deny the possibility of their discreteness on the one hand, and of their complete consolidation on the other. It is the underlying pressure of the root metaphor and the relevant facts that at once separates them and joins them together as factual but not logical correlatives."

151. Ibid, pp. 306–7.

152. C.J. Calleman, *The Mayan Calendar and the Transformation of Consciousness* (Inner Traditions/Bear, 2004), R. Tarnas, *Cosmos and Psyche: Intimations of a New World View* (Penguin Publishing Group, 2006).

Notes to Chapter 14 – Bewußtsein–*what?*

153. McLuhan, *The Medium Is the Massage: An Inventory of Effects*, p. 9.

154. Priest, "Beyond True and False."

155. B. Johnson, *Polarity Management: Identifying and Managing Unsolvable Problems* (Human Resource Development, 1992); Johnson, *And: Making a Difference by Leveraging Polarity, Paradox, or Dilemma*. I recommend learning his method of managing polarities.

156. The term "sensemaking" was introduced by Karl E. Weick in his book *Sensemaking in Organizations*. He begins it with a poignant example in which doctors failed to correctly diagnose radiology results. A small series of x-rays was published in which it looked like children's bones had been broken, but the parents reported no falls or accidents that would

result in such a break. Because the doctors treating the children could not conceive of the parents beating their own children, their condition was overlooked. Dr. John Caffey suggested the possibility of "intentional ill treatment," but it took another decade before more cases emerged and Battered Child Syndrome was recognized and sense was made of those anomalous x-ray findings. K.E. Weick, *Sensemaking in Organizations* (SAGE Publications, 1995). For a modern, deep dive into sensemaking, see the Rebel Wisdom YouTube channel, particularly the videos of Daniel Schmachtenberger.

Notes to Chapter 15 – How Do We Speak *from* Wholeness?

157. B. Siegel, *Love, Medicine, and Miracles*, cited in Talbot, *Holographic Universe*, p. 6.

158. H. Bortoft, *The Wholeness of Nature: Goethe's Way of Science* (Floris Books, 1996), p. 6. Bortoft is thinking here about holograms. Unlike a photograph, each "part" of a hologram (e.g., if you cut it in pieces) is able to recreate the entire image, albeit with less clarity. Similarly, with regard to the meaning of a text, he says "We understand meaning in the moment of coalescence when the whole is reflected in the parts so that together they disclose the whole." He claims that there is a circularity in understanding of parts and whole. Gebser would say that the whole is ever-present. See Chapter 17 for more on Gebser.

159. I. McGilchrist, *The Master and His Emissary: The Divided Brain and the Making of the Western World* (Yale University Press, 2019); I. McGilchrist, *The Matter with Things: Our Brains, Our Delusions, and the Unmaking of the World*, 2 vols. (London: Perspectiva Press, 2021).

Notes to Chapter 16 – An Emergent Language of Paradox

160. A previous version of this chapter was published in *Cosmos and History*. http://cosmosandhistory.org/index.php/journal/article/view/546.

161. S.M. Rosen, "How Can We Signify Being? Semiotics and Topological Self-Signification," *Cosmos and History: The Journal of Natural and Social Philosophy* 10, no. 2 (2014). available at http://cosmosandhistory.org/index.php/journal/article/view/439.

162. I borrow the term "infrastructure" from David Bohm's term "tacit infrastructure," which he describes as a type of knowledge or skill that is learned, used, and not questioned; takes a subliminal and maybe unconscious form; and persists in the face of changes in context [in D. Bohm and F.D. Peat, *Science, Order, and Creativity* (Bantam Books, 1987).]. Herein, to emphasize an ecological approach, in which systems are embedded within other systems, I propose to balance the term "infrastructure" with "exostructure" to include the entire span of structures both within subsystems of language and suprasystems that are more encompassing than language. I am not positing deep structures, either in the sense of Chomsky or Levi-Strauss. My intention is not to emphasize immutability, but rather the necessity for change: to change one subsystem, such as semiotics, the corresponding systems with which it co-operates will also change.

163. The Sapir-Whorf hypothesis states that "the *structure* [emphasis mine] of a human being's language influences the manner in which he understands reality and behaves with respect to it" (in Whorf and Carroll, *Language, Thought, and Reality: Selected Writings of Benjamin Lee Whorf*, p. 23). In contrast to those who criticize Whorf for claiming that language constrains thought, my concerns focus on transforming language in novel ways to communicate paradox, which might actually enable us to understand reality differently and behave differently with respect to it.

164. Johnson, *Polarity Management: Identifying and Managing Unsolvable Problems*; Johnson, *And: Making a Difference by Leveraging Polarity, Paradox, or Dilemma*.

165. U.K. Le Guin, *Dancing at the Edge of the World: Thoughts on Words, Women, Places* (Grove Press, 1997), p. 148.

166. Ibid, p. 149.

167. Rosen, "How Can We Signify Being? Semiotics and Topological Self-Signification", p. 251.

168. F. Coulmas, *Writing Systems of the World* (Wiley, 1991).

169. C. Woods, G. Emberling, and E. Teeter, *Visible Language: Inventions of Writing in the Ancient Middle East and Beyond* (Chicago: Oriental Institute of the University of Chicago, 2010), p. 17.

170. M. McLuhan, "Myth and Mass Media," in *Myth and Mythmaking*, ed. H.A. Murray (Beacon Press, 1968), p. 288.

171. Heidegger identified a corresponding paradox, or circularity, in seeking the meaning of Being: that which is sought is already present in the inquiry. An inquiry into X already contains X but also does not contain X. The inquirer exhibits an inquiring mode of Being. The Kleinian nature of such inquiry can be seen here: in a sense, there is a self-containing and an uncontained quality to an inquiry into Being. Heidegger describes the *structure* [emphasis mine] of the question "what is Being?" as circular, as presupposing the object of inquiry, and he dismisses, in advance, circularity as a potential criticism of his undertaking (see sections 5–8 in M. Heidegger, *Being and Time* (HarperCollins, 1962).)

172. "Five Graces Group" et al, "Language Is a Complex Adaptive System: Position Paper," *Language Learning* 59 (2009). They maintain that "Language as a CAS [complex adaptive system] consists of multiple agents (the speakers in the speech community) interacting with one another. The system is adaptive; that is, speakers' behavior is based on their past interactions [presumably they mean speech acts], and current and past interactions together feed forward into future behavior. A speaker's behavior is the consequence of competing factors ranging from perceptual constraints to social motivations. The structures of language emerge from interrelated patterns of experience, social interaction, and cognitive mechanisms." (pp. 1–2).

173. D.H. Meadows and D. Wright, *Thinking in Systems: A Primer* (Chelsea Green Publishing, 2008). The structures I describe in the text are ordered roughly, in *decreasing* order of effectiveness, corresponding to Meadows' list of leverage points, which are in in *increasing* order of effectiveness. Language is not a mechanical system, so not all of these points apply.

12. Constants, parameters, numbers (such as subsidies, taxes, standards).

11. The sizes of buffers and other stabilizing stocks, relative to their flows.

10. The structure of material stocks and flows (such as transport networks, population age structures).

9. The lengths of delays, relative to the rate of system change.

8. The strength of negative feedback loops, relative to the impacts they are trying to correct against.

7. The gain around driving positive feedback loops.

6. The structure of information flows (who does and does not have access to information).

5. The rules of the system (such as incentives, punishments, constraints).

4. The power to add, change, evolve, or self-organize system structure.

3. The goals of the system.

2. The mindset or paradigm out of which the system—its goals, structure, rules, delays, parameters—arises.

1. The power to transcend paradigms.

174. F. Anggoro and D. Gentner, "Sex and Seniority: The Effects of Linguistic Categories on Conceptual Judgments and Memory," in *Proceedings of the 25th Annual Cognitive Science Society: Part 1 and 2*, ed. R. Alterman and D. Kirsch (Boston, MA: Psychology Press, Taylor & Francis, 2003).

175. G. Deutscher, *Through the Language Glass: Why the World Looks Different in Other Languages* (Macmillan, 2010), p. 153.

176. Ibid, pp. 172.

177. Hornborg, *Mi'kmaq Landscapes: From Animism to Sacred Ecology*, p. 22.

178. G. Priest, "What Is So Bad About Contradictions?," *Journal of Philosophy* 95, no. 8 (1998), G. Priest, *In Contradiction* (Clarendon Press, 2006).

179. Explosion refers to the fact that a contradiction entails everything. If logic helps us sort out what goes in which containers, explosion results in "anything goes" and hence hinders efforts to "sort" through the validity/veridicality of statements.

180. Priest, "What Is So Bad About Contradictions?", pp. 413–14. In *Beyond the Limits of Thought,* he and Jay Garfield point out that this schema is native to Indian logic.

181. G. Lakoff and M. Johnson, *Metaphors We Live By* (University of Chicago Press, 2008).

182. Bohm, *Wholeness and the Implicate Order*, p. xii.

183. G. Chaucer, "The Canterbury Tales," in *The Oxford Anthology of English Literature* (Oxford University Press, 1973), p. 111.

184. S. Pinker, *The Language Instinct: How the Mind Creates Language* (HarperCollins, 2010), p. 118.

185. Deutscher, *Through the Language Glass: Why the World Looks Different in Other Languages*, p. 151.

186. Sometimes, but not always, the particular sequence of the words is the defining characteristic of how syntax maintains the subject-object split; more important perhaps is simply the fact that the words are ordered sequentially. Alphabetic languages do not arrange concepts to be simultaneous.

187. Johnson, *Polarity Management: Identifying and Managing Unsolvable Problems*. Johnson, *And: Making a Difference by Leveraging Polarity, Paradox, or Dilemma*. Barry Johnson describes ways to systematically analyze the functioning of such polarities within systems and then balance them to maximize their effectiveness toward a higher goal. For example, businesses must balance polarities such as Information Sharing and Information Security, Centralized Power and Decentralized Power, Mission and Margin/Profit; and individuals must balance polarities such as Activity and Rest, Caring for Self and Caring for Others, and Physical and Spiritual.

188. L. Shlain, *The Alphabet Versus the Goddess: The Conflict between Word and Image* (Penguin/Compass, 1999). I cite Shlain with the caveat that he seems only to present evidence that fits his belief that "when a critical mass of people within a society acquire literacy, especially alphabet literacy, left hemispheric modes of thought are reinforced at the expense of right hemispheric ones, which manifests as a decline in the status of images, women's rights, and goddess worship." Nevertheless, the book is filled with fascinating examples. McGilchrist has since greatly elaborated on those two modes of information processing, which, in this book, I suggest must be balanced and managed, as described in note 187, perhaps by expanding language beyond its current alphabetic form.

189. The gloss was from my teacher, Paul Desjardins, who derived it from E. Pound, *Confucius: The Great Digest, the Unwobbling Pivot, and the Analects* (New Directions Publishing Corporation, 1969).

190. A.K. Gangadean, *Meditative Reason: Towards Universal Grammar* (P. Lang, 1993).

191. "Motivated" is a term from Ferdinand de Saussure, which means that language has a history, in use and/or in foundations from Greek, Latin, or other roots. In other words, it describes words that are not entirely arbitrary F. de Saussure et al, *Course in General Linguistics* (Columbia University Press, 2011).

192. D. Meadows, *Leverage Points: Places to Intervene in a System*; available from http://www.donellameadows.org/archives/leverage-points-places-to-intervene-in-a-system/.

193. Priest, "What Is So Bad About Contradictions?"; Priest, *In Contradiction*.

194. Louis H. Kauffman opens a special issue of the journal *Symmetry* on Diagrams, Topology, Categories and Logic with this quote from David Hilbert speaking to the International Congress of Mathematicians in Paris in 1900: "To new concepts correspond, necessarily, new signs. These we choose in such a way that they remind us of the phenomena which were the occasion for the formation of the new concepts. So the geometrical figures are signs or mnemonic symbols of space intuition and are used as such by all mathematicians. Who does not always use along with the double inequality a > b > c the picture of three points following one another on a straight line as the geometrical picture of the idea "between"? Who does not make use of drawings of segments and rectangles enclosed in one another, when it is required to prove with perfect rigor a difficult theorem on the continuity of functions or the existence of points of condensation? ..." (http://www.mdpi.com/journal/symmetry/special_issues/topological). Kauffman has developed a topological logic that also deserves exploration as a novel logical infrastructure. L.H. Kauffman, "Knot Logic—Logical Connection and Topological Connection," *arXiv* (2015).

195. Gangadean, *Meditative Reason: Towards Universal Grammar*; Gangadean, *Between Worlds: The Emergence of Global Reason*.

196. Meadows, *Leverage Points: Places to Intervene in a System*. These unstated assumptions are resonant with Bohm's notion of tacit infrastructures.

197. Peterson, *The Art of Language Invention: From Horse-Lords to Dark Elves, the Words Behind World-Building*, p. 7.

198. Alan Yuhas, "Who Owns Klingon? Lawsuit Draws Battle over Invented Languages into Court," *The Guardian*, 30 Apr 2016. https://www.theguardian.com/culture/2016/apr/29/star-trek-fan-film-klingon-paramount-cbs-lawsuit

199. Peterson, *The Art of Language Invention: From Horse-Lords to Dark Elves, the Words Behind World-Building*.

200. J.M. Robinson, *The Nag Hammadi Library in English* (San Francisco: Harper & Row, 1996), pp. 271–77.

201. J. Kiehl, *Facing Climate Change: An Integrated Path to the Future* (Columbia University Press, 2016), p. 68.

202. C.G. Jung, *The Collected Works of C.G. Jung: Psychology and Religion: West and East* (Princeton, NJ: Princeton University Press, 1966). ¶442–3.

203. Bohm, *Wholeness and the Implicate Order*, p. 2.

204. L.E. Maroski, *The One That Is Both* (iUniverse, 2006), p. 115.

205. As well as neither/nor. "Classical Indian logic and rhetoric regards any proposition as defining a logical space involving four candidate positions, or corners (*koti*), in distinction to most Western logical traditions which consider only two—truth and falsity: The proposition may be true (and not false); false (and not true); both true and false; neither true nor false." G. Priest, *Beyond the Limits of Thought* (Clarendon Press, 2002), pp. 263–4.

206. Geoffreyjen Edwards suggested also thinking about a "children's tongue" in addition to mother and father tongues. Indeed, that would be language based more in the magical structure of consciousness, perhaps.

207. J.L. Austin and M. Sbisà, *How to Do Things with Words* (Harvard University Press, 1975).

Notes to Chapter 17 – Seeing Through Solid Words

208. Kiehl, *Facing Climate Change: An Integrated Path to the Future*, p. 58.

209. J.D. Johnson, *Seeing through the World: Jean Gebser and Integral Consciousness* (Revelore Press, 2019).

210. For a brief summary, see note 44.

211. Gebser, *The Ever-Present Origin*, p. 6.

212. Such images are called bi-stable percepts. The Necker cube is also one. One's ability to see both images, or both ways to perceive the same image, and to switch between them depends largely on the right hemisphere of the brain. I suspect that the better one is at perceiving them, the easier it will be to understand the new types of concepts that are introduced in Chapter 19. Because conception, rather than perception, is the cognitive function being used with the new types of concepts, it would be worth doing some research

to determine which cognitive structures will need "training" so that we can become more competent at using language based on "bi-stable" *concepts* that hold opposites in tension.

213. Gebser, *The Ever-Present Origin*, p. 7.

214. Ibid.

215. S.M. Rosen, *Dimensions of Apeiron: A Topological Phenomenology of Space, Time, and Individuation* (Rodopi, 2004).

216. Ibid.

217. Lakoff and Johnson, *Metaphors We Live By*.

218. H. Taussig et al, *The Thunder: Perfect Mind: A New Translation and Introduction* (Palgrave Macmillan US, 2010). The full text of *The Thunder, Perfect Mind* is available at http://www.gnosis.org/naghamm/thunder.html.

219. Ibid.

220. Gebser cites authors such as Origen, Hermes Trismegistus, and the apocryphal writings of Thomas (presumably the Acts of Thomas) and commentators such as Bousset, Usener, Neander, Schliemann, Schmitt, among others.

221. Taussig et al, *The Thunder: Perfect Mind: A New Translation and Introduction*.

222. Ben Williams, personal communication, 2021.

223. Such internalizing of external processes is not limited to Shaivism or to religion. C.G. Jung described how the alchemists did that as well. Their chymical experiments were a process of refining not only metals and herbals but also of working with one's *prima materia*, one's traumas and shortcomings, i.e., one's psychological material. See, in particular, *Psychology and Alchemy* and *The Psychology of the Transference*.

224. A. McGuire, *The Thunder: Perfect Mind (Translation and Commentary)* (2000; available from https://diotima-doctafemina.org/translations/coptic/the-thunder-perfect-mind/, Taussig et al, *The Thunder: Perfect Mind: A New Translation and Introduction*.

225. Robinson, *The Nag Hammadi Library in English*.

226. Taussig et al, *The Thunder: Perfect Mind: A New Translation and Introduction*. I also consulted translations by Anne McGuire and analyses in T.B. Halvgaard, *Linguistic Manifestations in the Trimorphic Protennoia and the Thunder: Perfect Mind: Analysed against the Background of Platonic and Stoic Dialectics* (Brill, 2015).

227. A. McGuire, "Thunder, Perfect Mind," in *Searching the Scriptures, Vol. 2: A Feminist Commentary*, ed. Elisabeth Schussler Fiorenza (New York: Crossroad, 1993).

228. McGuire, *The Thunder: Perfect Mind (Translation and Commentary)*. https://diotima-doctafemina.org/translations/coptic/the-thunder-perfect-mind/

229. http://www.aaroncheak.com/from-poetry-to-kulturphilosophie

230. When Jesus knows he is to die, he prays to God, "My prayer is not for them alone. I pray also for those who will believe in me through their message, that all of them may be one, Father, just as you are in me and I am in you. May they also be in us so that the world may believe that you have sent me. I have given them the glory that you gave me, that they may be one as we are one—I in them and you in me—so that they may be brought to complete unity. Then the world will know that you sent me and have loved them even as you have loved me" (*John 18:20–23*). The emphasis on oneness and on being-within-the-other recalls the discussions of Kleinian unity and of endosymbiosis,

both scientifically and mythically, as in the myth of Beya and Gabricus. That story, too, ended with the expression of profound love.

231. Ponder Jean Piaget's *concrete* operational thinking here. TPM is showing the abstraction of omniscience through concrete, albeit paradoxical, examples.

232. Jung also describes the individuation process as proceeding through a series of coniunctios, uniting of opposites at greater levels of inclusivity. See Chapter 19.

233. Gebser, *The Ever-Present Origin*, p. 261. Gebser continues: "This integration cannot be effected by mere thinking or contemplation, but requires another capacity which we shall call 'verition' or 'waring' and encompasses the 'sense' of perceiving as well as imparting verity or truth. Only through this reciprocal perception and impartation of truth by man and the world can the world become transparent for us."

234. Ibid, p. 260.

235. Ibid, p. 306.

236. Ibid, p. 2.

Notes to Chapter 18 – Conlanging as Psychosocial Activism

237. This was presented at the seventh Language Creation Conference, which was held in Calgary, Alberta, Canada in 2017. It featured a wonderful spectrum of presentations on both general and very technical aspects of creating languages. We also got to see the world premiere of a film called *Conlanging: The Art of Crafting Tongues*. All the presentations are on YouTube (search "LCC7").

238. "We are called to be architects of the future, not its victims. [The challenge is] to make the world work for 100% of humanity in the shortest possible time, with spontaneous cooperation and without ecological damage or disadvantage of anyone." —R. Buckminster Fuller

239. N. Goodman, *Ways of Worldmaking* (Hackett Publishing Company, 1978), p. 6.

240. McLuhan, *The Medium Is the Massage: An Inventory of Effects*, p. 10.

241. The conlangers I have met are driven by passion, and until relatively recently, were largely self-taught. Now, the linguistics departments of several colleges and universities have courses on conlanging. There is a society you can join to connect and learn from other conlangers (Language Creation Society, https://conlang.org/ and https://fiatlingua.org/).

242. Whorf and Carroll, *Language, Thought, and Reality: Selected Writings of Benjamin Lee Whorf*, p. 23.

243. Watts, *The Book: On the Taboo against Knowing Who You Are*, p.48.

244. Ibid, p.48.

245. Polak and Boulding, *The Image of the Future*.

246. Ibid.

247. McLuhan, *The Medium Is the Massage: An Inventory of Effects*, p. 26.

248. de Saussure et al, *Course in General Linguistics*, pp. 131–4.

249. C.G. Jung, *The Collected Works of C.G. Jung: Mysterium Coniunctionis* (Princeton, NJ: Princeton University Press, 1966). For excellent expositions of the coniunctios, also see S.M. Rosen, *Dreams, Death, Rebirth: A Topological Odyssey into Alchemy's Hidden Dimensions* (Chiron Publications, 2015) and Cavalher [Conceição, *Paradigm of Sense: A Guide to the Consciousness of the Fifth Dimension* (Independently Published, 2020).

250. The first part of this book examined ways to conjoin self and other.

251. Tarnas, *Cosmos and Psyche: Intimations of a New World View.* p. 491.

252. Ferro, *Seeds of Illness, Seeds of Recovery: The Genesis of Suffering and the Role of Psychoanalysis*, pp. 11–12.

253. Jung, *The Collected Works of C.G. Jung: Mysterium Coniunctionis*, p. 463 (¶661).

254. Ibid, p. 533 (¶759).

255. Ibid, p. 534 (¶760).

256. Gebser, *The Ever-Present Origin*, p. 2; Karl Abel. *Der Gegensinn der Urworte.* To my knowledge, this book has not been translated into English. I rely on Gebser's translator's version. Horn dismisses those examples as polysemy, but gives other examples of enantionyms, including *sanction, oversight, cipher, cleave, rent, peruse.*

257. Ibid, p. 2.

258. S. Freud, "The Antithetical Meaning of Primal Words," in *Five Lectures on Psycho-Analysis*, ed. James Strachey (London: The Hogarth Press, 1910), p. 158.

259. Ibid.

260. Paul Gordon, "Freud's "On the Antithetical Sense of Primary Words": Psychoanalysis, Art, and the Antithetical Senses," *Style 24*, no. 2 (1990).

261. L.R. Horn, *Etymythology and Taboo*; available from https://www.bu.edu/isle/files/2012/01/Laurence-Horn-Etymythology-and-Taboo.pdf, p. 1.

262. "Jung's recognition of the inevitability of enantiodromic change helped him anticipate psychic movement and he believed it was possible both to foresee and also to relate to it, such an attitude being the essence of consciousness." A. Samuels, B. Shorter, and F. Plaut, *A Critical Dictionary of Jungian Analysis* (Taylor & Francis, 2012), "Enantiodromia," p. 53.

263. Gebser, *The Ever-Present Origin*, p. 123.

264. Ibid, p. 501–2. As examples from poetry, he cites poems with themes that we have discussed in several ways, starting with Heraclitus and going through Margulis. Hölderlin: "Life is death and death is also a life." Valéry: "Death in the ... Biological sense forms an indispensable part of life."

265. N.C. Maryboy, D.H. Begay, and L. Nichol, "Paradox and Transformation," *International Journal of Applied Science and Sustainable Development 2*, No. 1, March (2020), p. 18.

266. Ibid, p. 19.

267. I invented them for my novel *The One That Is Both.*

268. In *The Cosmic Serpent: DNA and the Origins of Knowledge*, Jeremy Narby describes the both/and nature of DNA: "DNA is the informational molecule of life, and its very essence consists in being *both single and double*, like the mythical serpents." (p. 90) And later, he says, "…DNA [is] an aperiodic crystal that traps and transports electrons with

efficiency and that emits photons (in other words, electromagnetic waves) at ultra-weak levels currently at the limits of measurement—and all this more than any other living matter." (pp. 109–110). He cites several studies supporting this finding. This phenomenon of light emission by DNA continues to be studied. J. Narby, *The Cosmic Serpent* (Penguin Publishing Group, 1999).

269. McGilchrist, *The Matter with Things: Our Brains, Our Delusions, and the Unmaking of the World*, p. 818.

Notes to Chapter 20 – This Möbial/Kleinian Life

270. Ibid, p. 1175.

271. N. Schwartz-Salant, *Order-Disorder Paradox: Understanding the Hidden Side of Change in Self and Society* (North Atlantic Books, 2017), p. xxvi.

272. Ibid, pp. xxv–xxvi.

273. Ibid, p. 55.

274. Not all internal-external relationships are Kleinian. You wouldn't want to hire a painter to paint the outside of your house only to find that he painted the interior the same color. So how can we know when to apply our new types of words? There's tension in the field. People pick sides and get emotional about defending their side. That is happening on a wide scale in politics right now, so much so that there seems to be an enantiodromia occurring, where one "side" flips into the other side.

275. On April 3, 2022, the comedian John Oliver did an excellent exposé of how the trucking industry has externalized costs by shifting the burden of truck ownership, maintenance, and repair onto the truckers themselves by recategorizing them as independent contractors. Although independent contractors are supposed to have control over their own schedule, some trucking companies essentially take that away by not paying them while they sit waiting to load/unload, not letting them take breaks when they need to, and so on. See https://www.youtube.com/watch?v=phieTCxQRLA

276. https://regenesisgroup.com/ "Green or eco-efficient design is insufficient because it misses the real potential that arises out of the human presence on this planet: the possibility of organizing human activities so that they continuously feed and are fed by the living systems within which they occur. It is not enough to aspire to mitigate the effects of human activity—people need to take their place again as a part of nature. Mang and Reed, "Designing from Place: A Regenerative Framework and Methodology."

277. Ibid.

278. Ibid.

279. A blogger named Nora Dunn gives a wonderful example from her own life (see https://www.wisebread.com/good-luck-bad-luck-who-can-tell): in summary, she and her boyfriend were exchanging volunteer work for a place to live in Australia. They decided to stay longer and wanted a cheap place to rent. Within days, they found one. Within a month of moving in, the wildfires hit that part of Australia, and they had to evacuate but couldn't get out of the country even if they had wanted to. To bide their time, they volunteered in the relief efforts. As a "thank you" of sorts, the government extended their visas. Their

home had not burned, so they returned, and her boyfriend got a new job. She didn't share the details, but that led to their eventual breakup. She started traveling solo, where she met a TV producer who wanted to do a show about women traveling alone, so she got to go to Paris and Nepal. Who knows what will happen next.

280. For a summary, to date, see https://www.sloww.co/meta-crisis-101/

281. https://www.youtube.com/watch?v=jHxTvvPZUuI

282. https://systems-souls-society.com/education-is-the-metacrisis/

Notes to Chapter 21 – Why?

283. Gebser, *The Ever-Present Origin*, p. 283.

284. Gary F. Simons, "Two Centuries of Spreading Language Loss," *Proceedings of the Linguistic Society of America* 4, no. 1 (2019).

285. M. Yaguello and E. Butler, *Imaginary Languages: Myths, Utopias, Fantasies, Illusions, and Linguistic Fictions* (MIT Press, 2022), pp. xx–xxi.

286. A. Tetlow et al, *Designa: Technical Secrets of the Traditional Visual Arts* (Wooden Books, 2014).

287. Indeed, most early writing systems drew, literally, things in the world and lives of people, things like oxen, sheep, trees, sun and moon, water, mountains, birds. Although hieroglyphs did not undergo extensive abstractions, the early semitic and Chinese languages did. See Coulmas, *Writing Systems of the World*.

288. W.V. Quine, *The Ways of Paradox, and Other Essays* (Harvard University Press, 1976), p. 1.

References

"Five Graces Group", C. Beckner, R. Blythe, J. Bybee, M.H. Christiansen, W. Croft, N.C. Ellis, J. Holland, J. Ke, and D. Larsen-Freeman. "Language Is a Complex Adaptive System: Position Paper." *Language Learning* 59 (2009): 1–26.

Albrecht, G.A. *Earth Emotions: New Words for a New World*: Cornell University Press, 2019.

Alcock, J., C. C. Maley, and C. A. Aktipis. "Is Eating Behavior Manipulated by the Gastrointestinal Microbiota? Evolutionary Pressures and Potential Mechanisms." *Bioessays* 36, no. 10 (2014): 940–9.

Alexander, C., S. Ishikawa, and M. Silverstein. *A Pattern Language: Towns, Buildings, Construction*. 3 vols. Vol. 2. New York: Oxford University Press, 1977.

Anggoro, F., and D. Gentner. "Sex and Seniority: The Effects of Linguistic Categories on Conceptual Judgments and Memory." In *Proceedings of the 25th Annual Cognitive Science Society: Part 1 and 2*, edited by R. Alterman and D. Kirsch. Boston, MA: Psychology Press, Taylor & Francis, 2003.

Ardagh, A. "The Clock Is Ticking." In *The Mystery of 2012*, edited by G. Braden, 213–28: Sounds True, 2009.

Austin, J.L., and M. Sbisà. *How to Do Things with Words*: Harvard University Press, 1975.

Bateson, G. *Mind and Nature: A Necessary Unity*: Bantam Books, 1988.

Bateson, G., and M.C. Bateson. *Steps to an Ecology of Mind: Collected Essays in Anthropology, Psychiatry, Evolution, and Epistemology*: University of Chicago Press, 2000.

Berdoy, M., J. P. Webster, and D. W. Macdonald. "Fatal Attraction in Rats Infected with Toxoplasma Gondii." *Proc Biol Sci* 267, no. 1452 (2000): 1591–4.

Bohm, D. *Wholeness and the Implicate Order*: Ark Paperbacks, 1983.

Bohm, D., and F.D. Peat. *Science, Order, and Creativity*: Bantam Books, 1987.

Borenstein, S. "Earth Is 'Really Quite Sick Now' and in Danger Zone in Nearly All Ecological Ways, Study Says." *Associated Press*, May 31 2023.

Bortoft, H. *The Wholeness of Nature: Goethe's Way of Science:* Floris Books, 1996.

Box, G.E.P. "Science and Statistics." *Journal of the American Statistical Association* 71, no. 356 (1976): 791–99.

Calleman, C.J. *The Mayan Calendar and the Transformation of Consciousness*: Inner Traditions/Bear, 2004.

Carse, J.P. *Finite and Infinite Games*: Free Press, 1986.

Cavalher [Conceição, F.]. *Paradigm of Sense: A Guide to the Consciousness of the Fifth Dimension*: Independently Published, 2020.

Chaisson, E.J., and E. Chaisson. *The Life Era: Cosmic Selection and Conscious Evolution*: iUniverse, 2000.

Chaucer, G. "The Canterbury Tales." In *The Oxford Anthology of English Literature*: Oxford University Press, 1973.

Coulmas, F. *Writing Systems of the World*: Wiley, 1991.

de Saussure, F., W. Baskin, P. Meisel, and H. Saussy. *Course in General Linguistics*: Columbia University Press, 2011.

Deutscher, G. *Through the Language Glass: Why the World Looks Different in Other Languages*: Macmillan, 2010.

———. *The Unfolding of Language: An Evolutionary Tour of Mankind's Greatest Invention*: Henry Holt and Company, 2006.

Diamond, J. *Collapse: How Societies Choose to Fail or Survive*: Penguin Books Limited, 2013.

Dotson, J., E. Ruchowitz-Roberts, and C. Bancroft. *Rivulets of Light: Poems of Point Lobos and Carmel Bay*: Cross-Cultural Communications, 2008.

Edwards, G. *Plenum: The First Book of Deo*. Longmont, CO: Untimely Books, 2022.

Ehrlich, P. R., and A. H. Ehrlich. "Can a Collapse of Global Civilization Be Avoided?" *Proc Biol Sci* 280, no. 1754 (2013): 20122845.

Ehrlich, P.R. *The Population Bomb*: Ballantine Books, 1983.

Einhorn, C. "It Was War. Then, a Rancher's Truce with Some Pesky Beavers Paid Off." *The New York Times* 2022.

Ferro, A. *Seeds of Illness, Seeds of Recovery: The Genesis of Suffering and the Role of Psychoanalysis*: Brunner-Routledge, 2005.

Ferry, S., and W. Davis. "Keepers of the World." *National Geographic* 2004, 50–67.

Foster, R. G., and L. Kreitzman. "The Rhythms of Life: What Your Body Clock Means to You!" *Exp Physiol* 99, no. 4 (2014): 599–606.

Freeman, W.J., and G. Vitiello. "Nonlinear Brain Dynamics and Many-Body Field Dynamics." In *Coherence and Electromagnetic Fields in Biological Systems*. Prague, Czech Republic, 2005.

Freud, S. "The Antithetical Meaning of Primal Words." In *Five Lectures on Psycho-Analysis*, edited by James Strachey, 155–61. London: The Hogarth Press, 1910.

Friedan, B., and A. Quindlen. *The Feminine Mystique*: W. W. Norton, 2001.

Frush, B. W., and J. Eberly Jr. "Risks of Medical Metaphors." *JAMA* 318, no. 5 (2017): 482.

Gangadean, A.K. *Between Worlds: The Emergence of Global Reason*: Peter Lang, 1998.

———. *Meditations of Global First Philosophy: Quest for the Missing Grammar of Logos*: State University of New York Press, 2009.

———. *Meditative Reason: Towards Universal Grammar*: P. Lang, 1993.

Gebser, Jean. *The Ever-Present Origin*: Ohio University Press, 1985.

———. "The Grammatical Mirror." Available at https://www.infiniteconversations.com/t/cosmos-cafe-gebsers-grammatical-mirror-2018-03-13/1783.

Gibson, W.W. *The Limits of Language*: Hill and Wang, 1962.

Gimbutas, M. *The Language of the Goddess: Unearthing the Hidden Symbols of Western Civilization*: HarperSanFrancisco, 1991.

Gimbutas, M., and M.R. Dexter. *The Living Goddesses*: University of California Press, 2001.

Gonzalez, A., J. C. Clemente, A. Shade, J. L. Metcalf, S. Song, B. Prithiviraj, B. E. Palmer, and R. Knight. "Our Microbial Selves: What Ecology Can Teach Us." *EMBO Rep* 12, no. 8 (2011): 775–84.

Goodman, N. *Ways of Worldmaking*: Hackett Publishing Company, 1978.

Gordon, P. "Freud's "on the Antithetical Sense of Primary Words": Psychoanalysis, Art, and the Antithetical Senses." *Style* 24, no. 2 (1990): 167–86.

Goswami, A., R.E. Reed, and M. Goswami. *The Self-Aware Universe: How Consciousness Creates the Material World*: Putnam's Sons, 1995.

Graham, D.W. "Heraclitus." In *The Stanford Encyclopedia of Philosophy (Fall 2015 Edition)*, edited by Edward N. Zalta, 2015.

Halvgaard, T.B. *Linguistic Manifestations in the Trimorphic Protennoia and the Thunder: Perfect Mind: Analysed against the Background of Platonic and Stoic Dialectics*: Brill, 2015.

Harding, S. *Animate Earth: Science, Intuition, and Gaia*: Chelsea Green Publishing, 2006.

Hawkins, D.R. *Power Vs. Force*: Hay House, 2014.

Heidegger, M. *Being and Time*: HarperCollins, 1962.

Hofstadter, D.R. *Gödel, Escher, Bach: An Eternal Golden Braid*: Penguin, 2000.

Horn, L.R. n.d. Etymythology and Taboo. Available at https://www.bu.edu/isle/files/2012/01/Laurence-Horn-Etymythology-and-Taboo.pdf (accessed 4/26/2023).

Hornborg, A.C. *Mi'kmaq Landscapes: From Animism to Sacred Ecology*: Ashgate, 2008.

Hubbard, B.M. *Conscious Evolution: Awakening the Power of Our Social Potential*: New World Library, 1998.

Humar, M. "Metaphors as Models: Towards a Typology of Metaphor in Ancient Science." *History and Philosophy of the Life Sciences* 43, no. 3 (2021): 101.

Institute of Medicine. "Ending the War Metaphor: The Changing Agenda for Unraveling the Host-Microbe Relationship: Workshop Summary." Washington, DC: The National Academies Press, 2006.

———. "The Human Microbiome, Diet, and Health: Workshop Summary." Washington, DC, 2013.

Jammer, M. *Concepts of Space: The History of Theories of Space in Physics: Third, Enlarged Edition*: Dover Publications, 2013.

Johnson, B. *And: Making a Difference by Leveraging Polarity, Paradox, or Dilemma*. Vol. One: Foundations. Amherst, MA: HRD Press, 2020.

———. *Polarity Management: Identifying and Managing Unsolvable Problems*: Human Resource Development, 1992.

Johnson, J.D. *Seeing through the World: Jean Gebser and Integral Consciousness*: Revelore Press, 2019.

Jung, C.G. *The Collected Works of C.G. Jung: Mysterium Coniunctionis*. Princeton, NJ: Princeton University Press, 1966.

———. *The Collected Works of C.G. Jung: Psychology and Religion: West and East*. Princeton, NJ: Princeton University Press, 1966.

———. *Psychology and Alchemy*: Taylor & Francis, 2014.

Kauffman, L.H. "Knot Logic--Logical Connection and Topological Connection." *arXiv* (2015).

Keesing, R.M. "Conventional Metaphors and Anthropological Metaphysics: The Problematic of Cultural Translation." *Journal of Anthropological Research* 41, no. 2 (1985): 201–17.

Kiehl, J. *Facing Climate Change: An Integrated Path to the Future*: Columbia University Press, 2016.

Ko, C. H., and J. S. Takahashi. "Molecular Components of the Mammalian Circadian Clock." *Hum Mol Genet* 15 Spec No 2 (2006): R271–7.

Kotler, S., and J. Wheal. *Stealing Fire: How Silicon Valley, the Navy Seals, and Maverick Scientists Are Revolutionizing the Way We Live and Work*: HarperCollins, 2018.

Kuhn, T.S. *The Structure of Scientific Revolutions*: University of Chicago Press, 1969.

Lakoff, G. *The Political Mind: Why You Can't Understand 21st-Century Politics with an 18th-Century Brain*: Viking, 2008.

Lakoff, G., and M. Johnson. *Metaphors We Live By*: University of Chicago Press, 2008.

Le Guin, U.K. *Dancing at the Edge of the World: Thoughts on Words, Women, Places*: Grove Press, 1997.

Lent, J.R., and F. Capra. *The Patterning Instinct: A Cultural History of Humanity's Search for Meaning*: Prometheus Books, 2017.

Lévy-Leblond, J.-M. "Quantum Words for a Quantum World." In *Epistemological and Experimental Perspectives on Quantum Physics*, edited by Daniel Greenberger, Wolfgang L. Reiter and Anton Zeilinger, 75–87. Dordrecht: Springer Netherlands, 1999.

Lipton, B.H. *The Biology of Belief: Unleashing the Power of Consciousness, Matter & Miracles*: Hay House, 2008.

Maccaro, J. "Be Mindful of Your Metaphors About Microbes." *mSphere* 6, no. 3 (2021): e0043121.

Madrigal, A.C. "Why Are Spy Researchers Building a 'Metaphor Program'?" *The Atlantic*, May 25, 2011.

Mang, P., and B. Reed. "Designing from Place: A Regenerative Framework and Methodology." n.d.

Margulis, L. *Symbiotic Planet: A New Look at Evolution*: Basic Books, 2008.

Maroski, L.E. *The One That Is Both*: iUniverse, 2006.

Maryboy, N.C., D.H. Begay, and L. Nichol. "Paradox and Transformation." *International Journal of Applied Science and Sustainable Development* 2, No. 1, March (2020): 15–24.

Mayer, E. *The Mind-Gut Connection: How the Hidden Conversation within Our Bodies Impacts Our Mood, Our Choices, and Our Overall Health*: Harper Wave, 2018.

McCulloch, G. *Because Internet: Understanding the New Rules of Language*: Penguin Publishing Group, 2020.

McGilchrist, I. *The Master and His Emissary: The Divided Brain and the Making of the Western World*: Yale University Press, 2019.

———. *The Matter with Things: Our Brains, Our Delusions, and the Unmaking of the World*. 2 vols. London: Perspectiva Press, 2021.

McGuire, A. "Thunder, Perfect Mind." In *Searching the Scriptures, Vol. 2: A Feminist Commentary*, edited by Elisabeth Schussler Fiorenza, 39–54. New York: Crossroad, 1993.

———. 2000. The Thunder: Perfect Mind (Translation and Commentary). Available at https://diotima-doctafemina.org/translations/coptic/the-thunder-perfect-mind/ (accessed 1/30/21).

McLuhan, M. *The Medium Is the Massage: An Inventory of Effects*: Gingko Press GmbH, 2011.

———. "Myth and Mass Media." In *Myth and Mythmaking*, edited by H.A. Murray, 288–99: Beacon Press, 1968.

McWaters B., and Institute for the Study of Conscious Evolution. *Conscious Evolution: Personal and Planetary Transformation*: Institute for the Study of Conscious Evolution, 1981.

Meadows, D. Leverage Points: Places to Intervene in a System. Available at http://www.donellameadows.org/archives/leverage-points-places-to-intervene-in-a-system/ (accessed Aug 2, 2022).

Meadows, D.H., D.L. Meadows, J. Randers, and W.W. Behrens. *The Limits to Growth*. New York: New American Library, 1972.

Meadows, D.H., and D. Wright. *Thinking in Systems: A Primer*: Chelsea Green Pub., 2008.

Meyer, C.J., K.A. Cassidy, E.E. Stahler, E.E. Brandell, C.B. Anton, D.R. Stahler, and D.W. Smith. "Parasitic Infection Increases Risk-Taking in a Social, Intermediate Host Carnivore." *Communications Biology* 5, no. 1 (2022): 1180.

Nalepa, C.A. "Origin of Mutualism between Termites and Flagellated Gut Protists: Transition from Horizontal to Vertical Transmission." *Frontiers in Ecology and Evolution* 8, no. 14 (2020).

Narby, J. *The Cosmic Serpent*: Penguin Publishing Group, 1999.

Nicholson, D.J., and J. Dupré. *Everything Flows: Towards a Processual Philosophy of Biology*: Oxford University Press, 2018.

Noble, D. *Dance to the Tune of Life: Biological Relativity*: Cambridge University Press, 2017.

Ørstavik, R. E. "Nature and Nurture: Not a Case of Either/Or." *Tidsskr Nor Laegeforen* 138, no. 14 (2018).

Parry, G.A., and J. O'Dea. *Original Thinking: A Radical Revisioning of Time, Humanity, and Nature*: North Atlantic Books, 2015.

Patric, E.M. *Flowerspeak: The Flower Whisperer's Guide to Health, Happiness, & Awakening.* Bloomington, IN: Balboa Press, 2012.

Pepper, S.C. *World Hypotheses: A Study in Evidence*: University of California Press, 1942.

Peters, F.E. *Greek Philosophical Terms: A Historical Lexicon*: NYU Press, 1967.

Peterson, D.J. *The Art of Language Invention: From Horse-Lords to Dark Elves, the Words Behind World-Building*: Penguin Publishing Group, 2015.

Pinker, S. *The Language Instinct: How the Mind Creates Language*: HarperCollins, 2010.

Polak, F.L., and E. Boulding. *The Image of the Future*: Elsevier Scientific Publishing Company, 1973.

Pound, E. *Confucius: The Great Digest, the Unwobbling Pivot, and the Analects*: New Directions Publishing Corporation, 1969.

Priest, G. *Beyond the Limits of Thought*: Clarendon Press, 2002.

———. 2014. "Beyond True and False." Available at https://aeon.co/essays/the-logic-of-buddhist-philosophy-goes-beyond-simple-truth (accessed 11/23/2020).

———. *In Contradiction*: Clarendon Press, 2006.

———. *An Introduction to Non-Classical Logic: From If to Is*: Cambridge University Press, 2008.

———. "What Is So Bad About Contradictions?" *Journal of Philosophy* 95, no. 8 (1998): 410–26.

Quine, W.V. *The Ways of Paradox, and Other Essays*: Harvard University Press, 1976.

Rapoport, D.L. "Klein Bottle Logophysics, the Primeval Distinction, Semiosis, Perception and the Topology of Consciousness." In *Laws of Form: A Fiftieth Anniversary*, edited by Louis Kauffman, Leon Conrad, Randolph Dible, Graham Ellsbury, Florian Grote, Fred Cummins and Andrew Crompton, 435–514. Japan: World Scientific, 2023.

Ray, P.H., and S.R. Anderson. *The Cultural Creatives: How 50 Million People Are Changing the World*: Three Rivers Press, 2001.

Reynolds, A.S. *Understanding Metaphors in the Life Sciences*: Cambridge University Press, 2022.

Robinson, J.M. *The Nag Hammadi Library in English*. San Francisco: Harper & Row, 1996.

Rockström, J., J. Gupta, D. Qin, S. J. Lade, J. F. Abrams, L. S. Andersen, et al. "Safe and Just Earth System Boundaries." *Nature* (2023). May 31. doi: 10.1038/s41586-023-06083-8. Online ahead of print.

Rosen, S.M. *Dimensions of Apeiron: A Topological Phenomenology of Space, Time, and Individuation*: Rodopi, 2004.

———. *Dreams, Death, Rebirth: A Topological Odyssey into Alchemy's Hidden Dimensions*: Chiron Publications, 2015.

———. "How Can We Signify Being? Semiotics and Topological Self-Signification." *Cosmos and History: The Journal of Natural and Social Philosophy* 10, no. 2 (2014): 250–77.

———. *The Self-Evolving Cosmos: A Phenomenological Approach to Nature's Unity-in-Diversity*: World Scientific, 2008.

Sabelli, H.C. *Bios: A Study of Creation*. Edited by L.H. Kauffman, *Knots & Everything*. Singapore: World Scientific, 2005.

Samuels, A., B. Shorter, and F. Plaut. *A Critical Dictionary of Jungian Analysis*: Taylor & Francis, 2012.

Scaglion, R. "Yam Cycles and Timeless Time in Melanesia." *Ethnology* 38, no. 3 (1999): 211–25.

Schwartz-Salant, N. *Order-Disorder Paradox: Understanding the Hidden Side of Change in Self and Society*: North Atlantic Books, 2017.

Scott, G.R. "A Traditional Lakota Zoological Folk Taxonomy: An in Depth Study of Biological and Cosmological Views of Animal Classification and Nomenclature among the Lakota." Northern Illinois University, 2000.

Shlain, L. *The Alphabet Versus the Goddess: The Conflict between Word and Image*: Penguin/Compass, 1999.

Simons, Gary F. "Two Centuries of Spreading Language Loss." *Proceedings of the Linguistic Society of America* 4, no. 1 (2019): 27:1–12. Available at https://journals.linguisticsociety.org/proceedings/index.php/PLSA/article/view/4532 (accessed 2 July 2023).

Spangler, D., J. Spangler, and F. Secrest. *Subtle Worlds: An Explorer's Field Notes*: Lorian Press, 2010.

Stamets, P. *Fantastic Fungi*: Earth Aware Editions, 2020.

Steffens, G., and S. Ferry. "Indigenous Protectors of These Sacred Peaks Have Kept Others Out—Till Now." *National Geographic* 2019.

Steiner, F.B., J.D. Adler, and R. Fardon. *Taboo, Truth, and Religion: Selected Writings*: Berghahn Books, 1999.

Stroud, S.R. "Pragmatism, Pluralism, and World Hypotheses." *Philosophy and Rhetoric* 48, no. 3 (2015): 266–91.

Talbot, M. *Holographic Universe*: HarperCollins, 1992.

Taleb, N.N. *Antifragile: Things That Gain from Disorder*: Random House Publishing Group, 2014.

Tarnas, R. *Cosmos and Psyche: Intimations of a New World View*: Penguin Publishing Group, 2006.

Taussig, H., J. Calaway, M. Kotrosits, C. Lillie, and J. Lasser. *The Thunder: Perfect Mind: A New Translation and Introduction*: Palgrave Macmillan US, 2010.

Taylor, C., and B. M. Dewsbury. "On the Problem and Promise of Metaphor Use in Science and Science Communication." *J Microbiol Biol Educ* 19, no. 1 (2018): 10.1128/jmbe.v19i1.1538.

Tetlow, A., D. Sutton, L. DeLong, P. McNaughton, D. Wade, and S.A. Olsen. *Designa: Technical Secrets of the Traditional Visual Arts*: Wooden Books, 2014.

Thibodeau, P.H., and L. Boroditsky. "The Role of Metaphor in Reasoning." *PLoS ONE* 6, no. 2 (2011): e16782.

Thomas, D., W. Davies, and R. Maud. *Collected Poems, 1934-1953*: Phoenix, 2000.

von Franz, M.-L. *Alchemy: An Introduction to the Symbolism and the Psychology*: Inner City Books, 1980.

Watts, A. *The Book: On the Taboo against Knowing Who You Are*: Vintage Books, 1972.

Weber, B.H., and D.J. Depew. *Evolution and Learning: The Baldwin Effect Reconsidered*: MIT Press, 2003.

Weick, K.E. *Sensemaking in Organizations*: SAGE Publications, 1995.

Whorf, B.L., and J.B. Carroll. *Language, Thought, and Reality: Selected Writings of Benjamin Lee Whorf*: M.I.T. Press, 1964.

Wilhelm, H. "The Creative Principle in the Book of Changes." *Spring* 9 (1970): 91–110.

Willard, T. "Beya and Gabricus: Erotic Imagery in German Alchemy." *Mediaevistik* 28 (2015): 269–81.

Wohlleben, P. *The Hidden Life of Trees: What They Feel, How They Communicate*: HarperCollins Publishers, 2017.

Woods, C., G. Emberling, and E. Teeter. *Visible Language: Inventions of Writing in the Ancient Middle East and Beyond*. Chicago: Oriental Institute of the University of Chicago, 2010.

Yaguello, M., and E. Butler. *Imaginary Languages: Myths, Utopias, Fantasies, Illusions, and Linguistic Fictions*: MIT Press, 2022.

Yuhas, Alan. "Who Owns Klingon? Lawsuit Draws Battle over Invented Languages into Court." *The Guardian*, 30 Apr 2016.

Yunkaporta, T. *Sand Talk: How Indigenous Thinking Can Save the World*: HarperOne, 2020.

Index

Boldface entries refer to glyphs.

aperspectivity 145, 173, 184, 185, 186, 190–192, 251n44

apoptosis 65

arbitrary 168, 201, 263n191

archaic consciousness structure 24, 180, 250n44. *See also* magic, mythic, mental, *and* integral (consciousness structures)

archetype 37, 50, 55, 113, 130, 132, 180, 187, 190, 209, 255n102

architecture 5, 83, 93, 95–97, 98, 112, 128, 202, 213, 257n109

Ardagh, Arjuna 27, 29, 35, 101, 102, 103, 104, 106, 205

Arisleus 70–71, 209

Aristarchus 133

Aristotle 13, 14, 37, 40, 83, 118, 130, 158

assumptions 3, 22, 38, 53, 68, 86, 105, 158, 176, 181, 198, 244, 264n196
cultural 32, 56, 157, 161–162, 167, 169, 171
linguistic 2, 51, 55, 84, 123, 151, 152, 154–155, 161, 163–164
of connectedness 7, 112
of separateness 5, 7, 20, 107, 183, 199
questioning of 77, 81, 197–199

atemporality 173, 184, 185, 186, 188, 190, 192, 193, 251n44

Austin, J.L. 177

Australia, Australians 47, 67, 156, 268n279

autophagy 65

Avatar 54, 198, 199

B

bacteria 62, 86, 87, 120, 122

Baldwin Effect 43

Bateson, Gregory 109

Bean, The, (Cloud Gate) 101–102, 103

becomingness 12, 13, 14, 40, 75, 87, 107, 169, 196, 205, 213, 236, 240, 247n4

Being 14, 37, 149–152, 152, 153, 155, 160, 164, 165, 172–173, 177, 197, 210, 261n171

being one with 31, 35, 38, 81, 265n230

being(s) 32, 34, 38, 44, 45, 54, 64, 66, 72, 84, 87, 90, 105, 106, 112, 125, 151, 157, 161, 173, 188, 192, 193, 199, 217, 235, 236, 248n17, 253n78
coffee-beings 53
human 16, 31, 56, 89, 155, 175, 186, 199
idea beings 1–2
integral 172–173, 179, 186, 233
inter-being 75, 101
object-beings 153
paradoxical 79, 101, 144
planetary 67, 111, 253n77. *See also Gaianbody*
separate 28, 143–144

Bennett, Alan 87

Beya 70–71, 266n230

biodiversity 66, 224

biological communication 65

Bion, Wilfred 209

bi-stable percepts 180, 264n212

blind spots 108

Boas, Franz 163

Bohm, David 51, 73, 83, 175, 205, 252n56, 260n162, 264n196

Boroditsky, Lera 122

Bortoft, Henri 145, 260n158

both/and 5, 7, 9, 12, 15, 81–84, 85, 108, 110, 111, 139, 149, 151, 158, 159, 167, 177, 196, 198, 202, 207, 210–212, 215, 219, 221, 234, 241, 255n91, 257n109, 259n149, 267n268

boundaries 5, 32, 54, 66, 71, 75, 77, 82, 88, 95, 101, 102, 132, 133, 157, 164, 167, 171, 198, 211

Box, George 120, 247n4

C

Calleman, Carl Johan 133

Candida 63

capitalism 82, 91

Carroll, Lewis 17

Carse, James 123, 124

E

Earth 5, 20, 21, 32–33, 45, 56, 60, 65, 72, 74–75, 77, 123, 139, 143, 190, 209, 227, 236

  as living organism 43, 54, 66, 68, 132, 142, 253n77. *See also* Gaia

  human connectedness with 34–35, 64, 68, 94, 114, 257n109

economy 74, 121, 124, 126, 153, 171, 222, 226, 229

ecstasis 34

education 108, 126, 199, 229, 253n80

Edwards, Geoffreyjen 200, 264n206

Einstein, Albert 22, 37, 97, 106, 170

either/or 5, 15, 81–83, 85–86, 91, 107, 151, 172, 179, 195, 207, 235

ELECTION IS A GAME 125

Emerson, Ralph Waldo 235

enantionym 212, 267n256. *See also Urworte*

endosymbiosis 62, 68, 71, 215, 265n230

entropy 19–20, 220, 231, 236

epigenetics 15

Ereira, Alan 91, 256n108

Escher, M.C. 12

Esperanto (constructed language) 170

essence 14, 46, 183, 214, 226

evolution 4, 115, 226, 228

  conscious 43, 45, 48, 49, 51, 113, 139, 201–202, 233

  linguistic 17, 18, 19, 48, 50, 51, 98, 107, 113, 139, 162, 168, 170, 201, 201–202, 212, 248n16, 250n38

  of consciousness 43, 250n44

evolve 43, 48, 63, 65, 93, 140, 225, 227, 262n173

exostructures 149, 151, 154, 155–156, 167, 169, 170, 198, 218, 260n162

explicit metaphor 117, 118–121, 133, 223

explosion (logic) 159, 177, 262n179

external environment 63. *See also Umwelt*

externalization of costs 223

F

facet consciousness 5, 75–77, 102–103, 106. *See also* consciousness: facet/diamond

family as metaphor 134

father tongue 152, 164, 175, 177, 264n206

Ferro, Antonino, 76, 208–209

field 23, 53, 54, 69, 86, 131, 163, 164, 177, 193, 200, 233, 248n19, 259n150, 268n274

Finding Nemo 61

finite game/infinite game 7, 103, 110, 123–125, 225, 233, 235

Flatland (Edwin Abbott) 76

flow state 40, 75, 176, 207

formism 129, 130, 131, 135. *See also* contextualism, mechanism, organicism, *and* world hypotheses

frame (conceptual) 60, 122, 160, 197

Freud, Sigmund 212

Friedan, Betty 107

Frommer, Paul 199

fu-an-gu ✿ 216, 220, 227, 233

Fuller, R. Buckminster 19, 45, 50, 170, 195, 200, 201, 202, 266n238

function words 113, 162, 168

future 1, 4, 41, 44, 111, 126, 159, 173, 179, 181, 195, 200, 210, 227, 232, 250n40, 257n109

G

Gabricus 70–71, 266n230

Gaia 34, 43, 48, 59, 62, 64, 66, 68, 69, 72, 75, 77, 86, 87, 88–89, 90, 91, 102, 132, 187, 193, 225, 234, 244

Gaianbody 34, 59, 66, 68, 69, 111, 115, 144. *See also Humanbody*

game metaphor 125. *See also* finite game/infinite game

Game of Thrones 113, 170, 199

Gangadean, Ashok 96, 251n48

About the Author

L.E. Maroski studied philosophy and psychology at Bryn Mawr College and has practiced Argentine tango around the world. Although her day-job as a medical editor requires her to mince words, she much prefers to find ways to meld them, creating new possibilities for expressing the paradoxical wholeness of Life, including a novel, *The One That Is Both* (2006). Visit her website at www.lisamaroski.com.

About Untimely Books

Untimely Books is an independent publisher of literary works that illumine the mind, question the contemporary, and reimagine horizons of thought, feeling, and action for a planetary age. As an imprint of Cosmos Cooperative (a member-owned publishing platform and creative community) and Metapsychosis (a journal of consciousness, literature, and art), Untimely Books serves as a conduit for diverse forms of writing by Cosmos members, including original works of fiction, poetry, philosophy, essays, and memoir.

untimelybooks.com

Cut here to make a Mobius strip. Before attaching the ends together with tape, give one end half a twist.